# City Limits

RETHINKING INDIA
Series editors: Aakash Singh Rathore, Mridula Mukherjee,
Pushparaj Deshpande and Syeda Hameed

OTHER BOOKS IN THE SERIES
*Vision for a Nation: Paths and Perspectives*
(Aakash Singh Rathore and Ashis Nandy, eds)

*The Minority Conundrum: Living in Majoritarian Times*
(Tanweer Fazal, ed.)

*Reviving Jobs: An Agenda for Growth*
(Santosh Mehrotra, ed.)

*We the People: Establishing Rights and Deepening Democracy*
(Nikhil Dey, Aruna Roy and Rakshita Swamy, eds)

*The Shudras: Vision for a New Path*
(Kancha Ilaiah Shepherd and Karthik Raja Karuppusamy, eds)

*Her Right to Equality: From Promise to Power*
(Nisha Agrawal, ed.)

*Being Adivasi: Existence, Entitlements, Exclusion*
(Abhay Flavian Xaxa and G.N. Devy, eds)

*The Dalit Truth: The Battles for Realizing Ambedkar's Vision*
(K. Raju, ed.)

*Dreams of a Healthy India: Democratic Health Care in Post-COVID Times*
(Ritu Priya and Syeda Hameed, eds)

*The Great Indian Manthan: State, Statecraft and the Republic*
(Pushparaj Deshpande and Gurdeep Singh Sappal, eds)

*India's Tryst with the World: A Foreign Policy Manifesto*
(Salman Khurshid and Salil Shetty, eds)

VINTAGE

Vintage is an imprint of the Penguin Random House group of companies whose addresses can be found at global.penguinrandomhouse.com

Published by Penguin Random House India Pvt. Ltd
4th Floor, Capital Tower 1, MG Road,
Gurugram 122 002, Haryana, India

First published in Vintage by Penguin Random House India 2025

Copyright © Samruddha Bharat Foundation 2025
The copyright for the individual essays vests with the respective contributors.

All rights reserved

10 9 8 7 6 5 4 3 2 1

This anthology of essays is a work of non-fiction. The views and opinions expressed in the essays are those of the respective authors only and do not reflect or represent the views and opinions held by any other person. The essays in the book are based on a variety of sources, including published materials and interviews and interactions conducted by the respective authors with the persons mentioned in the essays. They reflect each author's own understanding and conception of such materials and/or can be verified by research and the facts are as reported by them which have been verified to the extent possible, and the publishers are not in any way liable for the same. The objective of this book or any of its essays is not to hurt any sentiments or be biased in favour of or against any particular person, region, caste, society, gender, creed, nation or religion.

Please note that no part of this book may be used or reproduced in any manner for the purpose of training artificial intelligence technologies or systems.

ISBN 9780670093052

Typeset in Bembo Std by Manipal Technologies Limited, Manipal
Printed at Thomson Press India Ltd, New Delhi

This book is sold subject to the condition that it shall not, by way of trade or otherwise, be lent, resold, hired out or otherwise circulated without the publisher's prior consent in any form of binding or cover other than that in which it is published and without a similar condition including this condition being imposed on the subsequent purchaser.

www.penguin.co.in

# City Limits

The Crisis of Urbanization

*Edited by*

# Tikender Panwar

**VINTAGE**
An imprint of Penguin Random House

# Contents

Series Editors' Note      vii

Introduction: The Hollow Promise of Neoliberal Urbanization
    Tikender Panwar      xiii

Right to the City: Unleashing India's Untapped Capital
    Ajay Maken      1

Demolition City: Planning Violations and the Erosion of Housing Rights
    Aravind Unni and Evita Das      23

Urbanization, Migration and Reclassification: A Special Focus on West Bengal and the City of Siliguri
    Asok Bhattacharya      47

On Homelessness
    Indu Prakash Singh      55

Conceptual Limitations: Analysing the Approach to Housing Projects for the Urban Poor
    Kanishka Prasad and Vertika Chaturvedi      68

New Governance Regimes and Urban Development
    Mathew Idiculla      83

Inclusive Urbanization
  *Romi Khosla*   102

The Urban Commons Outlook: A Vision for Transformative and Inclusive Indian Cities
  *Seema Mundoli and Harini Nagendra*   121

Whose Town Is It Anyway?: Urban Inequality in the Face of Climate Change
  *Vishnu M.J., Kavya Michael and Tanvi Deshpande*   135

Notes   149
About the Contributors   201
About Samruddha Bharat Foundation   207

# Series Editors' Note

Psychologists tell us that the only true enemies we have are the faces looking back at us in the mirror. Today, we in India need to take a long, hard look at ourselves in the mirror. With either actual or looming crises in every branch of government, at every level, be it central, state or local; with nearly every institution failing; with unemployment at historically high rates; with an ecosystem ready to implode; with a healthcare system in a shambles; with an education system on the brink of collapse; with gender, caste and class inequities unabating; with civil society increasingly characterized by exclusion, intolerance and violence; with our own minorities living in fear; our hundreds of millions of fellow citizens in penury; and with few prospects for the innumerable youth of this nation—in the face of all these increasingly intractable problems, the reflection is not sightly. Our true enemies are not external, not Pakistani terrorists or Bangladeshi migrants, but our own selves: our own lack of imagination, communication, cooperation and dedication towards achieving the India of our destiny and dreams.

Our Constitution, as the Preamble so eloquently attests, was founded upon the fundamental values of the dignity of the individual and the unity of the nation, envisioned in relation to a radically egalitarian justice. These bedrock ideas, though perhaps especially pioneered by the likes of Jawaharlal Nehru, Dr B.R. Ambedkar, M.K. Gandhi, Maulana Azad, Sardar Patel, Sarojini Naidu, Jagjivan Ram, R. Amrit Kaur, Ram Manohar Lohia and others, emerged as a broad consensus among the many founders of this nation, cutting across divergent social and political ideologies. Giving shape to that vision, the architects of modern India strove to ensure that each one of us is accorded equal opportunities to live with dignity and security, has equitable access to a better life and is an equal partner in this nation's growth.

Yet, today, we find these most basic constitutional principles under attack. Nearly all the public institutions that were originally created in order to fight against dominance and subservience are in the process of subversion, creating new hierarchies instead of dismantling them, generating inequities instead of ameliorating them. Government policy merely pays lip service to egalitarian considerations, while the actual administration of 'justice' and implementation of laws are in fact perpetuating precisely the opposite: illegality, criminality, corruption, bias, nepotism and injustice of every conceivable stripe. And the rapid rise of social intolerance and manifold exclusions (along the lines of gender, caste, religion, etc.) effectively whittle down and even sabotage an inclusive conception of citizenship, polity and nation.

In spite of these and all the other unmentioned but equally serious challenges posed at this moment, there are in fact new sites for socio-political assertion re-emerging. There are new calls arising for the reinstatement of the letter and spirit of our Constitution, not just normatively (where we battle things out ideologically) but also practically (the battle at the level of policy articulation and implementation). These calls are not simply partisan, nor are they exclusionary or zero-sum. They witness the wide participation of youth, women, the historically disadvantaged in the process of finding a new voice, minorities, members of majority communities and progressive individuals all joining hands in solidarity.

We at the Samruddha Bharat Foundation proudly count ourselves among them. The Foundation's very raison d'être has been to take serious cognizance of India's present and future challenges, and to rise to them. Over the past few years, we have constituted numerous working groups to critically rethink social, economic and political paradigms to encourage a transformative spirit in India's polity. Over 400 of India's foremost academics, activists, professionals and policymakers across party lines have constructively engaged in this process. We have organized and assembled inputs from *jan sunwais* (public hearings) and *jan manchs* (public platforms) that we conducted across several states, and discussed and debated these ideas with leaders of fourteen progressive political parties, in an effort to set benchmarks for a future common minimum programme. The overarching idea has been to try to breathe new life and spirit into the cold and self-serving logic of political and administrative processes, linking them to and informing them by grassroots realities, fact-based research and social experience, and actionable social–scientific knowledge. And to do all of this with harmony and heart, with sincere emotion and national feeling.

In order to further disseminate these ideas, both to kick-start a national dialogue and to further build a consensus on them, we are bringing out this set of fourteen volumes highlighting innovative ideas that seek to deepen and further the promise of India. This is not an academic exercise; we do not merely spotlight structural problems, but also propose disruptive solutions to each of the pressing challenges that we collectively face. All the essays, though authored by top academics, technocrats, activists, intellectuals and so on, have been written purposively to be accessible to a general audience, whose creative imagination we aim to spark and whose critical feedback we intend to harness, leveraging it to further our common goals.

The inaugural volume has been specifically dedicated to our norms, to serve as a fresh reminder of our shared values and principles, collective heritage and resources. Titled *Vision for a Nation: Paths and Perspectives*, it champions a plural, inclusive, just, equitable and prosperous India, and is committed to individual dignity, which is the foundation of the unity and vibrancy of the nation.

The thirteen volumes that follow turn from the normative to the concrete. From addressing the problems faced by diverse communities—Adivasis, Dalit Bahujans, Other Backward Classes (OBCs)—as well as women and minorities, to articulating the challenges that we face with respect to jobs and unemployment, urbanization, healthcare and a rigged economy, to scrutinizing our higher education system or institutions more broadly, each volume details some ten specific policy solutions promising to systemically treat the issue(s), transforming the problem at a lasting structural level, not just a superficial one. These innovative and disruptive policy solutions flow from the authors' research, knowledge and experience, but they are especially characterized by their unflinching commitment to our collective normative understanding of who we can and ought to be.

The volumes that look at the concerns, needs and aspirations of the Shudras, Dalits, Adivasis and women particularly look at how casteism has played havoc with India's development and stalled the possibility of the progressive transformation of Indian society. They first analyse how these sections of society have faced historical and structural discrimination against full participation in Indian spiritual, educational, social and political institutions for centuries. They also explore how the reforms that some of our epoch-making socio-political thinkers like Gautama Buddha, M.K. Gandhi, Jawaharlal Nehru and Dr B.R. Ambedkar foregrounded are being systematically reversed by regressive forces and the ruling elite because of their ideological proclivities. These volumes therefore strive to address some of the most glaring social questions that India faces from a modernist perspective and propose a progressive blueprint that will secure spiritual, civil and political liberties for one and all.

What the individual volumes aim to offer, then, are navigable road maps for how we may begin to overcome the many specific challenges that we face, guiding us towards new ways of working cooperatively to rise above our differences, heal the wounds in our communities, recalibrate our modes of governance and revitalize our institutions. Cumulatively, however, they achieve something of even greater synergy, greater import: they reconstruct that India of our imagination, of our aspirations, the India reflected in the constitutional preamble that we all surely want to be a part of.

Let us put aside that depiction of a mirror with an enemy staring back at us. Instead, together, we help to construct a whole new set of images. One where you may look at your nation and see your individual identity and dignity reflected in it, and when you look within your individual self, you may find the pride of your nation residing there.

*Aakash Singh Rathore, Mridula Mukherjee,*
*Pushparaj Deshpande and Syeda Hameed*

# Introduction

## The Hollow Promise of Neoliberal Urbanization

*Tikender Panwar*

### 'Will Live on Salt'

Bihar and Uttar Pradesh (UP) migrants refused to return to the cities of Rajkot and Surat in 'vibrant Gujarat'. The migrants said they were disowned by these cities. Such agony is not unique to migrants from UP and Bihar, as reported in the media; rather, this pain is universally felt across India.

A catastrophe of unparalleled proportions was witnessed during the lockdown period in India, which began on 25 March 2020 and continued for more than two months. The nationwide lockdown, announced by Prime Minister Narendra Modi , was a means to help us fight the 'war' against Covid-19. But the irony is that only four hours were given to the people to prepare themselves for the lockdown.

Why was it a catastrophe? This is because it exhibited the horrifying realities of urban India. It challenged the very foundation of urbanization in India. This period, without a doubt, proved and substantiated that our cities, over time, have become highly exclusionary and that our model of urbanization, i.e., urban planning and governance, is completely unsustainable.

Quite naturally, immediately after the lockdown was announced, millions of migrant workers started to walk back to their homes in rural India. Some of them walked for weeks on end. They set out on their journey back home because they knew that they would have starved to death had they stayed on in the cities. There are gory, heart-rending tales that emerged during those months. A migrant woman delivered a baby on the road while walking back home and then resumed her journey; sixteen migrant workers, for whom the only GPS guide to reach home was the railway track, were crushed to death by a goods train when they fell asleep on the track owing to fatigue and exhaustion.[1]

More than 400 non-Covid-19 deaths occurred in India during the lockdown period.[2] These deaths were because of hunger, accidents, exhaustion and even suicides. Apart from that, nearly 321 migrant workers died in road accidents while returning home; the victims were either walking on the streets or travelling en masse on other modes of transport, such as trucks.[3]

Amid such tragic reports, there emerged stories of exemplary relief work by individuals, groups, civil society organizations and even a few state governments. Kerala, for instance, ran thousands of community kitchens for migrant workers. Interestingly, in an affidavit filed by the Ministry of Home Affairs (MHA) in the Supreme Court of India, it was mentioned that 65 per cent of the total relief and shelter camps in India were run by the Kerala state. Ironically, in a few states like Gujarat, 74 per cent of the relief camps were run by civil society groups.[4] But such camps and noble interventions organized by individuals and groups just could not stop the process of 'reverse migration'. Why?

The answer lies in another question. Why is it that even for a few days or weeks, the cities could not hold their workers? The same workers who built these cities, its roads, parks, buildings, gardens, polished diamonds for the rich, spun cloth, wove it, provided food and so on. Was it just the fear of the coronavirus that catapulted them to the streets leading back to their homes, thus further exacerbating their vulnerability to the disease? Or was it our city development model that was responsible for this reverse migration march?

The Centre for Monitoring Indian Economy (CMIE) has released a report that has two important revelations.[5] Firstly, the urban unemployment rate during the Covid-19 lockdown period shot up to 27 per cent, and nearly 120 million jobs were lost. The second part has a greater implication. This part of the report deals with the rate of the urban worker's 'willingness to work'. This rate fell from nearly 70 per cent to as low as 34 per cent. Now this is astonishing. Most migrant workers in the urban centres do not just want to stay in the cities and work. They are determined to go back to their villages. They'd rather 'live on salt, but not return to the cities'. The underlying fact is that the Indian state has miserably failed to sustain the poor and marginalized migrant workers in the cities.

This exposes the hollowness of the claims made in the past—claims for sustainable urbanization, housing for all, smart cities, inclusive growth, etc. But why have the cities, which offer visions and aspirations for a better quality of life, better employment, education and healthcare, etc., become places of exclusion and even hatred for a section of the people?

Is it that Covid-19 precipitated a long-drawn, simmering discontent in the cities? Or was the reverse migration just a fallout of the pandemic, a temporary phase?

Let us try to explore more of this. And for that we need to understand the process of urbanization and city development in India over the last few decades.

## Urban India

According to the 2011 census, 32 per cent of India's population live in urban centres. If non-statutory towns are also considered, which are almost equal to the formal urban settlements (around 4500), then the people living in urban India are more than the number recorded in the census data.[6] The rate of increase in the urban population was recorded higher than that of the rural population in the 2011 census. There are nearly 40 per cent people living in urban agglomerations; however, the next census would record the exact numbers. Cities in India contribute 66 per cent to the national GDP, and nearly 90 per cent of the government revenue comes from urban India.[7]

Over the years, rather decades, especially since the late 1980s, one of the important features of Indian cities has been the humongous amount of surplus generated. There is expropriation of capital and the conventional mode of surplus generation has metamorphosed over the last forty years. There is nothing wrong in the generation of surplus in a capitalist economy; after all, the generation and appropriation of surplus happen to be its driving force. Hence, this is not a matter of great concern.

But what has happened in the recent period is unheard of even in a capitalist economy. In a capitalist economy, surplus wealth is generated in the production process. Therefore, every commodity so produced has an exchange value. But there are certain products that are considered to be of 'use value' for society and individuals and cannot be commoditized. Take, for example, water, education, health, etc. Is water a right or a need? According to the Washington Consensus, if water is a need, then the 'state' and its apparatus are not obliged to provide it.[8] The need can be fulfilled by many players, including large corporations in the market.

In fact, one of the major shifts in the portfolio of some of the large transnational corporations (TNC) over the past three decades globally has to do with the fact that they have shifted their investments from finance to utilities and services. The cities that are responsible for providing some of the essential services have either been coerced, or incapacitated in this regard, to allow the utilities to be run by large TNCs. The major share of capitalist appropriation or generation of surplus takes place in this form, and the cities are becoming facilitators to this.

What we are experiencing is the commoditization of basic services, such as education, health, IT, etc. Massive expropriation and appropriation of the surplus value is generated in this exercise.[9] While the process of concentration of capital was accelerating, there was actually a slowdown in the generation of new production and employment. So, in other words, the largest TNCs were generating their profits not because of production but because of the cannibalization of pre-existing production capacity.

Of the 100 largest TNCs by 2006, 20 per cent were into services; the earlier figure was just 7 per cent (1997).[10] In the United Kingdom, in 2008, outsourced public services accounted for nearly 6 per cent of the GDP, which was an increase of 126 per cent from 1997 to 2006.[11]

The post-neoliberal era has changed the character of capitalism, where maximization of profit takes place not owing to production but because of the predatoriness of capital, which is financial, like the bundling up of housing credit, commoditizing services and likewise. This has also changed the character of the class from essentially production to a varied form.

As Nik Theodore, Jamie Peck and Neil Brenner point out, neoliberalism is marked by 'deregulation of state control over industry, assaults on organised labor, the reduction of corporate taxes, the privatization of public services and assets, the dismantling of social assistance programmes, the enhancement of international capital mobility, and the intensification of inter-locality competition'.[12]

This phase of development is quite evident in Indian cities, accentuating inequity. Corresponding to this form of development, there has been fragmentation in the working class and its politics after the 1990s. The bargaining strength of the working class in the cities has reduced substantially. The cities are being transformed into centres of capitalist reproduction rather than production. More ancillarization and nuclearization has taken place in the production and social domains.

The informal sector, rather an overall informalization, has commanded the city affairs.

Most Indian cities have the following features:[13]

1. Distress migration is large. The agrarian crisis has increased demographic pressures. Instead of getting jobs in the organized sector, workers are pushed to finding jobs in the construction sector, or as rickshaw pullers, street vendors, etc.
2. Eleven million are employed in the organized sector, factories; 30 million in other organized-sector employment; and 12 million in the private sector. Regular employment in public sector has shrunk by 2 million.
3. The large army of unemployed people helps the ruling class to suppress the wages with no trend of increasing them. This is done to maximize profit.
4. Various methods are being used to suppress wages. Laws are being enacted or amended to further rob the workers. The Industrial Disputes Act, Trade Unions Act, and others are being diluted in the interest of capitalists. Similarly, special investment zones (SEZs) have discarded and, in fact, banned the formation of unions. The latest development in this area has been the decision taken by a few state governments to get rid of the some of the provisions of labour laws.
5. New methods are being adopted to loot the working class under the guise of modernizing them.

6. Even in the organized sector, massive outsourcing is practised. Many new categories have been formed: on-the-job trainees and long-term trainee employees (LTTE). In one Japanese firm, there are 1080 trainees and just seventy-three regular workers. In 2011–12, 77.5 per cent in the organized sector had no written contract with the employer; 2.43 per cent had a contract for just one year. The condition of women workers is worse. Among the women, 91 per cent had no written contract. Informalization in the formal sector has increased substantially. From 2003–04 to 2009–10, the share of directly employed workers grew by 5.4 per cent, whereas that of contract workers grew by 12.4 per cent, and the share now is above 30 per cent. Outsourcing is another important phenomenon being practised in the formal sector.
7. The unorganized sector constitutes 94 per cent of the total workers. Of course, this also includes agricultural workers. Their work differs in terms of skill, gender, caste, place of work, etc. The unorganized sector workers have very little protection related to their wages. In 2011–12, 93 per cent of the casual workers were not eligible for social security benefits. Because of the privatization of health services, this class of workers has been forced depend on huge debts.
8. Home-based workers, self-employed workers and scheme-based workers are all partial forms of employment, which is on the rise.

The cities are crying for large-scale investments for social and material infrastructure, but in the absence of public spending (the total urban expenditure is just 1 per cent of the GDP in the country compared to over 20 per cent in the capitalist world),[14] there is hardly anything to glorify about this shift. The partial support offered by smart and AMRUT (Atal Mission for Rejuvenation and Urban Transformation) cities, which demands an unclear and equal contribution from residents, has exacerbated existing vulnerabilities.

All of this has, over a period of time, led to a widening of the inequality gap in urban India. According to an Oxfam report,[15] in 2017, the gap between the top 10 per cent asset holders and the bottom 10 per cent in rural India was 500 times, whereas in urban India it was a staggering 50,000 times.[16] Today, just fifty-two individuals in the country hold wealth that is equivalent to the entire budget of the country.[17]

Three major areas have widened the inequity in the cities and precipitated the reverse migration flow. Firstly, the reduced capacity of the working people to bargain and reclaim their right in the city; secondly, the privatization of utilities and services such as health, education, etc., and thirdly, housing being a distant dream for working people.

The bargaining capacity of the working people vis-à-vis the employer and the state has reduced substantially. Bargaining strength meant a fair amount of redistributive policy and intervention for better living. However, with the change in the character of the working class in the cities, more so in the informal sector, this capacity has reduced. As Pratap Bhanu Mehta, in one of his recent articles, pointed out, 'It is a myth that India's labour laws increased Indian labour's bargaining power.'[18] As brilliant papers by Aditya Bhattacharjea of the Delhi School of Economics showed, Indian labour's wages have stagnated, there has been a massive decrease in strikes and lockouts since the 1980s, and factories with a hundred or more workers experienced more variability in employment than smaller firms. So the idea that Indian labour's bargaining power was an obstacle to India's industrialization is errant nonsense.

Another interesting report, published by Aziz Premji University, highlights the precarious condition of the worker in cities:

During the past three decades there has been a massive increase in the total wealth that has been generated in the country. The cities contribute roughly 70 per cent of it. However, the distribution of this wealth in the form of various social securities has weakened. According to the Azim Premji University's Center for Sustainable Development report, among the regular wage earners more than 57 per cent have been earning less than Rs 10,000 per month. Around 59.3 per cent casual workers are getting wages less than Rs 5,000. If another 25 per cent of wage bracket of Rs 5,001-7,500 is added then around 84.3 per cent casual workers are getting less than Rs 7,500 as wage.[19]

This is not the sustainable city-development model that leads to phenomenally high inequity.

Health, education and some other social security services have also robbed the urban worker from his asset-holding capacity. The health sector has performed particularly poorly—the current health expenditure of both state and Central governments is about 2.1 per cent of the GDP, against 1.6 per cent in the fiscal year 2021,[20] whereas the WHO's recommended minimum is 5 per cent.

Public health expenditures at 1.04 per cent of the GDP in 2012–13 is far below the average of low- and middle-income countries and the WHO's recommended minimum. Overall, the public health sector is in a state of neglect, while the private sector accounts for 80 per cent of outpatient and 60 per cent of inpatient care, making India one of the most privatized systems in the world.[21] Publicly financed health insurance schemes have been rolled out to mitigate the burden of out-of-pocket expenses on healthcare, but these programmes have left care provision open to private companies. Private hospitals benefit most from these publicly funded schemes, distorting the very structure of the health system by starving primary care facilities to the benefit of private secondary and tertiary care. And while health insurance has the explicit purpose of protecting patients from 'catastrophic' healthcare expenses, the actual depth of coverage under these schemes is poor.

One very visible manifestation of the private takeover of health services is the mushrooming of corporate hospitals. Hospital chains' revenues have grown exponentially in recent years. The rules of the game have shifted from promoting public health to mere profiteering as made possible by corporate-friendly regulations.[22]

Reclaiming the right to health, as reclaiming the right to food and water and housing, is essential for the sustainability of cities. But our health sector is turning out to be one of the primary sectors for profit maximization. The irony is that despite having a large share of outdoor and indoor patients, when it came to meeting the crisis of the pandemic, the private health sector was completely missing in action.[23]

Similarly, the education sector and service charges on other essential utilities have limited the urban worker's capacity to lay claim to assets and sustain himself. Take, for example, the water privatization drive, both direct and indirect. In the urban reforms process, the city governments are mandated to procure the cost of production of water from its citizens. The water production varies from city to city. It may cost Rs 10 per kilolitre, while in a mountain town, the cost may even jump to Rs 150 per kilolitre. It is just impossible for the citizens to bear such a huge burden, and the result is huge inequity even in water access. There is another form of privatization and cost escalation in water utility. And that is through the business of selling water-purifying gadgets, Reverse Osmosis (RO) machines,, etc. Though it is the mandate of the water supplier or the municipality responsible to distribute potable water, water companies end up amassing huge wealth on this issue. In a survey conducted in Delhi, the RO business was found to be as large as Rs 2500 crore per year.[24]

The onus of providing potable water falls on the Municipal Corporation of Delhi; if that is done with a formal protocol, massive wealth generated from the people can be saved.

Another important factor making cities unsustainable is the question of habitat. Housing in neoliberal capitalism is a commodity that does not become a universal right. Though the national and city governments made tall claims in Quito, at the Habitat III Conference, while approving the New Urban Agenda in 2016 on the right to adequate housing, the reality belies these claims. Paragraph 31 of the agenda states:

> We commit to promote national, sub-national, and local housing policies that support the progressive realization of the right to adequate housing for all as a component of the right to an adequate standard of living, that address all forms of discrimination and violence, prevent arbitrary forced evictions, and that focus on the needs of the homeless, persons in vulnerable situations, low income groups, and persons with disabilities, while enabling participation and engagement of communities and relevant stakeholders, in the planning and implementation of these policies including supporting the social production of habitat, according to national legislations and standards.[25]

## Gentrification as a Form of Exclusion

Our present-day city planning and development are rampantly leading to gentrification and further making housing beyond the reach of the common people; workers and especially those in the informal sectors do not even qualify. It is primarily for this reason that there has been a substantial increase in the number of slum residents. The major metro cities of India, and most Tier-1 and Tier-2 cities, have a large proportion of people living in slums—around 25–45 per cent of their total population.[26]

Raj Rewal, architect and urban designer, believes that urban design is a civic responsibility[27] and should not be privatized. In an interview given to an English daily, he pointed out that the Indian system, which allowed public buildings and social low-cost housing to be designed by architects through competitions, has devolved into the process of auctioning plots to builders without any urban design criteria. 'This has resulted in haphazard development. Akbar and Jai Singh, for instance, responsible for Fatehpur Sikri and Jaipur, had high standards of civic urban governance. In these cities, visual design with its humane concerns was honoured and implemented. Unfortunately, city planning in India has been largely handed over to international mercenary management consultancy firms, who have scarce knowledge of local issues.'[28]

The cities are given two options: gentrification or disinvestment. Though there are other options as well, the power of real estate pushes the cities towards this binary, and most cities choose gentrification. Ipsita Chatterjee, in her book *Displace: Revolution and New Urban Politics*, defines gentrification as 'the theft of space from labour and its conversion into spaces of profit'.[29] Gentrification is a process by which capital is reinvested in urban neighbourhoods, and poorer residents and their cultural products are displaced and replaced by richer people and their preferred aesthetics and amenities. Samuel Stein in his seminal work, *The Capital City*, explores why gentrification takes place in cities:

> As the complex process of deindustrialization unfolded, capital became both more mobile and, ironically, more grounded: tariffs dropped, firms internationalized and corporate globalization took hold while, at the same time, investments in land and buildings filled the literal and figurative space left by urban industrial flight. Real estate went from being a secondary to a primary source of urban capital accumulation.

This switch is the genesis of gentrification in the United States.³⁰

Still, the story of Indian cities is slightly at variance to the processes of real estate development and gentrification in the US. In India, the accumulation of capital happens through the process of dispossession. And the major issues here have been the eviction of the poor from the slums and the use of land meant for public purposes for real estate development.

Take, for example, the following transformation in the Delhi Development Authority's plan of action. According to D. Arsher Ghertner, in his article 'India's Urban Revolution: Geographies of Displacement beyond Gentrification':

> While the timing has varied from state to state, Indian cities have witnessed a gradual erosion of their socialistic land policies since the late 1990s. In 1999 the DDA launched its first commercial auctions, selling 'underutilized' land (parks, vacant land) that it had acquired for public purposes in order to generate revenue and encourage capital investment. In 2000 the DDA initiated its Freehold Conversion Program, which allowed leaseholders to obtain freehold rights, thereby setting in place a private property system—that is, land could be bought and sold in an unregulated market—for the first time since the DDA was established in 1955. When the Delhi Master Plan was updated in 2007, it cleared the books of the last remnants of the policy of socialized land by deleting the passages mandating land reservations for the urban poor. Fifty years ago the DDA was set up to prevent the speculative land practices of a developer named Delhi Lease and Finance. Today that same company, now known simply as DLF, has become the largest developer in Delhi (and in all of India), confirming the end of Delhi as a public city—a pattern echoed in the 'speculative urbanism' common across India (Goldman, 2011).³¹

The diminishing role of the Indian state in providing housing to its people and allowing real estate players to rule to roost was among the defining factors shaping the country's history after the 1990s. According to Professor Ravi Srivastava from the Institute of Human Development, 'For any developing nation, the bare minimum of 25 per cent of housing must be provided through public housing and the private or informal housing market can cater to the 75 per cent. However, in the Indian scenario, the condition is extremely precarious and the formal housing has fallen from 6 per cent to 3 per cent in the last six years during the Modi raj.'[32]

According to Gautam Bhan of the Indian Institute for Human Settlements, 95 per cent of slum houses do not require demolition and can sustain with minor alterations and reinforcements.[33] The state, in case it agrees to regularize the slums, can give a great fillip to the housing problem of the poor in the cities. Once land tenure rights are awarded to slum dwellers, there will be considerable improvement in the economic condition of urban workers.

Another notable feature of urban informal workers is that a large number of them are homeless. A recent survey conducted by the Indo–Global Social Service Society (IGSSS) at shelters for the homeless across Delhi found that 90–95 per cent living in these facilities are workers and not beggars. The majority of them are construction workers, or those working in the hospitality and other unorganized sectors. The Pradhan Mantri Awas Yojana announced by the Central government has failed to meet its targets and cannot be an alternative to public housing.[34]

In such a scenario, without strong affirmative action, the idea of a sustainable city will never become a reality. The democratization of surplus is crucial for our cities to be made liveable. It can happen through the collective strength of the working people and/or through policy interventions at the city, provincial and national levels. The flow of policy interventions can happen through strengthening the process of city development in a participatory mode. The 'right to the city', is not just a slogan for politicians; it is a call for action, where city planning and development are done in a participatory way, and where a common resident, too, can become a part of the planning process, besides laying claim to the assets and reclaiming urban spaces for themselves.

The city council can be one of the tools to achieve affirmative action and democratization of surplus. But the developments over the last six years have further robbed the capacity of our cities to govern themselves independently and democratically; at the most, they are turning out to be adjuncts of the provincial governments.

## Urban Governance: The Journey from 74th Constitutional Amendment to Smart Cities

This journey can be defined in one sentence as: 'From cities being managers to cities becoming entrepreneurs.' Such is the changed or metamorphosed role of the cities envisioned for city governance. K.C. Sivaramakrishnan, speaking of the smart city governance model, used to say, 'It is like writing an obituary of the 74th Constitutional Amendment.'[35] Cities are considered engines of growth in themselves, and this is what defines the desired role for them. The transformation of the cities did not just restrict the new economic paradigm, a model with land monetization as the core; rather, it transformed from privatization of the city's assets to privatization of governance in the smart city model. But before we speak of the smart city milestone, it is important to trace the journey of the 74th Constitutional Amendment.

The 74th amendment was brought in the year 1993 and became effective in 1995. The Indian Constitution was initially focused on the governance model at the levels of the

Centre and the state; an established model of governance in cities and villages was not constitutionally defined. The 74th amendment focused on a few important areas/subjects in this regard and mandated that a few functions, such as planning, civic utilities, etc., must be dealt with by the city, town and urban local bodies.

Under the 12th Schedule of the Indian Constitution, eighteen items were supposed to be transferred to the local bodies. Though there were aspersions cast at the inception itself, that the amendment spoke about empowering city governments without giving them financial power, nevertheless, it provided a space for cities and their leaders to engage.[36] A review of the amendment was done by a committee led by K.C. Sivaramakrishnan, a former bureaucrat and former chairperson of the Centre for Policy Research, Delhi, of which I was also a member. Once of the important findings of the review was that the cities and small towns across India, though governed by city governments, are actually controlled by state-run parastatals and are guided by consultant-driven policies. There are two functions out of the eighteen that are universally performed by the cities: issuing birth and death certificates, and garbage collection, i.e., solid waste management.

Leaving aside small towns and cities, which are anyway limited by their incapacity to perform, even large metropolitan cities are actually controlled by parastatals. Take, for example, Delhi. The land in Delhi belongs to the Delhi Development Authority (DDA), a parastatal, non-elected body, not answerable to the city government and directly controlled by the national government. The master plan of Delhi is not prepared by the city government; it is prepared and revised by the DDA. Similarly, in major Indian cities, the town planning/city planning is done by such development authorities: the Mumbai Metropolitan Region Development Authority, Greater Mohali Development Authority, Calcutta Development Authority and so on. The city plan is made at the behest of these non-political bodies, and a nexus is built up between the planners, consultants and the political class ruling either at the national or at state levels.

Large consultancy firms become part of the city development plans and can even become instrumental in writing the mobility, sanitation and greenhouse gas emission plans. Most of these plans have recommendations for capital-intensive technology, instead of low-cost, localized and decentralized solutions. Take two examples. There is a rush in the cities to manage solid waste through the consultant-driven advice of high-technological solutions. Irrespective of the fact that different cities are located in different geographical locations, and are of different sizes and density, one of the suggested solutions to manage solid waste in cities is to set up capital-intensive 'waste to energy plants'. What people don't realize is that such plants are not only ecologically unsustainable but are also financially untenable. City residents are then forced to pay user charges for these, which in some places are exorbitantly high.

The second example has to do with mobility and policies related to transit-oriented development. The consultants preparing city mobility plans for various Tier-1 and Tier-2 cities recommend metro rail as the solution to the mobility crisis.[37] The cost, i.e., capital and operational cost, is nearly five times that of a bus rapid transit system and its corridor. A large section of the population is excluded from the metro rail owing to the higher cost of travel. Similarly, there is encroachment on the right of pedestrians by subsidizing mobility for the middle class by laying big flyovers and widening the roads. The widening of the roads is done by acquiring land or even demolishing houses in the vicinity. Invariably, most cities opt for such proposals and solutions without realizing that, far from increasing the pace of mobility, such 'enhancements' end up slowing it down further. Quite interestingly, the consultants driving cities to such plans also promise high investments, provided their plans are approved in the desired manner. It is a strong nexus, which has made deep roots in the governance structure.

There are many other instances where either parastatals are running the utilities or the state has abdicated its responsibility and has passed this work to the private sector.

In 2019, a national-level roundtable on the 74th Constitutional Amendment Act was held at the IGSSS. It was called 'Looking Back at 25 years' and highlighted the issues missing from the 74th amendment, especially the issue of migration to the cities.[38] It also pointed out the need for a people's governance model of wards and *mohalla sabhas* for city planning.

A state-wise substantive review of the amendment was done by PRAJA in Delhi. According to Partha Mukopadhyay of the Centre for Policy Research:

> . . . the PRAJA work is a first real examination of how the 74th amendment has worked out across all Indian states, not from looking at the official documents but from actually talking to the people who are supposed to make it work. This kind of local empiricism is very valuable and unfortunately not enough is done in the implementation of the 74th constitutional amendment.[39]

If one looks at the trajectory of urban schemes in recent times—11th Finance Commission, Jawaharlal Nehru National Urban Renewal Mission (JNNURM), Smart Cities and AMRUT—invariably, in all these schemes, one finds a greater intervention of the Central government, though urban development is a state subject. The Central government, through these schemes, selected projects that were partially funded from the Central kitty, and an equal amount was to be generated by the state and the city governments. But going by the capacities of the state and city governments, it was virtually impossible for them to generate a matching grant, and hence they created an alternative methodology of generating revenue from land. The conditions put forward by the Centre further diluted the provisions of the 74th amendment.[40]

Speaking about this issue, Professor Amita Bhide of the Tata Institute of Social Sciences, Mumbai, said:

> As per the Grant Thornton evaluation study of JNNURM, which studied 25 states across the country, found that only 8 states had transferred all the functions in the 12th Schedule to the urban local bodies prior to JNNURM, and post-JNNURM 11 states were found to do so. If we start moving to specific aspects of this, then with respect to water supply and sanitation 10 states in the pre-JNNURM period and 1 state post-JNNURM. With respect to city planning, 8 states had transferred prior to JNNURM, and 2 states post-JNNURM. In terms of formation of District Planning Committees (DPC) which is supposed to be a critical part of coordinating resources at the district level, 11 states had done it in the pre-JNNURM period and 3 state post-JNNURM. With respect to formation of metropolitan planning committees, only West Bengal had done it in the pre-JNNURM states, and 2 more states were added to this list of implementing MPC's. Hence we see that . . . even a major program like JNNURM, which invested funds at such a large level was not able to adhere to the conditionalities per se . . .[41]

According to Ashima Sood, an urban researcher, the 74th amendment was passed to the background as part of the liberalization project, when the process of economic reforms was initiated through the IMF's conditionalities.[42] Decentralization has been playing out against such a backdrop. There is greater integration with the global economy and capital circuits. The deregularization of FDI coming into real estate is an open and stark example of this. With the 2002 guidelines for FDI in townships for construction and infrastructure in place, tremendous capital is pulled into the cities, and we see an integration with the global market. What this means is that the city has become a powerful tool for the state and Central governments.

As Ashima Sood says:

> The idea of competition between cities is central to policy imaginations which are reflected in AMRUT and Smart Cities Mission. AMRUT is a list of 500 of the best cities and Smart Cities constitute a smaller and much glorified category of 100 of India's best cities, and they have positioned themselves among the very best. We talk to policy makers at all levels [about] this vision of competitiveness among cities, and not only within India but internationally. Bombay competes with Shanghai, and Bangalore competes with Singapore, and this notion of competition is so central to policy vision that then the city is in fact a tool for certain kinds of economic logics to be put into motion. On one hand we have this vision of local democracy, a bottom-up perspective of the city of what the cities are like, but against them are powerful forces, which the state governments are very well aware of.[43]

A few years ago, in Hyderabad, Telangana, all the newspapers had a front-page advertisement announcing 'land on platter'—meaning the Government of Telangana was offering industries land on a platter. Therefore, these are forces that are working in contradiction to each other; they are definitely identifiable as adversaries to local democracy.

The notion of competitive cities is the nucleus to cities being entrepreneurs.

## The Smart City

The smart city concept represents a grave threat to fundamental rights and advances won by communities in the evolutionary history of city development. The smart city is an urban development plan that uses data points to automate citywide responsibilities, such as policing, traffic and energy. These plans transfer key decisions from local governments to multinational corporations, while privatizing many urban services traditionally governed by municipal officials. Bloomberg reported that the Internet of Things (IoT) represents a $19 trillion opportunity.[44] *Forbes* estimated that the smart city industry was expected to become a 1.5-trillion-dollar-plus market by 2020.[45] This new industry signals the privatization and financialization of public service provisions, and will accelerate the growth of inequality in our societies by bringing increased convenience and services to the wealthy few at the cost to the public as a whole. The technocratic smart city is curtailing individual freedoms and rights and leading us to an Orwellian future.

The smart city concept is a product of a particular phase of economic development, as stated earlier: this phase of capitalism is widely referred to as neoliberalism.

Smart cities are not merely information and communication technology stacks and policies implemented by the city alone. To deliver on the smart city's promises of value, a city or municipality must develop a complex community of participating organizations across public, private and social sectors. Each participant provides some form of value directly or indirectly and receives value in return. These exchanges of value can take forms such as services or benefits to a city's population, financial exchanges such as fees to technology partners for services rendered to cities, information such as data exchanged with cloud service providers, and intangible benefits such as increased citizen participation in policy creation.

There are many actors in this. These include large corporations known to coordinate with the US government security apparatus (in what's known as the 'NSA Prism' of Amazon, Google, Facebook, Apple, Twitter (now X), AT&T, Verizon,

Cisco and others), as well as industrial players such as IBM and GE, real estate developers and financiers, municipal authorities, public utilities and federal departments of commerce, among others.[46] The Smart Cities Council India, for instance, lists GE, IBM, Qualcomm, MasterCard, Alstrom, Verizon, Cisco, Enel, Microsoft and Thomson Reuters among its diverse set of smart cities technology and infrastructure service providers.[47]

Based on the principle of 'smart convergence', the smart cities' convergence is not restricted to the infrastructural level of the smart city ecosystem. Several of the largest and most prominent smart city technology service providers have taken on financier roles or work with financiers to fund smart city initiatives as well. This, of course, greatly increases the influence and control of each of these participants over smart city implementations, policies and data.[48]

In India, most of government funding allotted for smart cities is actually going into the manufacturing of smart enclaves for the professional class and the middle class (3 per cent of India's population), to separate them from the rest of the city, with its poverty and inconveniences.[49] The enclaves are being sold as utopias with smart grid and solar energy projects, smart metering, rainwater harvesting projects, solid waste management, e-governance, established networks of roads, footpaths, cycle tracks, smart parking and so on. But these utopias are meant only for a very small minority of the urban population. As Neeraj Jain has noted,

> There will be no investment in providing affordable healthcare for the poor by measures such as opening new government hospitals; there will be no investment in providing affordable education for the city's children and youth by opening more good quality government schools and colleges. The Smart City Plan has nothing to do with all this. All that is going to happen is that in the name of making the city 'Smart,'

the private sector will get an opportunity to invest in exotic projects like setting up ultra-modern bus stops and sensors to monitor traffic congestion on roads, and thus make huge profits.[50]

## Undermining the Municipal Authority

The smart city model, particularly in its current form as a top-down imposition of a largely Western technocratic solution to a range of different problems faced by developing countries, can be seen as a new colonial threat. In addition to the obvious economic benefit such a system gives these enormous corporations, there is the issue of their ability to shape cultures and societies. This is quite possibly the most dangerous problem these global conglomerates pose: the subversion of democratic processes and governance systems. For instance, municipal and state authorities' powers of governance are diluted in the interests of ensuring corporate control over developing the smart city.

In the Indian scenario, the smart city policy actively requires the democratically elected local authorities to cede governance powers to a private unelected entity (in the form of a Special Purpose Vehicle—SPV).[51] This has led to fears that these SPVs will misuse their authority, putting private interests before the needs or concerns of local stakeholders.

The importance of the local authority is primarily threefold. First, they represent the local people, generally by being elected and are therefore accountable to their voter base. Second, they tend to comprise the local citizenry, so that local cultures, sentiments, needs and requirements are better represented in urban planning. And third, they are, in general, required to act for the 'public good', as opposed to ensuring private profit. The privatization of democratic governance processes is also problematic, particularly given that 'private enterprises by their nature, pursue profits, and generally seek evasion of democratic procedure, rules, regulations and oversight to that pursuit'.[52]

Professor Alberto Vanolo notes, 'In the smart city, there is apparently little space for people at the margins, and this is particularly evident in cities of the Global South, where there is the risk of increasing the distance between the smart city and areas which exist off the map, off the grid, the so-called "informal city".'[53]

In an article about reimagining the future, environmental activist and author Chris Williams wrote, 'We should ask ourselves the question: What is the purpose of a city? Is it to facilitate and maximize capital accumulation? Or to facilitate and maximize human fulfillment, creativity and happiness?'[54] How we answer that question is determined by who holds social power and which human social values we see as imperative to the well-being of a society.

In the Indian case, many cities, even governed by the ruling party at the Centre, opposed this encroachment of the SPV model of governance. It is strange that the composition of the SPV is such that it is not answerable to the elected council of the city. The chief executive officer and the chairperson of the 'vehicle' is never a mayor of the city.

A review of the implementation of the smart city plan in India proves that it has become a major failure as reported in a query to a question raised in the Rajya Sabha.[55] The recent data collected by the NGO Wada Na Todo Abhiyan (Do Not Break Promises Campaign) has exposed the fallacy and the hollowness of the entire smart cities project.[56] The SPVs have released just 5 per cent of the total sum required for the project that is supposed to be implemented in the shortlisted smart cities. There is not much science required to understand what this means, as just 5 per cent would also quantify a commensurate dose of development in the respective 'smart' cities.

Both the Smart Cities Mission (SCM) and the Atal Mission for Rejuvenation and Urban Transformation (AMRUT) projects, launched in 2015, have faced significant challenges and criticisms in their implementation over the past decade in India. While official reports often highlight successes, independent analyses have pointed to various 'near failures' or significant shortcomings. The SCM was conceptually a flawed project that lacked a clear definition for a 'smart city' in the Indian context, an impulsive top-down approach without sufficient groundwork, and a failure to attract anticipated private and foreign investment. The local bodies, i.e., the city governments, were completely bypassed by the SPVs.[57]

The governance gaps (fragmented development due to independent SPVs), were massive and the weak Urban Local Bodies (ULBs) with insufficient expertise, limited private investment, funding shortfalls, execution delays, lack of urban planning, environmental issues and low citizen participation proved to be a complete misfit in the entire process.[58]

The AMRUT projects were slow in progress and the scheme's focus on a project-oriented approach instead of a holistic approach and potential overlaps with other schemes could not bring in integrated solutions. They were unable to address pollution issues and a non-inclusive governance structure lacking organic participation from elected city governments meant there was no real ownership of the entire scheme.[59]

## Why Could the Smart Cities Project Not Offload?

An important reason is that expecting private players to invest capital where there are no chances of returns is erroneous. They will merrily invest in bigger, metro-like cities, and are doing so, but will avoid smaller or Tier-2 cities. The financial capacity of the cities is so inadequate that more than 80 per cent of them are unable to pay the wage bill of their staff.[60] How can we imagine inviting big players in such cities? The government cannot abdicate its responsibility as a principal investor in such cities—especially when it comes to providing the basic minimum utilities, such as water, sanitation, electricity, roads, etc.

Another crucial factor is the way the smart cities project has been structured. The SPVs have taken control of the smart cities development project. These SPVs are too bureaucrat-centric, with a chief executive officer and a chairperson along with board members, where the elected institution has virtually no standing either to influence or guide them. As a result, the CEOs of the SPVs and the administration heads—mostly mayors—are at loggerheads. Ultimately, the project gets influenced from both the quarters, with neither owning it.[61]

The area-based development (ABD) and pan-city specification in which the smart cities were designed pose another issue. The ABD was supposed to focus on infrastructure projects in a dedicated area—either for retrofitting or for redevelopment or greenfield projects. The majority of cities have opted for redevelopment of their area. The ABD is a very small designated geographical area. Since it does not even comprise more than 2–5 per cent of the entire city, it draws hardly any interest from the residents of the city. It means that the city residents, too, are not very eager to see the fulfilment of such projects under the ABD. The pan-city development plan of the smart cities has focused mainly on the usage of high-speed connectivity to improve smart solutions either for transport or other utilities. Thus, 85 per cent of the budget—if available—would be usurped by just 5 per cent of the area.

## Plausible Alternatives

In the given scenario of the macroeconomic situation where cities are considered as shops and mere entrepreneurs, alternatives have to be advocated in different sectors. Instead of smart cities created to serve private interests, we need an 'Our City Movement' that elevates the needs of the commons. We need to build cities that are democratic and inclusive, that respect privacy and that preserve genuinely public spaces.

How can we build more resilient and more equitable cities? At the moment, smart cities and the Internet of Things are driven by an amoral logic based on Silicon Valley profit motives and a fetishization of technology (what the researcher Evgeny Morozov calls 'technological solutionism').[62] There is nothing inevitable about this, however. Technology will play an important role in urban planning and in constructing the commons, but technology is not the solution in itself, especially when that technology is based on the logic of the market. We can, instead, empower local governance and construct federated systems that enhance political and digital sovereignty.

In the case of smarter traffic management, sensors can detect breakdowns, round-trip time and route suggestions, but this technology doesn't help much if all the city roads are clogged. Instead, if the same investments were made to improve public transportation, such as elevated bus corridors, metro and train systems, the results could be better and serve more people.

Perhaps the smartest of the smart city projects needn't depend exclusively—or even at all—on sensors and computers. At Future Cities, Julia Alexander of Siemens nominated as one of the 'smartest' cities in the world the once-notorious Medellín. Its favelas were reintegrated into the city not with smartphones but with publicly funded sports facilities and a cable car connecting them to the city. 'All of a sudden,' Alexander said, 'you've got communities interacting' in a way they had never done before. Medellín was also named the most innovative city in the world by the Urban Land Institute.[63]

The alternative to the popularly promoted vision of the smart cities will not be a complete negation of technologies. That is neither possible nor pragmatic in an interconnected world. However, technology has to respond to the variety and diversity of city life. A democratic approach to reclaiming our cities for the greater common good should include some of the following features: use of open-source technologies rather than closed, proprietary, market-based systems; platform cooperatives; reclaiming the commons; distributive technologies and so on.

In the housing sector, the shining example of Solapur— where beedi workers, through their cooperative, reclaimed their space in the city and constructed nearly 20,000 houses for themselves—can be replicated. Instead of real estate ruling the roost, cooperative housing for the marginalized has to be a viable option.[64]

More rental housing and the creation of more labour hostels in the cities with a continuous engagement with the city governments have to be sought.

As Francesca Bria aptly writes:

> The new opportunities provided by digital technologies for participation, democracy, transparency and proximity to the citizens, could support a radical democratization of public institutions. However, they are being used for quite opposite aims, for instance promoting the Smart City that promotes 'cosmetic' involvement of citizens but that in reality puts forward a privatised, technocratic and business driven management of the City, pushing technology as the solution to structural problems that in reality require political and economic interventions and an innovative democratic approach.[65]

We want democratization of surplus back in society and a humanistic society for all people. We can construct smart city alternatives that prioritize 'interdependence rather than hyper-individualism, reciprocity rather than dominance, and cooperation rather than hierarchy', as Naomi Klein wrote in *This Changes Everything*.

The integration of technology and urban planning can exemplify the values of real freedom, justice and equality by creating digital-platform ecosystems that serve the masses, not the wealthy few. This is a huge, complex, audacious goal. It requires designing new ecosystems and merging technological innovation with policy expertise. But it is vital for the future of the planet.

We need to align all the open movements—access, data, information, software, operating systems, hardware, infrastructure—to start working on a coherent philosophy of action, with real scenarios and stories fully focused on these new architectures. Only a robust coalition comprising policymakers, technologists, planners and intellectuals can reverse some of the harm created by smart cities and build viable alternatives.

# Right to the City

## Unleashing India's Untapped Capital

*Ajay Maken*

Urbanization is an integral component of India's growth story. Urban areas (both cities and towns) generate over two-thirds of the country's GDP and account for 90 per cent of government revenues. The city in India is also becoming increasingly relevant as a political construct. One hundred and eight Lok Sabha constituencies have an urban population of more than 50 per cent, fifty-four have more than 75 per cent of the electorate residing in urban areas and another twenty-one are fully urban.[1] Additionally, cities in India now house a bulk of India's burgeoning population. To illustrate the point, India's urban population grew from 286 million (Census 2001) to an estimated 377 million.[2] India is projected to add 404 million people to its urban population between 2014 and 2050.[3] In fact, the annual growth in urban population in India between 2010 and 2015 was 1.1 per cent, the highest among the major economies.[4]

Urbanization in India has expanded rapidly as increasing numbers of people migrate to towns and cities in search of economic opportunity. Migrants make up a sizeable chunk of India's urban population, which was last recorded at 35 per cent.[5] (Incidentally, this survey was done for the first time by the United Progressive Alliance (UPA) government.) This has partly to do with sociological factors. For instance, caste, social networks and historical precedents play a powerful role in shaping patterns of migration in India. A large proportion of migrants come from the scheduled caste (SC), scheduled tribe (ST) and other backward caste (OBC) communities, who face discrimination at their villages. But many people also migrate to cities aspiring for a better life, with better livelihoods, incomes and education.

Yet, as the pace and scale of urbanization in India has mushroomed, the quality of life has rapidly deteriorated, especially for those at the bottom of the pyramid. Poor and vulnerable communities migrating into cities experience tremendous pressures caused by the profound economic, social and cultural disruption in their lives. When they come into cities, they are faced with unfamiliar and often hostile conditions. They struggle to feel included in the city and its mainstream activities. They are not afforded any space for the continued existence of their traditional community lifestyles and means of livelihoods, and are expected to transform themselves ontologically to 'fit in'. It has been rightly argued that migrants to cities share 'an experience of subjugation, marginalisation, dispossession, exclusion or discrimination'[6] and are often included into the city unfavourably. They face ghettoization, deepening socio-spatial hierarchies and growing disparities in income, housing and opportunities. They are sometimes unable to access public provisioning through fair price shops, public employment or other forms of social interaction.[7] They are also denied meaningful participation in their communities and thus lose out on the opportunity to fulfil themselves as human beings.[8] This obstruction (whether intentional or because of structural processes) excludes millions of Indians from positions of access and public benefits, as also from upward mobility. Consequently, their politics is still limited to *roti, kapada, makaan* (food, clothing and housing) and has not gone beyond these subsistence issues.

Just to cite one prominent example, it is an unfortunate reality that slums account for one-fourth of all urban housing.[9] On arrival into a city, many migrants are unable to afford proper housing and so, turn to live in slum settlements. Urban slum settlements are generally excluded from public-sector resources, severely limiting access of residents to formal education, healthcare services, and water and sanitation. Only about 47 per cent of the slum population has access to basic sanitation facilities (flush or pit), which means about 35 million people in urban India are living in unsanitary and potentially hazardous conditions. Of the total urban population, about 83 per cent have access to sanitation facilities.[10] Such conditions exacerbate the risks of waterborne diseases, such as cholera, and airborne diseases, such as influenza, pneumonia and tuberculosis. Just to illustrate the sheer enormity of the problem, in Mumbai, more than half the population lives in slums, many of which are situated near employment centres in the heart of the city, unlike in most other developing countries. Here are the figures for the population living in slums in our cities: 18.74 per cent in Delhi, 32.48 per cent in Kolkata, 18.88 per cent in Chennai, 17.23 per cent in Hyderabad and 10.02 per cent in Bengaluru.[11] What's equally shameful for a nation that seeks to be a global leader is that there are roughly 0.9 million homeless people in urban India, in addition to a slum population of roughly 65 million (or 17 per cent of urban India).[12]

This incapacity to actively participate in a city and its mainstream activities can first lead to social exclusion and, ultimately, to marginalization. Meeting the needs of India's soaring urban populations will therefore continue to be a strategic policy matter. Critical issues that need to be addressed are: poor local governance, weak finances, inappropriate planning, massive infrastructure shortages, inadequate public transport systems and major service deficiencies that include erratic water and power supply.

## The Moral Imperative of the State

Given that millions of Indians are struggling to find their place in modern cities, where public processes and utilities have been privatized and where development is driven primarily if not solely by corporations and markets, it is of the utmost importance that cities are inclusive for all Indians, and provide equitable opportunities to each so they can achieve fullness of life. It is, therefore, incumbent on the state to provide housing, education, transportation, jobs, community safety and security, neighbourhood sustainability, environmental justice, as well as the right to culture, celebration, rest and public spaces.

Yet, the state's commitment to urban citizens goes beyond basic rights and access to resources. In 'renewing access to urban life',[13] the state also has to find ways to empower urban citizens to shape the city as they see fit through rights to participation and active civil engagement. It must provide public goods and services that enable citizens to pursue their dreams and aspirations. Public goods and services include both pure public goods as well as goods of social value, for example, clean air, community parks, playgrounds and urban commons. Public goods are those that are required for all persons to be able to live with basic human dignity; they are an intrinsic part of the Directive Principles of State Policy[14] in the Constitution of India. There has been a series of rulings by the Supreme Court of India cumulatively recognizing many of these social and economic rights to be extensions of the fundamental right to life guaranteed under Article 21[15] of the Constitution. The most expansive interpretation of Article 21, which provides a constitutional basis for regarding a wide range of social and economic rights as fundamental rights, came from Justice P.N. Bhagwati:

> The fundamental right to life which is the most precious human right and which forms the arc of all other rights must therefore be interpreted in a broad and expansive spirit so as to invest it with significance and vitality which may endure for years to come and enhance the dignity of the individual and the worth of the human person.[16]

The Supreme Court has also interpreted this to be a positive right. Therefore, if a person enjoys a fundamental right to life, by the same token, she enjoys the right to all that makes a life with dignity possible, such as assured access to nutritious food with dignity, education and healthcare of a certain basic quality, decent work, decent shelter and social protection. Therefore, the state must guarantee equitable and mutually supportive allocation of the budget for the implementation of public policies and the provision of public goods and services. In this way, the idea of public good embraces the core democratic principles of dignity, equity, sustainability and solidarity. The definition of public goods is not static. It is a dynamic process, and it is imperative for policymakers to take adequate political and social action and push the frontiers of the notion of public good, and thereby continuously deepen these very principles.

## The City's Stark Reality

The groups most severely excluded from accessing public goods and services are almost always the same: women, Dalits, adivasis, Muslims and the poor. Members of these groups tend to be either excluded completely from access to public goods, or excluded on unequal and discriminatory terms compared to other sections of society. The consistent exclusion of these communities from just and equitable access to diverse public goods suggests that both in their design and functioning, state institutions, policies and laws tend to discriminate and exploit Indians based on gender, caste, class, religion and disability.

It is no coincidence that housing quality indicators from the 2011 Census[17] indicate significant differences based on caste and tribal status. SCs and STs, and among them, female-headed SC and ST households, have lower quality housing on average. While 53 per cent of all households nationally do not have a latrine within the premises, the figure rises to 66 per cent and 77 per cent for SCs and STs, respectively; and within them, to 78 per cent and 88 per cent for female-headed SC and ST households, respectively. About 82 per cent of all households in India have either open or no drains for wastewater.[18] In low-income and slum settlements in India, it is common to find a preference for male tenants, or witness the exclusion of tenants of certain regions of the country and even a binary inclusion of a particular community.[19]

This extends to other sectors as well, wherein citizens are unfavourably included on the margins of the city because of socio-economic variables. For example, between 2001 and 2011, an average of 1.4 crore people migrated into cities each year.[20] This sustained migration into cities has fuelled a corresponding demand for affordable housing. Affordable housing is at the heart of building inclusive cities. More than 90 per cent of the housing shortage in urban India is faced by economically weaker sections and low-income groups. In Mumbai alone, approximately 50,000 housing units are required per year. Yet, a 500-square-foot house in Mumbai costs over Rs 1 crore on average today. This is partly because housing is conceived as a commercial venture, not an essential public good, and partly because citizens routinely face discrimination on the basis of religion and caste.[21]

But it is equally true that the state also unfavourably excludes citizens, overtly and covertly. This is partly because some governance structures actively deny citizens equal access to the city and its promise. These tend to be granted or withheld on the basis of income, religious and caste determinants, and, in more recent years, on the basis of ideological inclination.

A classic example of the latter is the 2009 amendment to the Gujarat (Prohibition of Transfer of Immovable Property and Provisions) in Disturbed Areas Act, 1991, which mandates that citizens need to take permission from the state to sell property across religious lines. Contravention of this provision is treated as a cognizable offence with severe penalties.[22] This policy has ended up forcing Muslims and other minorities to live in ghettoes. These areas are reportedly characterized by poor sanitation, electricity, drinking water and other public amenities as compared to other areas. In Mumbai, too, there is a common and complex pattern of exclusion and self-segregation. Muslims have receded from mixed housing as a result of denial of rental and ownership access, and making a strategic retreat to Muslim-dominated localities.[23] This is not in the interest of national integration or indeed of the constitutional goal of fostering fraternity.

Similarly, the state excludes migrants in more direct and overt ways. Take the instance of the Indian Railways evicting slum dwellers from a slum cluster in Shakur Basti, without any notice on a cold day of December 2015.[24] During this demolition drive, an infant named Rookia died, allegedly buried under a bundle of clothes in her hut. Rahul Gandhi and I were the first ones to reach the demolition site. On being directed by Rahul Gandhi, I personally filed a petition on this matter in the Delhi High Court. My petition on 14 December against the Indians Railways pleaded that the Railways had no right to demolish slums without any notice and must alternatively rehabilitate the affected people. A division bench headed by Justice S. Muralidhar and Justice Vibhu Bhakru passed a detailed order on the same day. On 22 December 2015, the high court ordered the Delhi government to prepare a protocol that should outline the steps prior to, during and after the removal of slums. This protocol then became the basis of the Delhi Slum & Jhughi Jhopari Rehabilitation and Relocation Policy. Till the case was reserved for hearing, on 7 December 2018, Justice Muralidhar and his bench issued a series of interim orders and ensured that a proper Delhi Slum & JJ Rehabilitation Policy was in place.

On 23 March 2019, the division bench of Justice Muralidhar came up with a landmark judgment on *Ajay Maken vs Union of India*.[25] The judgment, authored by Justice Muralidhar, expanded on the right to housing and provided slum dwellers constitutional protection from forced and unannounced eviction. Placing much reliance on its previous judgment in *Sudama Singh*,[26] the court held that no authority shall carry out an eviction without conducting a survey and consulting the population that it seeks to evict. Further, the court held that no eviction shall be carried out without providing adequate rehabilitation for those eligible for it as per the survey. The court also observed that *slum-dwellers should not be treated as encroachers or illegal occupants but as people supporting the growth of the city*, forced to live in pitiable conditions due to the state's failure in providing adequate shelter. What was particularly fascinating and unique in the judgment was that the court invoked a particular phrase, pregnant with multiple meanings and possibilities, namely 'The Right to the City'.[27] In doing so, this judgment offered the means to address the numerous determinants that lead to exclusion/unfavourable inclusions. This judgment has now become a silver bullet of emancipation for slums across India.

Like slum dwellers have to deal with vested interests, relatively well-off urban citizens are also harassed and excluded by other unscrupulous interests. For example, the urban middle class and the lower-middle class are acutely vulnerable to the interests of self-serving builders/developers. Deeply sensitive to the fact that developers exploit the middle classes by delaying construction, revising rates, short-changing buyers over carpet area of flats, etc., the Real Estate (Regulation and Development) Bill (which established the Real Estate Regulatory Authority [RERA]) was spearheaded by the UPA government in 2012–13 under my stewardship as minister for housing and urban poverty alleviation. We did this primarily to protect the urban middle class and the lower-middle class from self-serving builders and developers. Among other things, the bill mandated that all statutory clearances had to be taken by builders before any project was launched, that developers do not divert money put in by prospective home buyers for other projects, that the promised carpet area and common areas are delivered to buyers and time-bound delivery of projects.

Yet, I faced tremendous resistance from the real estate developers' lobby and the land mafia, who tried very hard to scuttle the bill. They even seconded senior political leaders, who repeatedly tried to stall the passage of the bill for obvious reasons. Thankfully, I was backed to the hilt by the then UPA chairperson, Sonia Gandhi, and the then prime minister, Dr Manmohan Singh, who both saw the pressing logic of the bill. Both saw this bill as critical to safeguarding the interests of India's middle classes and were most concerned about ordinary home buyers facing problems from unscrupulous developers.

Prime Minister Manmohan Singh helped me manoeuvre the bill through the cabinet, which was almost unanimous on the urgency for RERA; and just to be doubly sure that the bill would see the light of day, the prime minister ensured it was introduced in the Rajya Sabha (where it could not lapse). When the bill was referred to the standing committee, I made it a point to ensure that Sharad Yadav, the then chairperson of the standing committee, and other members of the committee had the opportunity to meet members of resident welfare associations, numerous home buyers who had been victims of fraud committed by the builders and later landed up paying huge sums to the lawyers; so that they heard first-hand about the sheer scale of the problem. Consequently, the bill was cleared by the committee in record time. Unfortunately, the 2014 Lok Sabha election was just around the corner, and the bill was subsequently passed by the BJP government. Even though the BJP government has sought to take credit for this bill, what's more important to me is that ordinary people were provided a safety net by the state. Ultimately, we are all temporary actors on a vast stage, and it is enough that while we're there we did something meaningful and pro-people.

## The Indian City Pre- and Post-2014

To redress structural fault lines that exclude the poor and historically marginalized sections of society from a city, the UPA government spearheaded a number of progressive policies and schemes. Driven by the pro-people and pro-human rights approach instituted by the National Advisory Council (NAC), schemes like the Basic Services to Urban Poor (BSUP),[28] the Integrated Housing and Slum Development Programme (IHSDP)[29] and Interest Subsidy Scheme for Housing the Urban Poor (ISHUP)[30] focused on providing housing and basic amenities to the urban poor, especially to slum dwellers.[31] Similarly, the mass transport system in cities was developed expeditiously. In Delhi, the metro rail network advanced rapidly in 2012–13, and new projects were undertaken in Hyderabad, Bengaluru, Chennai, Mumbai and Kolkata.[32] Likewise, the Rajiv Awas Yojana (RAY)[33] aimed to create a slum-free India and provide financial assistance to states willing to assign property rights to slum dwellers (including current occupiers of slums). With a view to providing the urban poor access to institutional finance for affordable housing, the Credit Risk Guarantee Fund scheme was launched.[34] Finally, to enable street vendors to earn a decent livelihood and provide them with social security, the Street Vendors' (Protection of Livelihood and Regulation of Street Vending) Act, 2014, was enacted by Parliament.[35]

Furthermore, for the first time, a census of slums in India was undertaken in 2011.[36] It revealed that only 36.1 per cent (consisting of 49.65 lakh households) of slums in India were notified, that is, formally recognized, by some government, and were eligible for civic benefits. A whopping 63.9 per cent of slums (consisting of 87.84 lakh households) were in a legally grey area. Because they were not notified, the state does not provide for basic services for them, like clean drinking water, electricity and sanitation. For example, even though 3800 million litres of purified water is distributed in Mumbai per day, people living in buildings receive 150 litres per capita per day (LPCD)[37]. In stark contrast, those in small settlements (comprising 60 per cent of the total population) get 45 LPCD, while those in unrecognized settlements do not receive any.

Not being notified excludes them from any protection and rehabilitation, and makes them liable to be targeted by anti-poor governments. For example, recently, 200 *jhuggis* (households in slums) in Sarojini Nagar, Delhi, were almost demolished by the Union BJP government because the slum was not notified by Delhi's Aam Aadmi Party (AAP) government.[38] The Delhi government failed to come to the rescue of the poor slum dwellers and even opposed them in the high court, and it took the intervention of the Supreme Court to stop them. The story of the Sarojini Nagar jhuggis exemplifies the condition of many slums across India. That is why the Union government's 2012 memorandum on the RAY,[39] which was done under my stewardship, expressly allowed for development of all slums, irrespective of whether they were notified or non-notified.

Even before building on the RAY memorandum, I had spearheaded another policy change in the Master Plan for Delhi (MPD), which has proven to be a blessing for the urban poor and vulnerable. According to the 2011 Census, about 11.1 million units (or 12.4 per cent of the total national housing stock) across India lie vacant. They lie unused because they were originally bought for residential purposes but eventually diverted for commercial activities or for investments, etc. While 11.1 million may not seem much, compare it to the unused housing stock in 2011 to 1971, when only 1 million houses (or 9 per cent of the total housing stock) were vacant. Contrast this with the homeless and those who live in slums. This was because of a skewed land allotment policy, which did not adequately consider the vulnerable or poor. Surprisingly, even from a purely instrumental point of view, no housing mandates the creation of housing or any space for service providers who work in the same housing complex. This perforce pushes service providers to live in slums, with no protections. That is why, the MPD 2021 (para 4.2.3 of the Delhi Master Plan 2021, spearheaded by the UPA government in 2007) mandated that at least 15 per cent of the floor area ratio (FAR), or 35 per cent of the dwelling units (whichever is more), for every multistorey complex was reserved as housing for the economically weaker sections (EWS) of society. In the same section of the MPD 2021, resettlement of slums in the form of in-situ upgradation or rehabilitation was provided. Pursuant to the provisions of MPD 2021, the Delhi Development Authority took the initiative to rehabilitate slum and JJ clusters by identifying twenty-one sites, which were to be developed according to the public–private partnership model.[40] Just to cite a prominent example, while I was at the urban development ministry, it was decided that 2800 EWS houses (25 square metres each) were to be built in Kathputli Colony in Delhi, along with a primary school and community hall.[41] Similarly, we decided that 1122 EWS houses would be built to resettle slum dwellers in blocks E and F in Rohini Sector 18, around 1500 in Jailerwala Bagh and in many other places in Kalkaji, Vikas Puri, etc. However, despite these radical policy decisions, the pace of implementation was lethargic. This is partly because the efficient implementation of policies is still contingent on the active stewardship of conscientious political stakeholders, which is unfeasible given that ministers are often shuffled. There needs to be active ownership by the bureaucracy and rigorous accountability mechanisms to ensure that things get done. Failing that, different stakeholders continue to pass the buck to each other, and the nation suffers as a result.

Sadly, the NDA government has completely ignored this progressive policy. In fact, there are a number of regressive policies being spearheaded by the NDA government that are entirely anti-poor and certainly not in the national interest. To further illustrate the point, the Prime Minister Awas Yojana[42] (which is just the renamed PM-Rajiv Awas Yojana [PM-RAY]) has been contorted beyond recognition. While the PM-RAY provided for the development of, and delivery of civic services to, all slums (even non-notified ones), the Modi government has effectively absolved itself of all responsibility of ensuring the welfare of all non-notified slums, which are neither eligible for delivery of basic public goods and services nor for development. Accountability must also be fixed on the AAP government for failing to notify/formally identify a large number of slum clusters in Delhi, while they have been exploiting them for votes.[43] Reluctance of both the Union and state governments to bring the slum dwellers into mainstream society speaks volumes about their concerns for the urban poor population.

Deeply sensitive to the fact that the state has a key responsibility towards the urban poor, the UPA government had drafted two laws (Property Rights to Slum Dwellers Bill and the Union Territories Property Rights to Slum Dwellers

Bill) to give a legal right to shelter to the most vulnerable people in India. There is another, more fundamental reason for doing this. In explaining why some societies are productive and truly empower each citizen to achieve their fullest potential, Hernando de Soto[44] famously highlighted the mystery of missing capital. He argued that

> the poor inhabitants of [some] nations . . . do have things, but they lack the process to represent their property and create capital. They have houses but not titles; crops but not deeds; businesses but not statutes of incorporation. It is the unavailability of these essential representations that explains why people who have adapted every other Western invention, from the paper clip to the nuclear reactor, have not been able to produce sufficient capital to make their domestic capitalism work. This is the mystery of capital. Solving it requires an understanding of why Westerners, by representing assets with titles, are able to see and draw out capital from them.

What de Soto is effectively arguing is that some nations enable their citizens to access greater opportunities and assets by leveraging their existing assets, which include land, homes, inventories and skills. That is why entrepreneurs can use their properties or homes as collateral to secure credit for any business opportunity in many developed nations. But in India, we deny a vast section of our society the opportunity to seek credit or investments by denying them formal rights. This is a tremendous waste of human and financial resources. Admittedly, there are overlapping casteist, communal, patriarchal and anti-poor values at play, which deny people land titles, leadership roles and access to formal financial systems. Consider the case of slum dwellers. They have no title rights, and consequently are unable to leverage assets to secure credit for productive activities.[45] Just to illustrate how pervasive this problem is: about 70 per cent of people living in Delhi do not have freehold rights (i.e. do not have titles).[46] Imagine the possibilities if India is able to empower this untapped resource. By making assets bankable, we would indirectly be paving the way to unleash massive economic activities, while converting the informal sector into formal.

Keeping this in mind, we ushered in the Property Rights to Slum Dwellers Bill and the Union Territories Property Rights to Slum Dwellers Bill after extensive consultations with the Justice Mukul Mudgal Committee.[47] The provisions in these bills were designed to give slum dwellers property rights by ensuring a legal dwelling of carpet area of minimum 21 sq. m within 5 km of their place of livelihood (with provision for transit accommodation with minimum civic services for up to twenty-four months). Additionally, these houses were to be given to the female heads of households. Yet, because these model legislations were ushered in only towards the end of the UPA-2 government, these have been put in cold storage by the NDA government. If implemented, they can serve as pan-India models for property rights.

Similarly, prodded by the Arjun Sengupta Committee report's findings,[48] the UPA government was very sensitive to the fact that there is a high degree of informality that migrants face when they come into cities. They are subject to harassment and exploitation from vested interests. To redress this pervasive problem, the UPA government spearheaded the Street Vendors Act. To date, there is no act of this nature anywhere in the world. The Street Vendors Act was enacted to protect livelihoods and further promote the rights of these poor people. It recognizes vendors as an integral part of Indian cities, and grants legal protection to them against forced evictions, confiscation and harassment. Even though we faced tremendous pressure from vested interests, vending spaces equalling 2.5 per cent of the total population of every city in India was sought to be allocated to street vendors (and this could not be limited by bureaucratic high-handedness). This would basically mean that about 8–10 per cent of the total city's population would be covered. Any politically savvy government can leverage the certificates of vending to not just generate mass entrepreneurship but also create a massive source of revenue for the state government. Just to give one example, the total population of Delhi is about 2 crore.[49] By the provision of this act, Delhi can officially allocate 2.5 per cent of its population certificates and have 5–6 lakh formal vendors. If certificates are granted at a nominal annual fee of Rs 1000, at one stroke, the government would regularize 5 lakh vendors, earn annual revenue of Rs 50 crore from just one city, and give vendors livelihood security (thereby protecting them from illegal harassment from local authorities).

Furthermore, no zone can be declared as a no-vending zone if the government doesn't do a formal survey and allocate vending zones. This means that no government can evict any person unless it does a comprehensive survey (due to be done every five years by the town vending committee) and then gives certificates of vending. This was to be survey-based and not application-based. This put the onus on the municipal administration, and more specifically on the Street Vendors Committee (of which 40 per cent were to be street vendors who were to elect their own representatives). The onus was not on the vendors to go and apply with municipal administrations.

Yet, neither the state nor Central governments have followed the law since the UPA government passed it. Despite the Street Vendors Act, vendors have been harassed, attacked and evicted by municipal authorities across the country. For example, it took the BJP government seven years to notify the rules under the Street Vendors Act. This delay has been misused by various governments that have violated the law. For example, the act mandates a survey of all street vendors by the town vending committees. In the absence of rules, state governments are unilaterally conducting the survey and imposing unattainable rules based on applications (rather than survey). Similarly, it is a violation of the act to bulldoze structures without completing legal formalities. The demolitions in Jahangirpuri were challenged in the Supreme Court, and a stay order was issued. Despite the stay, demolitions continued, leading to further legal action. The Supreme Court extended the stay and sought responses from the North Delhi Municipal Corporation (NDMC) and Delhi Police.[50] The municipal authorities did so knowing full well that the people living in Jahangirpuri are largely the poor and vulnerable, mostly working as informal workers. To make already vulnerable people further insecure and unsettled is just inhumane.

But the municipal authorities and Delhi government agencies have continuously shown a propensity to violate acts that support and empower the poorest of the poor.[51] Recently, it violated the Street Vendors Act in arbitrarily instating a rule that street vendors would need to show ten-year domicile certificates to ply their trade. This is blatantly illegal, for it forces street vendors to furnish papers to a bureaucracy bent on soliciting bribes to verify them. Similarly, licence fees for street vendors have become prohibitive, and for some strange reason, the Delhi government has made licence fees that street vendors have to pay contingent on the class of colonies where they ply their trade. Therefore, a class A colony is categorized as posh, and hence, street vendors would have to pay a higher fee to ply their trade there. This is plain elitist and ends up deterring lakhs of street vendors. This puts nearly half a million Delhi citizens (since street vendors constitute 2.5 per cent of the city's population) at risk, since they continue to live under the constant threat of eviction because the Delhi government and the civic agencies have been unwilling to implement the Street Vendors Act.

It is easy to suspect that the Delhi government purposely failed to recognize street vendors because of deliberate collusion with vested interests. That is why it has not yet conducted a city-wide survey of street vendors because of which a large number of them have been excluded from availing benefits from schemes like the PM SVANidhi Yojana. The yojana strives to provide affordable loans of up to Rs 10,000 to more than 50 lakh street vendors.[52] Yet, because the Delhi government has not done a survey of street vendors, few can actually benefit from the yojana. Even those who do are excluded on particularist grounds. That's why, of the Rs 4386.01 crore funds disbursed (till December 2022), only 10 per cent have been allocated to the minorities, 19 per cent to Dalits and only 3 per cent to adivasis.[53] In Delhi alone (in the same time period), of the 1.14 lakh applications approved, 5 per cent of funds in the PM-SVANidhi Yojana went to the minorities, 1 per cent to adivasis, 12 per cent to OBCs and 15 per cent to SCs.[54] The survey of street vendors under the PM-SVANidhi Yojana is to be conducted by urban local bodies. In Delhi, this would mean the various municipal branches of the National Capital Territory of Delhi, which includes the Municipal Corporation of Delhi (MCD) and New Delhi Municipal Corporation (NDMC). Both of these were controlled by the BJP at the time. Clearly, minorities, adivasis and Dalits have been excluded from this scheme.

But such exclusionary policies are not limited to state and municipal governments. They extend all the way to the Union government. For example, the NDA government's Pradhan Mantri Awas Yojana (PMAY), which aims to provide affordable housing to the poor, is continuously failing in meeting its stated targets. Despite allocating Rs 1.8 lakh crore, PMAY-U has not solved deep-rooted issues associated with the housing market in India.[55] As on 25 June 2024, only 84.02 lakh houses of the sanctioned 118.64 lakh houses had been completed.[56] Furthermore, in India's 4000 cities, just about 7.92 lakh houses have been built under the scheme. That is less than 10 per cent of the total urban housing need. This is despite a hike of almost Rs 3000 crore (from Rs 4175 crore in 2015–16 to Rs 6853 crore in 2019–20) for the PM Awas Yojana. Part of the problem is that fund utilization for the scheme is a dismal 36 per cent.[57] In stark contrast, in the preceding five years, the UPA government had built 1.23 crore urban houses and 89.65 lakh houses as part of rural households,[58] averaging 24.7 lakh houses per year.[59]

Similarly, the NDA government's ambitious Smart Cities Mission failed to achieve the targets and has managed to complete only 17 per cent of the total worth of projects sanctioned under it since its launch in 2015.[60] Despite increasing budgetary allocation, five years after the mission's inception, not a single project has been completed in twenty-eight cities. In fourteen cities, only one project has seen its conclusion.[61] This is partly because the Smart Cities Mission neither empowers Urban Local Bodies (ULBs) nor does it ensure citizen participation. The mission adopts a very narrow view of urban development, with an overwhelming majority of its funds going for the redevelopment of a tiny fraction of each city. Instead of creating systems wherein citizens can suggest things that would be most beneficial for their neighbourhoods, the mission empowers various multinational firms that are ramrodding urban design experiments that are incongruent with Indian cities and their realities.[62] This is in stark contrast to the 74th Amendment, which deliberately seeks to empower ULBs and the people. It also negates the hard work undertaken by the UPA government, whose JNNURM scheme created economically productive, efficient, equitable and responsive cities.

This ramrodding of top-down and exclusionary schemes has continued unabated. The NDA government's much touted Swachh Bharat Mission-Urban (SBM-U) aimed to build home toilets for 12 million urban households, 25 million public toilets and 30 million community toilets at a cost of Rs 62,009 crore.[63] Yet, the scheme has only managed to get 68.86 lakh toilets constructed,[64] without giving users any access to water or sewage systems. Most of the constructed toilets lie unused or are used more as storage sheds rather than toilets. A related scheme which actually aimed to provide universal access to water supply and sewage management in 500 cities by 2020 remains a pipe dream. Launched in 2015, the Atal Mission for Rejuvenation and Urban Transformation (AMRUT) has seen only 15 per cent of the funds allocated to it being utilized.[65] Additionally, as of January 2019, more than half of the projects are nowhere near completion. This inordinate delay has resulted in an increased lack of basic drinking water and sewerage facilities in the cities.

Additionally, neither the Swachh Bharat Mission nor the AMRUT scheme do anything to redress the problem of manual scavenging, which continues to thrive unabated. They also do not address the challenge of solid waste management. Even now, more than half of our waste is not segregated and is dumped in landfills. *Swachhata* must not be envisaged just in terms of infrastructural responses to the problems, but as calculated policy and societal responses required for cleaner and sustainable cities.

## Conclusion

When the state absolves itself of its core responsibilities to citizens, it is incumbent on political parties and civil society to take the lead in putting pressure on the state. Only then can the state be held accountable and hopefully be nudged to course-correct. In that spirit, I filed a petition (case) concerning the demolition of Shakur Basti on railway land, where the Delhi High Court invoked the idea of the 'Right to the City' to uphold the housing rights of slum dwellers. This case led to the framing of a humane protocol for slum relocation and also the Delhi Slum Rehabilitation Policy, 2015, providing safeguards against forced evictions of slum residents.

I believe that this landmark judgment offers us an opportunity to reimagine the role of the state and its relationship with the citizen. This radical reimagining would mean first acknowledging that sovereignty is shared between the state and the individual, and that the state must practise restraint in exercising its powers. In this normative framework, the state must make citizens central to urban governance. Doing this would mean re-hauling top-down governance solutions like the special purpose vehicle (SPV), which was formed to implement the Smart Cities Project.[66] Apart from excluding both citizens and political representatives from planning, the SPV completely outsources financial management and the delivery of services to private contractors. In fact, many SPVs that govern cities today are registered as companies; they are not accessible to citizens and supersede elected local bodies.[67] The SPV is a classic example of the NDA government imposing an unviable technocratic solution that violates the 74th Amendment, outsources and commercializes governance while excluding citizens from having any say regarding their own lives.

That is why I firmly believe that every Indian should have an inalienable right to the city. Building upon the Rights-Based Paradigm that the NAC spearheaded, this needs to be statutorily codified as a bundle of human rights that secures equality, inclusion and social justice. This right would include adequate and dignified housing, food, health, security and sustainable livelihood opportunities. It would also remove barriers for full inclusion in the social, economic and political life of a city. Just to cite one example, the ration card (which is a means to accessing public goods and services as well as a source of identification) is today location-specific. A citizen may be able to access food and other public goods in his/her place of domicile but won't be able to do so in the city. This requires a structural policy change that necessitates dialogue with all the three tiers of India's federal structure and consensual governance. Sadly, that kind of dialogue is completely absent in India today, and the Union government has positioned itself antagonistically against both the state and municipal administrations.

Finally, a city can provide for everybody. But to do that, it must be shaped and reshaped by *everybody*. That is why the right to the city is critical to ensure urban governance is inclusive and puts citizens at the centre. Once citizens are empowered and included to shape their lives, we can collectively forge a city that can fulfil the needs and aspirations of every urban citizen. Policymakers need to remember and strictly follow the principle that sovereignty is vested in every individual, and that each citizen has equal rights to the natural bounties/resources of a nation. Given this, the state must provide for each citizen, especially if they don't have the means to live well. Only then can each Indian achieve fullness of life.

# Demolition City

## Planning Violations and the Erosion of Housing Rights

### Aravind Unni and Evita Das

*The authors gratefully acknowledge the courageous efforts of community collectives, civil society actors and social movements—particularly Navnirman Manch (Indore), the National Alliance for People's Movements (NAPM – Delhi), and Ghar Bachao Ghar Banao (Mumbai)—whose brave advocacy against state excesses on urban communities has been instrumental in making this piece possible.*

## Introduction

Indian cities have always been a contested terrain. Urban planning in the conventional sense—top-down and state-led—has never been implemented, except for a few, sparse examples of planned Indian cities.[1][2][3] The visible manifestations of state-led planning have been the conflicts with urban informality[4] and people's settlements.[5] While most of the post-Independence (new) urban centres accommodated the informalities, since the 2000s the contestations have taken a different turn. In the changed sociopolitical context of neoliberalized Indian cities, informality and settlements are viewed with antipathy, as aberrations that are meant to be removed from city centres to make way for the impending world-class cities. There is a wide existing body of research that has argued for the dramatic increase in evictions; the discourse on urban planning, the courts and the jurisprudence are all undergoing a change to view the slums (*bastis*)[6] as illegal—as settlements that need to be cleared to make way for more ordered, better developed Indian cities.[7][8][9][10] Also, it is not a matter of coincidence that slums are majorly Dalit and Bahujan dominated.[11] Our cities are segregated, and this anti-slum sentiment, much more visible after 2014, is further deepening the divides in our cities. The last decade has also seen the COVID pandemic, which also saw furthering of the anti-poor discourse under the garb of COVID protocols and regulations.

It is in this context that this essay attempts to sketch the contours of the altered Indian city after 2014, when, for the first time, the urban aspiration was catapulted to the centre stage and became an election cry. This was the beginning of a renewed focus on the urban landscape, resulting in a host of schemes starting from the Smart Cities Mission (SCM)[12], specifically focusing on cities and their development, and also on the urban component of schemes like the Pradhan Mantri Awas Yojna (PMAY)[13] and Swachh Bharat Mission (SBM)[14].

While it is pertinent to ask how (in)effective these schemes are, the focus should also be on the impact of them on the psyche of the Indian city and how the larger public discourse around smart cities was used to demolish people's settlement in Indian cities. It is what this piece aims to achieve. Today, it is widely believed that the discourse on urban planning has been altered after 2014, leading to more exclusionary development.[15][16][17][18][19] The cases presented here, from Indore, Mumbai and Delhi, are an attempt to capture, comprehend and delineate this altered imagination of cities. They expose the transformed nature of urban life and urban planning through examples of slums and their erasure, while negating their housing-land claims using urban planning. These struggles also reveal the possible trajectories of efforts to reclaim the urban centres.

## The Case of C.P. Shekhar Nagar, Indore

> 'About 3000 people from low-lying areas of Indore have been evacuated to safer locations after heavy rains continued to pound the city since late on Tuesday evening.[20]

It was during the rains of July 2015 that C.P. Shekhar Nagar was again featured in the news.[21] As in the case of slums, it is only during such episodic intervals that the state realizes their presence. The district administration, citing the rains, had issued a high alert for all low-lying areas. Slums, including C.P. Shekhar Nagar, which abutted the Kahn River were badly affected. Even though Shekhar Nagar, among the older slum communities of Indore, had seen numerous threats and even partial removals, the rains and subsequent flooding proved fatal. Unlike previous instances, Shekhar Nagar over the next six months saw human rights violations[22]—employing the language and tenor of urban planning.

The genesis of the basti of C.P. Shekhar Nagar is enmeshed within the history of Indore. The city is part of the Malwa region, which developed as 'Mini Bombay'—as it is called because it is the commercial capital of Madhya Pradesh—and attracts people from across castes, usually in the form of migrants associated with different occupations. The residents of this settlement mostly belong to the Matang[23] community, which is a Dalit community with origins in Maharashtra.[24] The migration waves in the 1950s–1960s in search of employment led to the emergence of a settlement along the banks of the Kahn River.

The strategic accidental location of this settlement, in what was then the centre of Indore, also aided in its development and opened access to new opportunities for the residents.

Like any informal settlement in Indian cities, C.P. Shekhar Nagar grew incrementally over a period of time. In 1976, under the Gandi Basti Unmulan Abhiyan (slum eradication campaign), the residents of C.P. Shekhar Nagar were given ration cards; at that time there were around 600–700 families living in this slum and their main occupation was collecting waste. Soon they were also provided with electricity connections and a piped water supply, roads were laid inside the basti and some common facilities, such as a community hall, school and other basic amenities, were also put in place.[25] Under the Madhya Pradesh Nagariya Kshetro Ke Bhoomihin Vyakti Adhiniyam, 1984, around 1000 families were given land entitlement (*pattas*).[26] The land titles were again renewed in 2003, after thirty years. In the meantime, residents obtained all other identity proofs, such as voter ID cards, Aadhaar cards and so on.[27] This additional yet continuous growth is also noted in the government and official documents that recognize the settlement to have a majority of pucca structures, interspersed with public amenities.[28]

## *Prelude and Eviction*

It was in 2013 that the Indore Municipal Corporation (IMC) prepared the Slum Free City Plan of the Indore Metropolitan Area. The Government of Madhya Pradesh had earlier identified Indore, Bhopal, Gwalior, Jabalpur, Ujjain and Sagar as 'Priority Cities' and initiated action under the now defunct Rajiv Awas Yojna (RAY).[29] City-specific strategic interventions to make cities 'slum-free' were employed by the more proactive of the cities[30], such as Indore, which created a database that analysed the settlements on a priority basis. A blueprint for the evictions was prepared and followed in the subsequent years under the convergence of the SCM, SBM and PMAY. It reduced people-built settlements to tenable and untenable binaries, and mapped these based on indices that were arbitrary, ignoring the ground reality. And it identified that almost half the slums in Indore were located within conflicting land-use zones.[31] [32] [33] [34]

Come the rains of July and August 2015, the flood situation worsened in Indore. But the blame and the axe fell on the informal settlers and their communities abutting the river. This five-decade-old settlement was bulldozed under the orders of the National Green Tribunal (NGT). The NGT ordered the removal of all structures up to 30 m from the riversides in the name of conservation and safety for the residents, and for the 'well-being' and 'greater good' of the city.[35] [36]

> *After 25 years of unsuccessful attempts, the Indore Municipal Corporation (IMC) has finally managed to clear CP Shekhar Nagar and shift its residents to other locations.*[37]

Thus went the media headlines. It was a congratulatory message to the authorities who had successfully managed to 'clear' and 'shift' the residents to 'other' locations. On 16 August 2015, the IMC evicted 800 families living in C.P. Shekhar Nagar following the implementation of an order of the NGT related to riverbanks.[38] This led to a protracted court battle. The high court stayed the evictions on multiple grounds;[39] nevertheless it has been reported that IMC authorities and the district administration continued to carry out the evictions surreptitiously, disregarding the high court's stay order against the forceful eviction of slum dwellers.[40] This violation has also been brought to the court's notice.[41] Meanwhile, the IMC officials claimed that the relocation drive (read eviction) was carried out 'peacefully and successfully', even though resistance to the demolition was met with lathi charges and coercions.[42] In spite of the legal status of the tenure[43] and security through numerous years of habitation, the final lot was entirely demolished by October 2015, almost four months since the first wave of evictions.[44]

The location for the resettlement 16 km away from the city centre goes against the principles of justice and has made the communities more vulnerable. A series of housing inventory was built in the periphery of the city, in areas that had been lying vacant, constructed under the Basic Services to the Urban Poor (BSUP) component of the Jawaharlal Nehru National Urban Renewal Mission (JNNURM), first phase. While they got a place to stay, their source of livelihood was taken away. The waste pickers and the informal-sector workers, whose income depended on the original location and the ease of access to livelihood options it provided, have been adversely impacted.[45] Not many people are happy to have been resettled to the new location because of its distance from the centre, and the poorly built structures (G+3)—called 'multies'[46] by the residents—have been built without any basic amenities in them. They lost the benefit of using their home's horizontal spaces for work purposes as and when needed. The residents were uprooted and their right to water, education, sanitation, healthcare services, livelihood opportunities and their relationship with city life were undermined.[47]

## *The Backstory*

In 2014, with the election of the BJP-led NDA government, a slew of urban schemes was introduced. One among those was the Smart Cities Mission (SCM). It came as part of Narendra Modi's onslaught on the public imagination and as a continuation of the 'Gujarat Model'. Launched with a lot of fanfare and expectations, the SCM, by 2015, metamorphosed and achieved a more plausible, actionable form, if not an articulate one. The smart city was defined as 'one having provision of basic infrastructure to give a decent quality of life to its citizens, a clean and sustainable environment and application of smart solutions, keeping the citizens at the centre'.[48] Under the SCM, the IMC, along with its SCM's Special Purpose Vehicle (SPV), had reimagined, among a host of other interventions, the rejuvenation of river systems in Indore.[49] This rejuvenation plan, unlike the holistic ecologically centred revival of rivers, included mostly the cosmetic beautification of water systems that painted informal settlements as reasons for floods and the city's misery.[50] What's more startling is that, despite the state's historical recognition of the settlement, the state machinery itself went ahead and approved the demolition drive, violating people's basic human rights, and it was stated in the court that the 'persons who are around Khan river have been forcibly dispossessed'.[51] The demolition took place on only one side of the river where the basti was situated,[52] leaving the other side of 30 m as it is; it comprised studier-looking concrete structures and shops constructed by the corporation. According to Clause 3.A and 4 of the Madhya Pradesh Patta Act, families evicted under public-interest reasons must be restored possession, and the land acquisition act also mandates compensations, particularly when the affected families belong to SC/ST communities. However, in this case, the forceful eviction and resettlement of the community far from their homes and livelihood not only disrupted their lives but also their rights conferred by these legal protections.[53] A report by Housing and Land Rights Network (HLRN) in 2018 (three years after the PMAY roll-out), documented demolitions of at least 41,734 houses and forced evictions of 2,02,233 people across the country. These staggering numbers compel us to ask: Why have evictions increased post the PMAY roll-out? Are these evictions being carried out to fill long-abandoned dwelling units, like in JNNURM and in the PMAY constructed units with just a few basic amenities? Is this the way to make world-class cities, where the historically oppressed communities and the urban poor are pushed away from the city centre, left out of the state's vision of urban development, no longer accounted for in the city's vision? These questions find some resonance in the case of C.P. Shekhar Nagar.

The site where once Shekhar Nagar stood is now to be redeveloped as a park.[54] The eviction and forced housing of people in unhabitable tenements destroyed their livelihoods and damaged the social fabric that they crafted brick by brick over three generations. This process is emblematic in the SCM approach of urban development. As stated earlier, SCM's rejuvenation of rivers classified the settlement as informal, providing the pretext for eviction. In doing so, it violated the long-standing tenurial security, bypassed democratically drafted master plans and undermined the state's own housing policies.

Evictions based on human rights violations and discriminatory planning are just not the story of one community in Indore. This is replicated across the country in multiple forms, leading to multiple violations.[55] [56] Indore, the ninth-largest city in India, with over 20 lakh people, has shown 'phenomenal' progress in rankings in central schemes.[57] It was ranked 117 in 2014, has secured the first position from 2017 onwards in the Swachh Survekhshan Report.[58] [59] But these rankings do not guarantee a life of dignity or freedom from arbitrary evictions.[60]

## The Case of Mahul, Mumbai

Mahul is an industrial zone, located in the eastern suburb of Chembur in Mumbai. The place derives its name from a small *gaothan*[61] called Mahul. This is arguably one of the most polluted areas in the city, and is surrounded by chemical refineries, fertilizer plants, petroleum companies and other industrial units. In the past decade, the aspirational middle classes and bureaucrats have aspired to transform Mumbai into a 'world-class' city by floating vision plans that have resulted in massive eviction and demolition drives in the name of urban renewal, road widening, river beautification, airport expansion and other infrastructure projects. The implementation of these projects, too, has meant the reorganizing of the city, including shifting of populations, mainly those living in settlements (slums) to what have been called resettlement and rehabilitation (R&R) sites.[62] Mahul shows us the (in)visible effects of these drives. The overarching objective of these development projects has been to overhaul the crumbling infrastructure of the city and to give a boost to the economy.

Mumbai has seen the creation of nearly thirty-two R&R colonies over two decades. The process has consolidated in the last ten years. All have come about in the eastern fringes of the city. These colonies have an estimated number of 56,000 tenements providing housing to more than 3 lakh people.[63] [64] The process of resettlement has resulted in a city beyond imagination, as the impacts of resettlement are not restricted to the R&R sites but affect the social and demographic fabric of the entire city. It is essential to note that the shifting of populations has not been uniformly carried out across the city. The disposed are huddled and pushed towards the most polluted peripheries. One such project is the demolition of settlements along the 160-km-long Tansa pipeline, a major source of water supply for Mumbai where several settlements had developed over the last fifty years.[65]

## Green Wheels Along Blue Lines: Building Walls and Jogging Tracks

In 2006, a PIL was filed by the NGO Janhit Manch, seeking the demolition of housing structures within 10 metres of the Tansa water pipeline that provides water to Mumbai. The prayers filed in the PIL sought the removal of 'illegal structures around the main pipelines'. The case gained currency after the terrorists' attacks of 2008 and captured the attention of the public and courts. The Bombay High Court, in 2009, directed, 'to protect the pipelines, remove the hutments and ensure that the water, which is used by the citizens of Mumbai, is safe, and to ensure that these pipelines do not become a target for persons to attack the citizens of Mumbai, we feel that it needs concerted effort and a well-thought-of policy by various agencies, including the Government of Maharashtra.'[66] The committee constituted under the court orders had prepared a draft plan for the protection of the Tansa pipeline, also proposing a rehabilitation plan for the families that would be displaced. This proposal included the cut-off date of 2000, the estimated number of families to be displaced and possible site of rehabilitation, and also a few possible locations. Mahul did not figure in the original list of locations for resettlement. The court also said that the directions issued in this PIL were not confined to the main pipeline which carried water from Tansa Lake, but the same extended to all the water trunk mains carrying water from the lakes to the city. It is important to note that while the court was apprehensive and discerning in its analysis of the water pipelines, it did not discuss how slums are a reality in Mumbai and how the state had not provided housing to a vast majority of its residents. Nor did it address the issue of how water procured from the outskirts of Mumbai's metropolitan region was depriving marginal tribal communities and limiting their access to water resources.[67]

The Brihanmumbai Municipal Corporation (BMC), as in other cases, went into a slumber, only to be woken up again after the Bombay High Court pulled it up for non-compliance of orders, setting a deadline for the work and asking the civic body to submit a progress report.[68] Since then, citing court orders and the threat to people's lives, they have engaged in a spate of evictions along the Tansa pipeline.[69] It was only after 2016 that the BMC, sensing opportunity and impetus to act, drew up a plan for building walls, as well as cycle and jogging tracks around the water pipelines. With the proposed action plan as a framework, the BMC, Mumbai's governing body, commissioned a Rs 300-crore project titled 'Green Wheels along Blue Lines' to secure the 10 m buffer from the pipeline in order to safeguard the pipeline,[70] employing Section 33(10) of the Monopolies and Restrictive Trade Practices (MRTP) Act, which has provisions about resettlement and rehabilitation. But the principle of the action plan that was drawn up by the committee was ignored. Over the past decade, the residents say, the city corporation has shifted over 5500 families (roughly 30,000 people) to Mahul from their settlements that were deemed 'illegal', in Ghatkopar, Chembur, Powai, Vakola and Bandra (East) along the Tansa water pipeline.[71]

## The Rehabilitation Site and Deaths

The Mahul tenements comprise seventy-two buildings and 17,025 dwelling units that aim to provide housing for approximately 86,000 inhabitants. The buildings are packed so densely that many of the flats never see direct sunlight.[72] Sewage leaks from overhead drainage pipes and fills the narrow alleyways between the buildings, often seeping into the underwater tanks that supply drinking water. Most of the people living here, evicted from slums to clear the grounds for infrastructure projects, were given one-room flats by the government. The residents are now known as Project Affected Persons (PAPs).

Here in Mahul, the tenements are flanked by large chemical industries such as Tata Power, Bharat Petroleum Corporation Limited (BPCL) Refineries and other treatment facilities. In 2015, the NGT observed that 'there is perceptible threat to the health of residents of Mahul due to prevailing air quality in the area'. The NGT based its judgement on a KEM Hospital report (2014) that noted that the adverse health symptoms of the residents were similar to those caused by toluene diisocyanate exposure.[73] The report also recorded a high number of respiratory illnesses in the area. Given the toxic air in the region, these residents have been battling respiratory diseases like asthma, tuberculosis, rashes and a range of skin allergies. In the three years of the immediate shifting in Mahul, over 100 people are reported to have died due to pollution-related complications. This becomes an added burden to the families who have been displaced; many have lost their livelihoods and now have to face the brunt of increased expenses on travel, education and healthcare.[74] The building complex was also heavily criticized for not having basic services and provisions. Incidentally, Mahul's tenements weren't originally commissioned for the Tansa-evicted people. These buildings were meant for the 'Brimstowad project'—one of the many city renewal projects that displaced numerous families to Mahul in 2013.[75]

## The Protest

It was the third massive phase of demolitions in 2017 that saw more than 5000 houses demolished and many PAPs come together.[76] Ironically, this happened not at the site of eviction but after they were evicted and in the R&R sites. Later that year, in November 2017, the people who were shifted to Mahul from various areas along the pipeline organized themselves under the Mahul Prakalp Grast Sangharsh Samiti (Mahul PAP Struggle Committee), to fight for a just rehabilitation. They went on to file a writ petition in March 2018 demanding the same, saying that Mahul is a critically polluted and uninhabitable region. On 8 August 2018, in an interim order, the Bombay HC ordered the Government of Maharashtra to either relocate the Tansa pipeline-affected persons to a habitable place or compensate them enough so as to enable them to rent a house in Mumbai.[77] There was a significant delay in implementing the court's order. The PAPs converged and initiated the Jeevan Bachao Andolan on 28 October 2018 and occupied a footpath in Vidyavihar in protest. They said that they were better off on the footpath, where they had lived before the evictions, than at the rehabilitation sites. In April 2019, the Bombay High Court acted towards their previous order by directing the Maharashtra government to deposit Rs 15,000 per month as rent and an additional Rs 45,000 as refundable deposit in the bank accounts of the residents and other PAPs.[78] Soon after this order, in May 2019, the BMC approached the Supreme Court for a stay on the Bombay High Court order and the Supreme Court granted an interim order to the stay stating, 'there shall be stay of the operation of the impugned order and judgment passed by the High Court'.[79] Despite earlier judicial observations repeatedly describing Mahul as a toxic hell and an uninhabitable area, this notice came as a setback. In response, the residents staged a protest in 2019, which continued for more than 200 days.[80]

The andolan initiated by the people of Mahul questioned the very understanding and basis of rehabilitation. Rehabilitation should mean that people's standard of living is increased, or at least maintained. Protracted court hearings and public outrage led the SC to lift its stay order[81] and ensure the Bombay High Court order remained unchallenged:

> . . . we direct that no family required to be rehabilitated as a consequence of slum clearance would be shifted to the PAP colonies in Mahul or Ambapada and those who have been rehabilitated at the said two colonies under the slum rehabilitation schemes would be offered accommodation elsewhere and till alternative accommodation is made available they would be paid ₹15,000/- per month as transit rent with security deposit of ₹45,000/- upon the family rehabilitated through its head filing an application seeking to move out and upon the condition that upon receipt of the security deposit and commitment to be paid transit rent, if no other alternative accommodation is provided, the family moves out.[82]

In other words, it directed the state government and BMC to find more humane accommodation for the 5500[83] families who were made forced residents in Mahul and to pay an adequate amount of rent for the families to rent a place of their own.

While this has been a relief for the forced residents of Mahul, over these six years of struggle, many have lost their lives to the toxic air, lost family breadwinners or become too sick to work after moving to Mahul. The relocation is still happening in batches,[84] which means people have no choice but to endure this toxic hell while political negotiations and paperwork drag on. Mahul is still being considered to receive PAPs from the city despite the known implications.[85] These considerations continue, even though Mahul is widely recognized as unfit for habitation, and despite the fact that existing residents continue to struggle to make a living, protect themselves from disease and find a decent source of livelihood, having been uprooted from their homes under the guise of 'rehabilitation and resettlement'.

## The Case of Kathputli Colony, Delhi

The Kathputli Colony was a settlement of street performers in the Shadipur Depot area of Delhi. It was home to more than 4000 families. As the name suggests, it was inhabited by members of different communities of street performers, such as magicians, snake charmers, acrobats, singers, dancers, actors, traditional healers and musicians, and especially puppeteers or *kathputli* (puppet) performers. It was also largely stratified along the lines of the geographical origin of its residents.[86]

The colony had emerged in the 1950s as a cluster of makeshift tents in an open field on the fringes of Delhi, set up by itinerant puppeteers from Rajasthan initially; then more performing groups from Andhra Pradesh and Maharashtra came here. The tumultuous 1970s saw the worst demolitions in Delhi, especially close to the Kathputli Colony. This prompted the communities to self-organize and set up institutions for their welfare and development.[87] By the 2000s, and then with the advent of the metro line a few years later, the Kathputli Colony came under the scanner of the authorities and the pressures of urban renewal. Eviction was gradually ruled out as an option as the settlement was recognized in the 675 JJ clusters (slum pockets) in the Delhi government list.[88] [89]

## The Planning

The Kathputli Colony saw numerous attempts for its (re)development by different actors. Resettlement and upgradation plans were offered to its residents, who were unwilling to move from the site, thereby thwarting the state's plan to initiate slum development. It was in 2009 that the Delhi Development Authority (DDA) announced the in-situ development of Kathputli Colony. DDA is the primary planning authority in Delhi, under whose control most of the slum communities come, including Kathputli Colony. It was the 2007 master plan that introduced the idea of monetizing slum land and cross-subsidizing housing tenements for slum dwellers.[90]

The Master Plan 2021, adopted in 2007, states that around 40 per cent of Delhi's housing could be satisfied through redevelopment/upgradation of existing areas in Delhi.[91] The plan also states that the 'overall responsibility for provision of land and facilitation of adequate housing to meet the projected demand lies with the DDA'. Inspired by Mumbai's Slum Rehabilitation Authority (SRA), the master plan hoped to kindle the interest of private players in addressing the housing needs of the city.[92] This was in the context of increasing abdication of responsibility on the part of the state when it came to housing for the urban poor. After a detailed selection process, a famous private developer was picked to undertake the project. On 6 October 2009, DDA awarded its first slum redevelopment project—5.22 hectares of land allocated for Rs 6.11 crore and the obligation to rehabilitate the Kathputli Colony—to the developers, with an expected total cost of Rs 254.27 crore. They announced the construction of 'Delhi's first true skyscraper' on the Kathputli Colony plot. With a planned height of 190 metres, the towers would be fifty-four floors of luxury flats, equipped 'with skyclub and helipad', according to the developer's advertisements.[93]

The Kathputli in-situ slum rehabilitation was imagined as a three-step process. First, the residents of Kathputli who qualified for the project would move from their current settlement to a transit camp. Second, the slum cluster would be removed and the construction of high-rise apartments—and a luxury skyscraper—would begin on site. Finally, within the next three to five years, the transit camp residents would move back into the settlement, next door to the expensive towers. A project scheme later adopted by the DDA in its agreement with the developers said that the number of Economically Weaker Section (EWS) houses required to be constructed was 2800. This contract also details out the units, sizes, specifications and site layout. Apart from the responsibilities relating to the EWS housing, developers would have the right to construct and sell up to 170 houses at commercial rates. This bonus lies at the centre of the DDA's incentive scheme for attracting developers.

Though seemingly clear, the execution of the above mentioned three steps was marred by irregularities that the communities were not able to navigate. The project proposal and detailed project report (DPR) were finalized even before conducting a survey of the community. People in general had to depend on the *pradhans*—traditional leaders of the community—for decision-making. The cut-off dates were also arbitrarily set to only increase the viability of the scheme and to include a certain percentage of families so that they agreed to the redevelopment project. Starting with 2007, the cut-off date was then extended to 2009 and then finally to 2015, which resulted in a changed number of beneficiaries of the subsidized housing.[94]

It was estimated that around 25–30 per cent of the residents were left without houses in the redevelopment process. A lack of project clarity and non-availability of information in the public domain also meant that people had no scope to contribute to the project. The surveys were also surreptitiously carried out. Multiple rounds of surveys had been done with the changing set of cut-off dates leading to chaos within the community. It was also clear that the survey was flawed and did not take into consideration the dense nature of the settlement. It left out the higher storeys where separate families were staying. The design itself had problems: the dense, high-rise construction for slum dwellers ignored the unique needs of the community and their livelihoods. The builders added an office complex and mall on its 'share' of 35 per cent of the land, while they were allotted only 18 per cent in the contract. They then raised the height of the 2800 EWS flats to fifteen storeys. It enraged the residents as they didn't want such a tall dwelling unit and change in plan.[95] [96]

## The Evictions

The Kathputli Colony was rife with rumour-mongering since the last survey was carried out in July 2017 with the revised cut-off dates. It is said that the DDA, following 'due procedures', pasted some notices regarding the impending eviction and the final list of eligible families. The procedure, it was argued, left many confused, and over 4000 families were unaware and kept in the dark about the lists and eligibility. The authority did not provide adequate notice to the residents and rendered several families homeless. The residents of the Kathputli Colony also witnessed a similar demolition drive in January 2017, in the peak of Delhi's winter.[97]

On 30–31 October 2017, led by the DDA and with a huge police deployment, the eviction of the Kathputli residents began. DDA used violence and tear gas to demolish over 2000 homes over a period of ten days for the proposed in-situ redevelopment project. The process, which began at 10 a.m. and lasted till 6 p.m., flattened 1000 houses, while 2000 more remained. DDA made hurried provisions for 2800 temporary houses in a camp in Anand Parbat.[98][99] What was astonishing was the amount of violence unleased by the establishment and police.[100] The area was under complete clampdown and even the press was not allowed access to the demolition site to cover the plight of the people. In a rarity, tear gas and a lathi charge were employed to frighten people into accepting the alternative accommodations. While the people scampered for accommodation amid the confusion and coercion, the DDA continued with the demolitions.[101][102]

On 31 October 2017, numerous civil society organizations approached the Delhi High Court on the grounds of non-compliance of eviction procedures and inconsistencies within the eligibility lists; they highlighted that a massive number of people had been evicted and rendered homeless in Delhi winters.[103] A complete stay on demolition was sought and the high court, noting gaps in the DDA's claims, enforced a blanket stay on demolitions for two weeks, bringing respite to the affected families and communities.[104][105]

In a surprise move, a day later, the DDA moved the high court, seeking relief so that the 'development' project could continue. Modifying its stay order, the Delhi High Court on Wednesday allowed the DDA to demolish the houses of only those residents of West Delhi's Kathputli Colony who were eligible for relocation and had moved out 'voluntarily'.[106][107] This proved to be a disaster as, under this pretext, in spite of court orders protecting non-voluntary residents, the DDA continued to demolish the leftover structures in the settlement. As the demolitions went further, the court too was unwilling to entertain requests for a stay or further scrutiny of the demolitions. The DDA kept using its extensive resources and community networks for coercion and cleared the settlements house by house.[108] While those considered 'eligible' for housing at the Kathputli Colony (2800 families) were moved to an overcrowded transit camp without adequate space and basic services, about 492 families were forced to do a makeshift arrangement to Narela, a resettlement site located 40 km away on the outskirts of the city. Those found 'ineligible' (754 families) were rendered homeless. Eventually, both the later groups struggled to stake claims individually and most remained without any compensation or alternative accommodation.

## Kathputli Colony Now

The Kathputli Colony is Delhi's first in-situ redevelopment project and was pitched to be a model for the coming years in other slum communities. Even a decade after its commencement, there are many aspects of the project that remain unclear, both for the residents of Kathputli and for the wider public.[109] Strong signals were sent by the minister for urban development and lieutenant governor of Delhi, who flagged off the Kathputli redevelopment foundation ceremony as chief guest, while the Kathputli residents were busy struggling in the courts to retain their claims.[110] This stressed on the significant shift and a changed reality that community claims and stay orders on projects are a thing of the past. Now the debate will be about individual claims, compensation and the mere terms of the same, of whether one is eligible or not, but development cannot be stopped.

## Conclusion

If good, effective planning is about better-designed, inclusive and liveable cities, Indian cities are proof that our urban planning model has not really worked. It has caused more problems than it has actually solved and is distant from the aspirations of the people who built and inhabit the city. The debate about whether Indian urban planning results only in exclusion and violation, or Indian cities are deliberately unplanned, is decades old. But the even the old pretence and benevolence with a degree of accommodation associated with the state, which permitted and allowed the informalities in urban centres, has dwindled.

Though housing a substantial percentage of urban population on a minuscule portion of urban land, in cramped and dense settlements, slums historically have been seen as sites of accommodation for groups that are oppressed in rural areas and wish to move to urban ones. Now, the last decade has shown that Indian cities will increasingly attack and remove them from their core. Arguably, this led to a planned exclusion, dispossession and erasure of urban poor and historically oppressed groups from the city's centre.

It is also extensively well argued that the Indian city has employed urban planning as a tool of exclusion and has been co-opted by global capital, which also aligns with the desire of separation within the cities based on caste and class lines. Akin to caste-based segregation, Indian cities have now seen the emergence of R&R sites across the bigger cities and gradually the smaller ones. All waiting with vacant flats to welcome and segregate the underclass of the city from the world-class, and thereby operating to further segregate and displace the urban poor and historically oppressed groups to the peripheries of cities. They are akin to Dalit *tolas* in villages: at the peripheries, under-serviced, devoid of amenities and far from the fancier, better-developed areas—thus depriving the present and the next generations from the right to further their lives. All this shows us how urban planning in Indian cities has lost its moral compass.

Increasingly, it is evident that the urban poor populations are pitched as impediments to development and are considered to be in opposition to the betterment of the city. Earlier notions of sacrificing for the 'greater good' have been replaced by demonizing the slums and oppressed communities and heightening the stakes of development to national importance. In recent years, judicial responses have often aligned with or failed to critically interrogate state-led actions targeting vulnerable urban populations—groups that are frequently portrayed as impediments to the broader goals of urban development. In cases such as those from Indore and Delhi, actions against slum settlements have proceeded even when they appear contrary to people's sentiment.[111]

This trend suggests a judicial deference to state narratives that frame such displacements as necessary trade-offs for long-term developmental goals, particularly under flagship schemes like the SCM. State-led urban planning provisions and laws delegitimize and paint communities and people's settlements as illegal. Bourgeois environmentalism, supported by elite NGOs and civil society organizations, has adopted an even more lethal tone, painting the urban poor and historically oppressed communities as not just illegal bodies, but as hazards to public safety in a life-threatening manner. All this while, despite the visible violence in Delhi and Indore, and the deaths of people in Mahul, the court orders effectively suggest sacrifices are necessary for development.

The last few years have also shaken many age-old beliefs of urban contestations and reinforced some existing ones. It was always expected among communities and civil society actors that once settlements become old, with acquired services over a period, they get de-facto protection along with occupancy rights from such evictions. That belief stands completely altered. Today, generations-old communities are being cleared and their settlements demolished. The newly declared smart cities are leading this rejection of long-held imagined occupancy, customary and other legal rights. And it is becoming tough to fight this trend.

The state has now gone beyond the rhetoric of who is legal and illegal; it is pushing the dispossession model with a development agenda—that 'we are demolishing to develop'. This allows the state to be ruthless and continue to pursue its agenda of urban planning and smart cities while sidestepping the legal, constitutional rights of the land. What is more disturbing is the ad-hocism in its approach to planning, where master plans—that are a more democratic and legally sound city-making process—are completely being ignored, for gains that are short-term and hollow, as opposed to holistic long-term development. SCM is leading the removals, flanked by PMAY and SBM that are operating in the guise of offering housing and cleanliness in the cities. Through the SPV, SCM is also destroying the little capacity of urban local bodies that exist, such as measures that underwrite the decentralization principles in the 74th Constitution Amendment Act.

It's also critical to note the collaborative role that the media and civil society plays in propagating this myth. They paint schemes, whether good or bad, as though they were for the betterment for all, towards national interest and beyond all criticism. Civil society has increasingly echoed the state's development agenda, where the eviction of settlements has turned into a process of rehabilitation and resettlement. This shift has overshadowed the communities' ongoing struggles and demand for land rights, with the discourse on the semantics of land rights being erased. The resistance against such urban policies are viewed with suspicion. The urban fabric has been completely devoid of people, their politics, their struggles and their narratives. The displaced people in our cities are reduced to being PAPs and the enormity of displacement is reduced to numbers and figures. This is something our cities will have to bear witness to and a price we must pay for development in the coming years.

The last few years have also seen a consolidation of a 'false image of the city' that we have created for ourselves. This has been aided by imported images of developed cities of the global north that can be sold easily to the political elite and by the vocal, aspirational Indian middle class. They are setting the standards for what we want and how we want our cities to be. It is not realized that this imagery rests on violence, violation and co-option of urban planning to serve the purposes of a few, and not the majority of residents who are in need. This needs to be countered with the reimagination of cities that are inclusive, sustainable but frugal, and use resources effectively. Adopting a notion of protecting, regulation and reinforcing people's settlements can be a means to go forward.

There is a need now to reclaim the cities, but that will not be possible without reclaiming the tool of urban planning coupled with the politics of land rights, that in the present is bereft and deprived of the idea of social justice. This will only happen if a host of actors—including the people, civil society and communities themselves—save urban planning from the hands of an expert few, top-down and centralizing practices, and make it a more egalitarian tool, redirecting us to a broadened definition of urban development for all; thereby bringing social justice, land and housing for all as a cardinal aspect of our planning and cities.

During the pandemic, we witnessed an accelerated drive of evictions. While people were ordered to stay home and struggled to survive, the business of eviction continued as usual, often justified under the pretext of illegal encroachments. In a post-Covid time-space, we have witnessed the further use of urban planning, Centre-led urban development schemes and spectacles like the G20 Summit in India, to unleash a wave of evictions and dispossession in scores of cities. The unsaid understanding of how international events are meant to make Indian cities world-class gets picked up by contending city governments and state governments competing to outdo each other. It is all the more critical that in the coming years, alongside the humanitarian challenges of addressing the needs of the historically oppressed sections, there will be daunting questions of sustainability and climate emergency that need to be addressed, which is also possible where people themselves are (re-)making their cities. Or else like other crises that are taking over as alibis for furthering the oppression and marginalization through planning, climate action will be (if not already) co-opted by the powerful for unequal cities. This democratization of urban planning coupled with radical people's resistance, struggles and aspirations on the ground level are the only way our cities can be salvaged and saved.

# Urbanization, Migration and Reclassification

## A Special Focus on West Bengal and the City of Siliguri

*Asok Bhattacharya*

We know that in terms of urban population, India ranks second after China. But in terms of percentage of urban population, India's rate of growth is even slower than that of many other developing countries. As per the census report of 1991, India's rate of urban population was 25.7 per cent, which increased to 27.8 per cent as per the census report of 2001. It further increased to 31.2 per cent in 2011. As per the census report of 1951, the total number of cities and towns in India was about 2000. In 2011, these numbers increased to 8000.[1] We know there are three factors of urbanization. One is natural birth rate, the second is reclassification and the third is migration. Urbanization is closely linked with modernization, industrialization and the sociological process of rationalization. It is considered to be an inevitable part of economic development and transformation. Urbanization is inescapable in the present scenario. In India, there are two kinds of towns: one is statutory, the other non-statutory.[2] Non-statutory towns are called census towns (CT) or peri-urban areas.

Urbanization is related to diversion of workforces from agriculture to non-agricultural activities. During the nineteenth and twentieth centuries, urbanization used to occur due to industrialization only. This may be called the first generation of urbanization. But twenty-first-century urbanization is the urbanization of developing countries. This may be called urbanization of the third generation, which is based on service sectors where agriculture is becoming non-remunerative. During the twentieth century, urbanization played a positive role in creating jobs, particularly in the developed capitalist or industrial countries. But in the current century, especially as a result of neoliberal economic policies, urbanization is not playing positive roles in socio-economic development in comparison with the last century. Because of the pursuance of neoliberal economic policies, cities are gradually losing manufacture-based industries.[3] These industries have lost the capabilities of absorbing the surplus workforces of rural areas. The present economic growth does not support job creation or labour-intensive projects.

A huge number of production-based industries have either shifted outside cities or towns, or are in the process of shifting. In place of these industries in most big or medium-sized cities, various service sectors are growing, such as banking, insurance, BPO, KPO, information technology-based services, high-end entertainment centres, commercial centres, malls, hotels and restaurants, real estate, etc. These sectors need highly skilled workers and knowledge, and a younger generation of workforce. The migrated workforce cannot be matched for these jobs in terms of skills. Even unskilled workforces, who were engaged in mills or productive units earlier, have been compelled to leave cities due to a lack of opportunities and suitable jobs. The surplus agricultural labour is not being attracted by the cities because of a lack of job opportunities. In the 2011 census report, we can see the trend of declining population in the capital region of Delhi, Chandigarh, the Mumbai suburbs, Hyderabad, Chennai, Ahmedabad, Kolkata, etc., due to less in-migration from rural areas.

Natural birth rates in the cities are also declining gradually.[4] Now, the important factor of urbanization is reclassification of rural areas and the emergence of new census towns. These towns are playing an important role in adding urban population to many states of our country.

\* \* \*

Now, to come to the trend of urbanization in West Bengal, especially during the last decade. The percentage of urban population in West Bengal is more than the national average. As per the census report of 2001, urban population in West Bengal was 27.97 per cent, and by 2011, it increased to 31.87 per cent.[5]

Interestingly, the contribution of statutory towns in the total urban population of West Bengal decreased between 2001 and 2011, from 24.17 per cent to 23.11 per cent.[6] As per the census report of 2011, the percentage points of difference between statutory and non-statutory towns was 3.80 per cent in 2001, and it increased to 8.76 per cent in 2011. The contribution of non-statutory or census towns in adding the total urban population in West Bengal, during the last decade, was 66 per cent, the highest in India. In Maharashtra, it was 16 per cent and in Tamil Nadu it was 25 per cent. In the 2021 Census, West Bengal was expected to see a reclassification of approximately 300 census towns. Simultaneously, about ninety-two census towns were predicted to be declassified. This suggests a net increase in the number of census towns, as more were reclassified than declassified.

If we come to the numbers of towns in West Bengal, we find that in 1991 these numbers were 382, in 2001 this figure decreased to 375, but as per the census report of 2011, it again increased to 909, and the growth rate over the previous census report was 142.4 per cent. The main contribution towards this increase was from non-statutory towns or census towns. In terms of the percentage of population in some towns in West Bengal, the contribution of towns populated between 5000 and 10,000 increased to 10.5 per cent from 4.3 per cent; the contribution of towns of 10,000–20,000 also increased from 5.1 per cent to 9.3 per cent, but in the case of towns with a population between 1 lakh and 5 lakh, the share decreased to 38.91 per cent from 48.9 per cent. Regarding the contribution of cities with a population of more than 10 lakh, the share declined to 19.2 per cent from 24.9 per cent. But this picture in Maharashtra, Gujarat and Karnataka was different, where the percentage of urban population increased in big and medium towns or in metro cities, in contrast to the small and medium towns or census towns.[7]

In West Bengal, it was found that urban population growth in the last decade was highest in the district of Howrah.[8] There are six districts in West Bengal where the growth of urban population was higher than what was recorded in the previous census report, and the district of Darjeeling was among this high category of urban-populated districts.[9] Why was there such a speedy increase of urban centres or urban markets? Simply because a huge percentage of the population of West Bengal discarded agriculture and joined in non-agriculture activities during the last decade. There may be different views on such growth of peri-urban areas in West Bengal. Some are of the opinion that this is the result of the distressed condition of agriculture and its gradual transformation to a non-remunerative nature. In some people's opinion, in West Bengal, this was the result of the success of land reforms, particularly Operation Barga,[10] and also the success of the implementation of the three-tier system of panchayats during the Left Front regime.

Further, on other factors adding to the overall urban population, we can see that West Bengal is surrounded by three sovereign countries, Bangladesh, Bhutan and Nepal. The North-east region also lies in proximity to West Bengal. Political instability in these countries and the surrounding states caused a huge exodus from these regions to West Bengal.[11]

Siliguri is surrounded by these three countries (at distances spanning between 7 and 50 km) and some other states have been riven by political instability. Siliguri is the only emerging metro city in this region. Geographical areas of this city consist of two districts, Darjeeling and Jalpaiguri. There is also the factor of prolonged political instability in the Darjeeling hill areas.[12] Most of the urban inhabitants of Siliguri belong to erstwhile East Bengal, or present-day Bangladesh, and also to Nepal, Bhutan, Assam and other North-eastern states. Besides, business communities, mostly the Marwaris, migrated to Siliguri in huge numbers and settled here permanently. Many migrant labourers, who belong to tribal communities, were brought by the British to work in the tea garden areas of north Bengal 200 years ago, from the districts of Chota Nagpur, Santhal Parganas and Odisha. Now they have settled permanently in the adjacent tea gardens. Many Gorkha labourers were brought in from the western part of Nepal by the British. Besides these, a multitude of poor people regularly migrate to Siliguri in search of unskilled or any other jobs. Economic activity in and around Siliguri is very robust, in comparison to other cities and towns of the surrounding states and districts, even though this does not result in creating new jobs.[13]

There was a time when a good percentage of the population of Siliguri were Nepalese. But gradually, this decreased with the passage of time. During the period of the political instability in the Darjeeling hill areas and North-eastern states, the in-migration of the Nepalese people again increased.[14] A huge number of Bengali people migrated to Siliguri due to the politically unstable situation and violence in Assam. This may also be an impact of the disputes related to the National Register of Citizens (NRC) in Assam as well. Most of these people are engaged in petty or medium businesses. Many young and educated people are being absorbed in the service sectors with low-paid jobs and are settling in Siliguri permanently. A large number of Bihari people migrant to Siliguri from the northern part of Bihar. They are engaged in unskilled labour jobs across the city. A good number of migrant workers can be seen in Siliguri; they are largely temporarily engaged in construction-related works, earth works, etc., and are from the districts of Maldah, Uttar Dinajpur, Purnia, etc. Usually, they are not permanent settlers, and go back to their native districts after the work is over.

If we analyse the trend of the growth of urban population in Siliguri over the last two decades, we find that the percentage increase of population in Siliguri between 1991 and 2001 was about 50 per cent. From 2001 to 2011 it came down to nearly 10 per cent.[15]

If we look at the ward-wise population in Siliguri, we will find that out of the forty-seven wards, the population of twenty-three either declined or remained stagnant or increased marginally during the decade of 1991–2001. During this decade, the percentage growth of population of ward numbers 4, 31, 32, 33, 34, 35, 36, 37, 38, 39, 40, 41, 42, 43, 44, 45, 46 and 47 increased from 100 per cent to 300 per cent. But during 2001–2011, the increase of population in these wards was minimal, except in ward 46. In ward 4, where the percentage increase of population during 2010–20 was less than 3 per cent; this increase was about 200 per cent for the 1991–2001 census. As a whole, during 1991–2001, the increase of population in Siliguri was about 50 per cent, but in the last decade, this figure was less than 10 per cent, i.e., 1 per cent per annum. It is seen that the rate of increase of population in seventeen wards newly added by the Siliguri Municipal Corporation is higher than that in the other wards.[16]

* * *

These statistics prove that economic activities during the last decade in Siliguri were not helpful in job creation in labour-intensive industries. The overall economic activity and economic growth rate in Siliguri might be high, but this was in the service sector, where the erstwhile workforce or migrated workforce is not suitable to be absorbed.[17] Because of that, the rate of in-migration in Siliguri is declining. A huge number of rickshaw pullers or van pullers used to migrate to Siliguri until a few years ago, from the districts of Coochbehar, Jalpaiguri, Uttar Dinajpur and north Bihar. But more recently, auto rickshaws, *totos* (diesel-run large autos), city buses and privately owned two- or four-wheelers have been introduced in large numbers. Hence, services of the migrant workforce are becoming redundant. They have had to go back to their native villages. A good number of poor people who earlier used to live in shanties or in non-notified slums shifted to peri-urban areas, which have now become easily accessible due to the improvement in road connectivity. They can easily commute from the peripheral areas to Siliguri.[18]

To attract people from outside, economic activity in the city, particularly in secondary sectors, has to be increased. Though the real estate or construction sectors in and around Siliguri are growing fast, these lack the capacity to absorb the huge numbers of unskilled surplus workforces from rural areas. In Siliguri, the rate of economic activity may have grown fast, but, as per the census report of 2011, the rate of urbanization and the rate of job creation are slow. The contribution of migration in adding to the urban population in Siliguri is now negligible. As stated before, whatever migration takes place here now happens mostly due to the situation arising out of political instability in the surrounding countries and states but not due to economic activity. Besides, the cost of land and living costs are also high in Siliguri's urban areas.

Siliguri, a rapidly growing town in northern West Bengal, serves as a vital gateway to the North-east and a key hub for trade, tourism and transportation. Despite its strategic importance, the town faces significant challenges, including unplanned urbanization, traffic congestion, frequent flooding and inadequate infrastructure. Yet, Siliguri also holds immense opportunities due to its location near international borders and potential for economic growth through cross-border trade and ecotourism. The resilience of its people is evident in their adaptability, entrepreneurial spirit and strong community networks, which help them navigate hardships and continue striving for a better, more inclusive future.

# On Homelessness

*Indu Prakash Singh*

> The city has turned into a battlefield where the strong wrestle down the weak and the rich exploit and tyrannize over the poor.
> —Kahlil Gibran

Delhi is no exception to what Kahlil Gibran says about cities. Compared to other cities of India, Delhi actually fares the worst in terms of the way the poor are treated. Among the poor, the homeless (which includes children, women, the elderly, destitute, disabled, mentally challenged, men, etc.)—i.e., the people who sleep on pavements, rickshaws, handcarts, *rehr*is (carts), railway platforms, flyovers, in parks, under bridges, etc.—are really in a vulnerable position.

This is not to say that slum dwellers fare any better. But from the point of view of a homeless person, slum dwellers at least have a place to sleep in—good or bad, small or dingy, doesn't matter too much. Also, in contradistinction to the homeless, slum dwellers do form a constituency for political parties, whereas the homeless have no ration card or voting rights in the city. Which is why they are in a condition of extreme deprivation and neglect, and are facing social ostracization. And this has given rise to the myths and misconceptions about the homeless, spawning and abounding. Little wonder why the gap between the homeless and the rest of society has increased manifold. We all know that the lack of social interaction is what generates fear, inhibitions, prejudices, hatred and contempt. The homeless are the worst victims of this process of marginalization (pushed out from the rural economy to the urban economy), leading to social apartheid.

## From Rural Poor to Urban Homeless

Politicians, bureaucrats and economists don't tire of repeating, day in and day out, that the glamour and privileges of metropolitan cities like Delhi pull people from the hinterlands. Their blinkered perception is far removed from the reality.

The homeless in Delhi are migrants, mainly from UP, Bihar, West Bengal, Rajasthan, MP, etc., who left their homes in the village due to extreme distress. They are pushed out of the rural economy, as there is no work for them; they are redundant as their skills, of weaving, crafts etc., do not fetch a living, and they have no or little landholding. Recurrent droughts and floods, too, have made agriculture impossible. Some are also socially persecuted, divested of property—by their relations or dominant castes.

So, there are a host of personal and economic reasons for this migration. Our villages remain starved of any tangible development, with much of the investment going into scams of all kinds. Everybody has been a beneficiary but the poor. Such is the condition in villages that even the primary health centres have operating theatres that aren't operational. The education situation is bleak.

So, most of the homeless are basically the rural poor, who are pushed out of their villages and reach the nearest city in order to address their poverty. The homeless are not a monolithic category. They have their unique problems, and in order to solve some of those, they are compelled to lead a precarious life, be they children, women, men, elderly, disabled or destitute. The Covid-19 pandemic particularly highlighted the pitiable condition the so-called migrants, the homeless, live in across the nation.

## Informal Economy

Many men are engaged as labourers: handcart pullers, loaders, rickshaw pullers, casual workers, etc. They are paid below the minimum wages. While both labouring men and women contribute to the growth of Delhi (that's the reason we call them CityMakers[1]) and subsidize our costs of living (by providing cheap labour), they get nothing in return, except insults and indignities heaped on them day in and day out. Few are able to save and send money back home.

Most of the children are engaged in rag-picking, pushing handcarts, working at street eating joints, etc. Women, disabled and elderly, are mostly destitute, with no one to take care of them. Many have been thrown out by their kindred, while others have grown old living on pavements. Dhanetri of Bihar was thrown out by her sons after the death of her husband. And at seventy years of age, she is left with no option except to beg at railway stations. Women and children are the most vulnerable among the homeless. While men can sleep anywhere they are able to, women have to watch out—they either sleep on the busy pavements of Paharganj or at railway platforms, temples, mosques, gurdwaras, churches, etc. Most children and women end up as victims of sexual exploitation, which is very common.

## Police Brutality

Among the myriad problems encountered by the homeless, the most brutal is regular police beatings. We ourselves have witnessed this and have challenged the police over this. Govind, a seven-year-old child in a night shelter, is nursing the dream (or nightmare?) of growing up to be like Hitler (he said so when asked what he wanted to be when he grew up). When asked why he wanted to be like Hitler, he remarked angrily, 'I was beaten by belts and boots by a Delhi Police constable. I couldn't walk and speak for over a week. I want to be a Hitler and kill all the policemen. They beat us every now and then.' One fails to understand what our police personnel are trying to do. And who has given them the authority to beat children and other homeless people mercilessly? Are the police above the law, or is there a law that governs them as well?

## The Myth of Criminality

If Govind grows up to be what he wants to be, that would justify the myth spread by the police—that criminals live on pavements. But nobody is born a criminal. Who will punish the constable who has ruptured the sensibility of a seven-year-old child? No one knows how many more children might become victims of this cop's brutality and nurse similar ambitions as Govind.

Whatever the police might say, we have a different reality to highlight. During our rapid assessment surveys, on countless night-outs on Delhi's streets from 7 p.m. to 6 a.m., from 2000 onwards, we have had women volunteers and colleagues with us. We went to all the so-called crime pockets of Delhi—be it Dholak Walon ki Basti, Majnu ka Tila, Yamuna Bazaar, ISBT, Anand Parbat, Inderpuri, etc. We didn't face any untoward incident. While Delhi tops in the entire country in criminality, definitely the criminals are not the ones living on the pavements of Delhi. Delhi Police should go beyond its most comfortable paradigm of solving crimes by arresting the homeless.[2] And the homeless neither have identity cards nor any guarantors nor any advocates who can represent them. Remember the 2008 blasts in Delhi? One blast got averted due to the sense of responsibility and exemplary courage shown by a balloon-seller child near Regal Cinema. He was awarded the Child Bravery Award in 2007–08. We are in touch with his family, who stay in Rajiv Chowk, New Delhi. This boy, who is an adult today, is still homeless, with his family staying in the DUSIB Shelter Complex, near the Bangla Sahib Gurudwara, Baba Kharak Singh Marg.

## Data

In 2000, we counted 52,765 (estimated over 1 lakh, assuming that for every one homeless person we counted, we missed one) homeless people in Delhi; in 2008, a study done by the Indo Global Social Service Society (IGSSS) numbered the homeless at 88,410 (estimated over 1.5 lakh). The census figures are underestimates. As per them, these were the number of homeless in India and Delhi in 1991 and 2001:

| Year | Census (national) | Census (Delhi) | AAA | IGSSS |
|---|---|---|---|---|
| 1991 | 12,00,000 | 29,000 | – | – |
| 2001 | 19,43,476 | 24,966 | 52,765 (June 2000) | 88,410 (May 2008) |

The above figures show how the census underestimated the figures.[3] We were not just witness to the 2001 census, but rather we provided training to the charge officers under whom the enumerators operate. The 2001 census was a total farce in this regard. We and the media reported about it in great detail. The same was the case in 2011, in many cities: Delhi, Mumbai, Chennai, Hyderabad, Kolkata, Bengaluru, Patna and Lucknow, among others. The next census, which was supposed to happen in 2021, got delayed due to the Covid pandemic. But we have to be vigilant in the next census and ensure that the exact numbers of the homeless, across the country, are captured in the data. We are also part of the Global Homelessness Data Initiative (GHDI) of the Institute of Global Homelessness (IGH) with UN-Habitat. The exact numbers are crucial for any planning and intervention.

The issue is glaring. Can we keep disputing the numbers of the homeless? The rampant evictions going on in Delhi and across the country (whether in the name of beautification, world-class city, erstwhile JNNURM, Commonwealth Games or the 2020 railway line clearances, environmental purges [Khori and others]) have increased homelessness. We all are required to address it. Can we remain mute spectators or will we join the homeless in their fight for their right to live and work with dignity?

Thankfully for us, the Delhi High Court intervened suo motu in 2010, and that changed the course for us in Delhi, with a large number of shelters coming up in the city. Our petition, WP 572 of 2003, filed in 2003, along with WP 55 of 2003, filed by E.R. Kumar, got activated in 2013. Owing to that, shelters have been coming up across the country.

We had our urban poverty group in the National Advisory Council, 2011–12. The National Urban Livelihood Mission (NULM) emanated from the deliberations of this group. Now, the specific criteria of 50 sq. ft living space per person is the bare minimum ensured in all the 24/7, all-year shelters for the homeless.

The 24/7 free shelters in Delhi are for everyone—pregnant and lactating mothers, chemically dependent women and men, families, children, women, men, disabled, elderly, people with mental issues, recovering patients, etc. Shelters for transgenders is the desiderata. The same should be made available across the country. In 2000, the government allocated Rs 1 crore for shelters (these were called night shelters; we clamoured for these being twenty-four-hour shelters, which they have become now) for the homeless for the whole nation. Today, under the NULM we have Rs 1000 crore. We have come far but still have a long way to go.

We need to have shelter complexes (shelters for families, women, men, children, chemically dependent [for de-addiction], recovery shelters) like the ones in Delhi near the side of Bangla Sahib Gurudwara, Jama Masjid and Sarai Kale Khan. And the shelters have to be in the concentration areas of the homeless, not far away from the hub of activity, food points, amenities, hospitals/health centres, source of livelihoods, etc. We need a policy for the homeless.[4]

It's time that all schemes and master plans are converged to empower the CityMakers, rather than pauperize them. And all the government departments should work with a missionary zeal to ensure human rights to all, especially the deprived, destitute, marginalized, stigmatized, excluded and exiled people and communities. Let them, too, belong to India, rather than decay in non-India.[5]

The work that we have done with the homeless, since 1999, makes it amply clear that courts have an important role in proffering justice. Courts are the last resort to put the Constitution of India to greatest use. Yes, there is inordinate delay in getting justice. But once a verdict is given, the governments have to abide by it. The same bureaucrats who would have done nothing to address homelessness were perforce made to deal with it with the intervention of the Supreme Court of India and the Delhi High Court. When laws are non-existent, or are silent on certain matters, courts using their jurisdiction and jurisprudence can usher in justice, especially when all other institutions of governance have failed. The law indeed is a potent tool to decimate poverty; it can be a harbinger of development and good for all, leaving no one behind.

Today, we are seeing the blatant misuse of governance by the Union government and the governments in states run by the Union government's party. On the slightest pretext of any protest, bulldozers are used to bring down the homes of 'protestors'. This is against the Constitution of India and the laws of the land, as well as the Universal Declaration of Human Rights, 1948. The National Register of Citizens (NRC) and the Citizenship (Amendment) Act (CAA) are tools that turn large numbers of Indians homeless. Over two decades since 1999, we have tried hard to create homes for the City Makers/homeless residents, with the support of civil society, media, judiciary, some proactive governments (like the one in Delhi) and the CityMakers themselves. We all need to resist the move across the world to generate homelessness by laws, wars, Islamophobia, lynchings, killings, etc. Organizations like the Institute of Global Homelessness, Chicago, are playing an important role in raising advocacy to end global homelessness and are taking the issue to the portals of the UN, UN-Habitat and other international bodies.

Gandhi, Martin Luther King Jr and Nelson Mandela have taught us that our lives are intertwined, and we need to work for the common good of all, especially the marginalized, oppressed, exiled, poor—people confined to the fringes of our country's policies and schemes. Now is the time to bring them centre stage.

Join us! To transform Delhi and the country, and the world—to build caring and happy cities. To create homes for the homeless.

## Annexure

The following constitutional and international instruments, declarations, covenants, conventions and charters are binding on India and need to be adhered to:

## Relevant provisions in the Constitution of India and international binding instruments regarding the right to housing[6]

### A: Constitution of India - Fundamental Rights

Article 21: The right to protection of life and personal liberty except according to procedure established by law.

Article 14: The right of every citizen to be treated equally before the law or be given protection of the laws within the territory of India.

Article 15 (1): The right of every citizen to be protected against any discrimination on grounds of sex, religion, race, caste or place of birth.

Article 19 (1) (d): The right of every citizen to move freely throughout the territory of India.

Article 19 (1) (e): The right of every citizen to reside and settle in any part of the territory of India.

Article 19 (1) (g): The right of every citizen to practice any profession, or to carry on any occupation, trade or business.

### A1: Constitution of India - Directive Principles

Article 39 (1): State policy to be directed to securing for both men and women equally the right to an adequate means of livelihood.

Article 42: Provisions to be made by the State for securing just and humane conditions of work and for maternity relief.

Article 47: Duty of the State to raise the level of nutrition and the standard of living and to improve public health.

## B: International Binding Instruments

### Article 25(1), Universal Declaration of Human Rights, 1948

Everyone has the right to a standard of living adequate for the health and well-being of himself and of his family, including food, clothing, housing and medical care and necessary social services, and the right to security in the event of unemployment, sickness, disability, widowhood, old age or other lack of livelihood in circumstances beyond his control.

### Article 12, Universal Declaration of Human Rights, 1948

No one shall be subjected to arbitrary interference with his privacy, family, home or correspondence, nor to attacks upon his honour and reputation. Everyone has the right to the protection of the law against such interference or attacks.

### Article 17, International Covenant on Civil and Political Rights, 1966

No one shall be subjected to arbitrary or unlawful interference with his privacy, family, home or correspondence, nor to unlawful attacks on his honour and reputation.

### Article 11 (1), International Covenant on Economic, Social and Cultural Rights, 1966

The States Parties to the present Covenant recognize the right of everyone to an adequate standard of living for himself and his family, including adequate food, clothing and housing, and to the continuous improvement of living conditions. The States Parties will take appropriate steps to ensure the realization of this right, recognizing to this effect the essential importance of international co-operation based on free consent.

## Article 5, International Convention on the Elimination of All Forms of Racial Discrimination, 1965

In compliance with the fundamental obligations laid down in article 2 of this Convention, States Parties undertake to prohibit and to eliminate racial discrimination in all its forms and to guarantee the right of everyone, without distinction as to race, colour, or national or ethnic origin, to equality before the law, notably in the enjoyment of the following rights:

(e) Economic, social and cultural rights, in particular: (iii) The right to housing;

## Article 14, Convention on the Elimination of All Forms of Discrimination against Women, 1979

2. States Parties shall take all appropriate measures to eliminate discrimination against women in rural areas in order to ensure, on a basis of equality of men and women, that they participate in and benefit from rural development and, in particular, shall ensure to such women the right:
(h) To enjoy adequate living conditions, particularly in relation to housing, sanitation, electricity and water supply, transport and communications.

## Article 27, Convention on the Rights of the Child, 1989

1. States Parties recognize the right of every child to a standard of living adequate for the child's physical, mental, spiritual, moral and social development.
2. The parent(s) or others responsible for the child have the primary responsibility to secure, within their abilities and financial capacities, the conditions of living necessary for the child's development.
3. States Parties, in accordance with national conditions and within their means, shall take appropriate measures to assist parents and others responsible for the child to implement this right and shall in case of need provide material assistance and support programmes, particularly with regard to nutrition, clothing and housing.

## Article 16, Convention on the Rights of the Child, 1989

No child shall be subjected to arbitrary or unlawful interference with his or her privacy, family, home or correspondence, nor to unlawful attacks on his or her honour and reputation.

The child has the right to the protection of the law against such interference or attacks.

## Article 9, International Labour Organization Social Policy (Non-Metropolitan Territories) Convention, 1947

Measures shall be taken to secure for independent producers and wage earners conditions which will give them scope to improve living standards by their own efforts and will ensure the maintenance of minimum standards of living as ascertained by means of official enquiries into living conditions, conducted after consultation with the representative organisations of employers and workers.

In ascertaining the minimum standards of living, account shall be taken of such essential family needs of the workers as food and its nutritive value, housing, clothing, medical care and education.

# Conceptual Limitations

## Analysing the Approach to Housing Projects for the Urban Poor

*Kanishka Prasad and Vertika Chaturvedi*

Numerous families across India's urban landscape continue to live in conditions unfit for human habitation. A lack of access to opportunities for work and resources in rural areas has been the cause of large numbers of occupation-based migration to urban areas, resulting in conditions of abject squalor in a large proportion of residential dwellings being built and inhabited across India. In 2011, 377 million people (31 per cent of India's population) lived in urban centres, of which as many as 65 million (or 27 per cent) lived in squatter or slum settlements.[1] The Economic Survey of 2017 noted that, on the one hand, migration to urban centres had been almost double of what the Census of 2011 had predicted, while on the other, districts in India that housed the lowest 40 per cent of our population received only about 29 per cent governmental funding.[2]

For the poor and in particular, the urban poor, there has been both a critical lack of housing and a general lack of access to the benefits sanctioned under governmental schemes and grants. Over the past seven decades since Independence, various kinds of schemes have been made to subsidize the development of residential quarters for the economically weaker section (EWS) and lower income group (LIG) categories in urban India. These have included resettlement schemes that involved upgrading of existing settlements by interjecting critical supply and services systems, relocation to new and often distant sites, sites-and-services schemes that provided the site and financial incentives for the construction of individual homes, and, more recently, in-situ rehabilitation schemes that rely on encouraging private developers to build a certain percentage of these homes in exchange for permission to build additional commercially lucrative built-up area.[3]

However, it is important to note that these categories of economic classification are based on arbitrary definitions of annual family income being derived typically from median incomes with no universally accepted standard,[4] yet what becomes clear is that these sections of society are the ones engaged largely in temporary, insecure and informal employment and so are exposed to great vulnerability. This results in scant availability of resources to meet even their most basic human needs and further means a great difficulty in garnering adequate means to develop any reasonable dwelling, let alone a pucca (or permanent) one. But conversely, a large proportion of the budgetary allocation towards schemes ostensibly made to help these marginalized sections remain at best underutilized. The most recent scheme, the Pradhan Mantri Awas Yojna (PMAY), which subsumed previously running projects of the United Progressive Alliance (UPA) government's Jawaharlal Nehru National Urban Renewal Mission (JNNURM) and inherited some of its shortfalls, achieved only a 12 per cent completion rate even after reducing its original target from 2 crore dwellings to 1 crore, and only a 33 per cent release of actual allocated funds (as per pre-pandemic figures).[5] Previous schemes have faltered because they have not considered the aspect of livelihoods. As a result, in due course, the resettled residents have tended to sell or rent the allocated shelter and return to squatter settlements in the vicinity of potential work opportunities. The singular definition of the permanent or pucca shelter, symbolized by the reinforced cement concrete (RCC) cast in-situ slab as the proverbial 'roof over one's head', with its universal aspirational appeal, primarily for its associative and connotative value, further leaves these already disenfranchised families to deal with prevalent constructional materials, techniques and market agencies. This means that more often than not, the modest governmental loan or subsidized grant proves grossly insufficient to effectively accomplish the brief.[6]

The UN, in its Global Report on Human Settlements of 2003, notes how the private real estate development and finance markets have also typically focused only on the needs of the middle and upper-middle urban home seekers with monthly family incomes exceeding Rs 60,000, whereas a typical slum family would have by comparison a monthly income of only about Rs 7500.[7] Governmental figures reported at the launch of the PMAY, with its ambitious target of housing for all by 2022, reflect a shortfall of 19 million urban homes of which as many as 56 per cent were said to be in the EWS category.[8] Yet over the last dozen years (from 2005–2017) the JNNURM, Rajiv Awas Yojna and the PMAY cumulatively had provided only 1.1 million dwelling units.[9] This number has since swollen to about 8.5 million units as per the PMAY (urban) website's claims[10], but a cursory scan of advertisements in popular dailies, journals, electronic media and web portals reveals a trend among developers and banks to offer as 'discount' the PMAY subsidy being given by the government, of Rs 2,67,000 on bank loans for two-bedroom and larger apartments in tower-like developments catering to the middle and upper-middle classes. This practice was sought to be curtailed by some state governments,[11] yet continues and gains significance in the context of the recent trend of declining supply and sales in the affordable housing sector in spite of such incentives.[12] Compounding this situation of crisis in terms of housing stock is that nearly 12 per cent of all built houses in urban India, in fact, lie vacant.[13] There is great disparity and lack of equitable distribution of resources both in terms of availability of land as well as access to input finances to develop residential housing stock in urban areas. Cities such as Mumbai have almost 15 per cent of total housing stock vacant, while Gurgaon and Pune, which have been developed as real estate hubs driven by multinational corporations, have as much as 20 per cent of the total housing stock lying vacant.[14] This presents a scenario of disparity where a third of our urban population (as mentioned earlier) lacks access to any resources to build themselves a house and is forced to live in complete squalor at risk to their and their families' health, while one-sixth of our population in the more affluent classes can actually afford two or more tenements, the second of which is held vacant. This growth is again largely fed by the housing loan market that, on the strength of high-paying corporate jobs, enables growing numbers of even middle-class families to invest in second properties at the farthest fringes of an ever-expanding urban sprawl.

This characterizes the quintessential model of urban development driven by market speculation that spurs a persistent demand for housing by promoting the aspiration of an urban lifestyle while at the same time adding sectors of land and built blocks further and further away from the initial urban centre. The urban sprawl in India, in recent years, has seen two significant governmental interventions at two distinct periods and under distinct administrations, namely the JNNURM, 2005, and the Smart Cities Mission, 2015. In different ways, they envisaged a push towards such a systemic urbanization and the 'elevation' of cities of differing hues towards such a homogenized view of that which is to be considered a world-class city. The JNNURM[15] was conceptualized as a joint initiative of the Ministry of Urban Employment and Poverty Alleviation (MoUEPA) and the Ministry of Urban Development (MoUD). The co-authorship of these two ministries indicated a policy thrust that poverty alleviation may be achieved by providing the impetus for greater urbanization by encouraging upgradation projects in existing urban centres, and also the elevation of smaller towns or rural areas to the status of emerging urban centres.

The JNNURM in its overview proposed a simultaneous thrust on developing and augmenting urban infrastructure while also focusing on delivering basic services to the urban poor. It proposed that the MoUD would take up projects of public infrastructure, including water supply and sanitation, solid waste management and road and surface transport, while the MoUEPA would focus on the task of targeting urban services at the urban poor.[16] The mission wished to focus on improved urban governance by increasing the role of the urban local body (ULB) as a tool for increased community participation in urban developments while increasing transparency and accountability within its functioning by deploying the City Development Plan (CDP) as a framework for planning interventions.[17] It suggested that resource management was to be the key focus while giving a major boost to urban development by making the process of grant of licence for building activity much more streamlined. It suggested an increased use of renewable sources of energy to supplement existing non-renewable electric supply, rainwater harvesting as a mandatory tool for groundwater recharge and a greater use of recycled water. While trying to focus on a welfare state approach to urban poverty alleviation, it significantly suggested the repeal of the Urban Land (Ceiling and Regulation) Act of 1976, thus permitting consolidation of land parcels in the hands of private individuals (developers) and the enactment of complementary and supplementary municipal laws within a regional and state frame, in order to incentivize private investment in real estate development.[18] Large-scale developers and construction companies were encouraged to purchase portions of land and seek consolidation to drive urban housing development and 'incorporate private sector efficiencies' in the sector.[19] It proposed the grant of 'assistance' by way of additional 'viability gap support' funding to ensure the 'commercial viability' of proposed development projects being executed by private enterprises.[20] In order to incentivize developments of this scale, greater floor area ratio (FAR), more lenient developmental norms and simpler processes for gaining approvals were encouraged for enactment as part of state-level reforms, thus allowing the developer to build more floor space than previously permitted while simultaneously recommending that 20–25 per cent of all urban land development in housing be dedicated to the service of the EWS/LIG categories.[21]

The more recent Smart Cities Mission of 2015,[22] driven this time by the MoUD alone, focused much more on the e-governance aspect of the first scheme and envisaged a greater role for technology-driven systems that would map people and services in a series of real-time Geographical Information System (GIS)-based models. This tracking of goods, services and people as visualized by the international consulting firm McKinsey and Co. would, in theory, give the agencies of public administration much greater control and a much reduced response time to ameliorate the issues of their citizens.[23] Disbursing all forms of services electronically, whether it be medicine, education, energy, transport, water and access to local government, was to be encouraged. The issue of housing, however, appears to have shifted from a stated commitment to upgradation and provision of affordable housing (particularly for LIG and EWS) to being a more general call for 'expanding housing opportunities for all'.[24] The government, from being a proactive driver of socially sensitive urban development, is conceived to have a reduced role of 'choreographer' or one who coordinates the disparate actions of other private actors acting in self-interest.[25] Outsourcing of production, including even the generation of the technological models and maps being followed by the applicant smart cities in the hope of achieving an automation of delivery is the perceived way forward.[26] The mission defines the position of consulting agencies (CA) and handholding agencies (HA)—such as the World Bank, Asian Development Bank, DFID, UN Habitat, etc.—as contributors and drivers of the process of generating project proposals and concepts.[27]

The mission also introduces, as part of the Smart City Proposal (SCP), the preparation of which is to be aided by these CAs and HAs, a City-Wide Concept Plan[28] that would be based on an overview of existing City Development Plans (CDP), masterplans, sanitation plans and mobility plans. When addressing the proposed projects within the urban space, it continues with two approaches from the earlier development approaches— one for the brownfield or older parts of the city that are to be rejuvenated by being retrofitted with newer services, while the other, for more distant peripheral zones of existing cities, to be treated as fresh greenfield developments with an in-built conception of these ideals. The mission document, however, introduces a third approach permitting the redevelopment of significantly large portions of the city by razing the existing constructions to the ground with a mixed land use and with higher floor space index (FSI) to generate greater density of occupation.[29]

The indications in these two schemes mooted by the two major political dispensations of India are that the country has been set on a path of rapid urbanization. Both schemes reveal a reliance on enabling private developers and promoting public-private-partnership (PPP) models in urban infrastructure development; and they see a significant role of private consulting firms in the conception of development briefs and agendas. However, the corporate interests of these developers, based on preconceived notions of economic viability, are served by catering to the affluent economic classes. The redevelopment project of the Kathputli Colony in the Shadipur area of north-west Delhi by Raheja Developers is a case in point. This redevelopment project included the development of a luxury condominium tower called Navin Minar, comprising serviced apartments ranging between 2300 sq. ft and 7200 sq. ft[30] on the understanding of cross-subsidized development of 2800 dwelling units for the in-situ resettlement of families living in the Kathputli Colony.[31] The colony of primarily travelling performers from Rajasthan that pre-dated Independence was razed in 2016 to make way for these two developments, but after numerous delays, the project remains incomplete to this day, forcing these families who were removed from their homes to continue living in a squalid transit camp nearby.[32] Additionally, the development of a luxury tower with such lavish square footage per apartment belies the very intent of promoting a greater FAR and FSI to achieve greater occupation density, particularly in the case of housing. With the focus of developers on building more high-rise developments but comprising primarily of units having a greater individual floor area for luxury living, urban developments of this kind tend towards even lower occupational densities.

These two schemes represent the intention of the government and governmental agencies in promoting the project-based model of development and funding, with project execution largely in the hands of private funding agencies or international aid agencies. We discuss in the next section the case of East Kidwai Nagar residential redevelopment to show how, in the process, by paying lip service to the masterplan yet not conducting rigorous impact assessment studies, the projects under these schemes executed by governmental agencies but driven by international consultants have managed to undermine the work of planning agencies of the past and present. Successive masterplans were drawn up keeping in mind present-day growth as well as projected growth trajectories for the entire urban and suburban region, and thus continued to hold out the hope of a sense of cohesiveness in the urban pattern and efficiency in resource management over time. Recent masterplans of Delhi–NCR, for 2021 and 2041, envisaged the all-round development of the National Capital Region in order to have dispersed urban settlements to simultaneously cater to the demands it faces given its international and regional prominence along with a unique multi-agency governance structure and yet decongest its already overburdened limits. These documents incentivized the adoption of alternative sources of water and electrical power, particularly renewable sources.[33] However, with the introduction of new documents,[34] like the city-wide concept plan representing a parallel developmental agenda promoted by an alien consulting company impacting the redevelopment of significantly large portions of the city without clearly specifying the procedures for transport and environment impact assessment, the focus appears to have shifted from ensuring an effective implementation of the overall vision of the masterplan document to the execution of visually impactful projects. In Delhi, the debates around the East Kidwai Nagar (also cited in the Smart City Mission document as an example of a redevelopment project)[35] and Nouroji Nagar–Sarojini Nagar developments, with large residential and commercial components, bear witness to this trend. These developments, executed by the National Buildings Construction Company (NBCC) for the Government of India, have been done with the primary thought of maximizing the estimated market potential of the land in question by adding commercial spaces that can be leased for offices[36] to the programme brief, rather than with the intent of developing a residential space for government functionaries in a holistic and inclusive manner. This notion of returns on investment as being the prime driver of the project was belied once again when the revenue department of the government was asked to step in and lease 60 per cent of the developed commercial space after the NBCC reported finding few takers for the developed commercial space.[37]

Corporate interests driven by bottom-line performance and statistical analysis of demand data push the majority of developers to promote projects of high monetary return projections without any consideration for social upliftment. The project had previously been disallowed in 2012 by the Delhi Urban Arts Commission (DUAC), calling the seventy-six towers that make up the residential development to be a 'vertical slum'.[38] This was noted in a Delhi High Court order in a petition filed by lawyer Aman Lekhi in 2021,[39] that cited how the DUAC had twice rejected clearance to the project objecting to the repetitive blocks with a height of 150 ft as having an 'adverse impact on Delhi's character and environment' and how the 'scheme presented destroy[ed] the emerging future urban design form and architectural character'. The court judgment merely cites that the revised plan submitted to the DUAC in 2013 was approved by it without going into the details of why it was hurriedly granted permissions the subsequent year in the face of such stern and fundamental critiques earlier. Menon and Kohli are of the opinion that that was done citing an urgency of demand, without a detailed environmental impact assessment; even after it received legal rebuke from the National Green Tribunal (NGT) and DUAC for cutting almost 85 per cent of the 3300 existing trees and insufficient action towards compensatory tree planting and other afforestation commitments.[40] The project has faced much litigation both in the NGT that cited NBCC for felling of 16,500 trees in the area, and the civil courts, including the Delhi High Court, which temporarily stayed the grant of possession for the commercial spaces in 2018.[41] While the litigation seems to have yielded little by way of legal censure, it may be noted that flawed assumptions about critical aspects of the impact of the project, whether in terms of traffic (for which the NBCC relied only on the foreign consultants' traffic assessment and sought no independent audit), water demand or overall environmental impact have characterized the conception and design of this development and were sought to be reassessed by the courts with the aid of experts.[42] Yet the private consultant responsible for the masterplan and design, Chapman Taylor, continues to advertise it as one of their premier projects that has been presented and discussed at COP-21 held in Paris 2015 as a model of sustainable urban development.[43]

The dominant narrative of urban development thus appears to be shifting increasingly in favour of private developments and large-scale individual building projects conceived, in letter and spirit, on the basis of the requirements of international funding agencies and their consultants. This means that cities that are today projected to be beacons of prosperity have little to offer the weaker sections of society who continue to be compelled to settle in slum or squatter settlements.

The UN Habitat (Slum Almanac 2015–16)[44] defines the slum as a place composed of households that are characterized by the existence of one or more 'household deprivations'. These deprivations are listed as i) lack of access to supply of water, ii) lack of access to proper sanitation, iii) lack of sufficient living area, iv) lack of housing durability, and v) lack of security of tenure. According to this definition, UN Habitat estimates that as many as 1 billion people live in a slum or slum-like tenements globally. As noted earlier, slum rehabilitation schemes that often involved relocating the squatters failed to foresee adequate forward and backward linkages to employment opportunities for them at the new site, leading to situations where allottees would sell their resettlement apartments only to return to shanties either in or near the place of previous residence. This in more recent times has given way to the trend of in-situ slum rehabilitation, but as reported by inhabitants of the Kathputli Colony still awaiting their homes, they experience a lack of trust in the process of redevelopment when the developer is allowed leniency in spite of numerous delays with no accountability.

While these slum or squatter settlements are viewed as problems by the majority of urban administration and planning agencies, it is important once again to look at the positive role that these settlements may play by according a sense of autonomy and self-determination to their inhabitants. In conclusion, we wish to discuss some trends in this direction and look at whether these may provide an alternative definition for terms like dwelling, house, settlement and housing.

*Architectural Design* magazine in 1968, edited by architect and product designer Charles Eames, refers to an older study (covered in its August 1963 issue) of an 'architecture-without-architects'.[45] One of the key contributors to this volume and, through his professional experiences in Latin America and Africa, to this movement in housing and its design, was British architect John F.C. Turner. An architect from the Architectural Association of London in 1954, Turner worked with the design and construction of architectural projects in the public sphere and with the housing design of squatter settlements in Peru between 1957 and 1965. In the 1970s, he was a part of urban studies research at both the Massachusetts Institute of Technology (MIT) and at Harvard. Over the past six decades or more, he has advocated for an autonomous system of design and construction in the case of housing in general and in the case of squatter settlements in particular, by trying to redefine dwelling as an activity (so a verb) as against its noun form representing a finite end state housing unit limited by its deterministic preconception by a professional architect who is alien to the processes of living and production adopted by its inhabitants.[46] He made this case by highlighting this as the core misunderstanding between the professional and the client, as seen in his experience of building a school in Arequipa, Peru.

The clients, the district council of Tiyabaya working on a Ministry of Education grant, were given a design for the proposed school by Turner and Peruvian architect Luis Filipe Calle as representatives of the Office of Technical Assistance to the Popular Urbanizations of Arequipa (OATA).[47] The structure proposed by the duo using local materials and technologies, in an attempt to maximize space utilization, climate response, spatial performance as well as the monetary resources made available by the governmental grant, was first extensively quizzed and then only grudgingly passed by the council. Subsequently, however, during execution, the material was changed to being reinforced cement concrete for the structure to reflect the aspirations of the council members. What this actually meant was that in place of building the proposed workable school well within the given grant amount, the council struggled even to complete the first classroom. Finally, the school and the council were spared the logical conclusion of their decisions, as an earthquake in the region literally buried the matter.[48]

This incident amply demonstrates the chasm between what a habitation needs to be and what the technocrats imagine and execute it to be. In *Freedom to Build*,[49] Turner makes the argument that the preconceived biases of public administration about housing in particular manifest themselves in the articulation of design language in the building by-laws or code. This he argues to be a restrictive enumeration of abstract norms about dwelling units that actually imply certain assumptions about dwelling itself. Turner further argues that these assumptions contribute greatly to the failure of housing schemes, primarily because they lack a nuanced understanding as well as the ability for a calibrated response to the act of dwelling. Additionally, they lack the flexibility to allow for the evolution of this conception of the act of dwelling with time. He demonstrates how governmental funding of projects, based on a predictive model converted to a prescriptive solution, falls woefully short of meeting the house owner's needs, as it fails to appreciate the potential strengths and divergences of each particular family and their dwelling unit, be it in terms either of number of occupants or nature of usages. He notes how house owners even in the lowest income bracket may over time incrementally spend on their dwelling unit twice or thrice as much as the allocation and per-unit construction cost of any publicly funded housing or redevelopment scheme.[50]

While Turner advocates a near complete withdrawal of the state or developmental agency, granting full autonomy to the owner of the dwelling to construct, shape and manage their habitat, Chilean architect Alejandro Aravena, winner of the Pritzker Award 2016, in his project for social housing in Iquique, Chile, makes a case for partial autonomy. His project gives residents 'instead of a full good house they cannot afford, half a good house they can'.[51] In a similar vein, Indian architect Ashok B. Lall propounded a four-part matrix for the built structure of the chassis, the infill, the accessory and the auxiliary representing respectively the main structure, the walling material to enclose space, additional spaces (like balconies and verandas) attached to the main space and lastly, the elements of ornament like awnings and coverings that render spaces more functional. Lall's proposal suggested that the first two parts of the matrix fall in the scope of the developer, which can either be a private or a public agency, while the latter two would grant each owner partial autonomy to shape their individual tenement as part of a high-density low-rise affordable housing scheme.[52] The present Ministry of Rural Development, under the Pradhan Mantri Awas Yojana-Gramin (PMAY), proposes an IIT Delhi and UNDP report titled *Pahal*[53] containing a set of dwelling unit design solutions that are categorized by various types of climatic and topographical regions in eighteen selected states of India. These solutions cater to the specific needs of the particular region and incorporate the use of regional materials and technologies.

In this way, some architects and urban designers appear to be making small departures from the urge for a singular and inflexible solution of past schemes to a range of more dynamic and localized regional solutions. Yet the question of whether this is enough of a departure from the established order of the prescriptive solution, and whether this too would yield non-personal and culturally alienating dwelling units that may be easily abandoned by the inhabiting family for even minimal financial inducement, still needs to be addressed. If private enterprise is to be encouraged, it must be done in an increasingly democratic manner, offering true empowerment to each owner upon every dwelling unit to decide the nature and detail of her own habitation and community, irrespective of her social and economic class. Such a methodology of design characterized truly by free choice would yield a level of engagement with the process and the resultant personalization of the end solution, enabling users to gradually build bonds with the emerging architecture and so make them less likely to abandon it. Further, the use of new materials and innovative usages of existing ones must be encouraged to yield a level of frugality and efficiency of material and energy usage. In the context of an impending global climate crisis, these must form the key drivers to an innovative aesthetic and design, which are essential tools to also tackle the burgeoning urban dwelling crisis.

# New Governance Regimes and Urban Development

## Mathew Idiculla

India's embrace of economic liberalization and globalization in the early 1990s has transformed the trajectory of urban development in a fundamental way. Though urbanization was viewed with suspicion in the early years of independent India, cities are now increasingly being promoted as the 'engines of economic growth'.[1] The new economic policies of 1991 and other subsequent economic reforms have not only transformed the nature of urban development but also the governance architecture of Indian cities. With India adopting an economic growth-centric idea of urban development, new institutions in the form of Special Economic Zones (SEZs), industrial townships and smart cities are gaining ascendance across the country. This essay seeks to clarify and explain the transformation of the governance architecture of urban development in India by examining the emergence of such new institutions.

This essay characterises SEZs, industrial townships, smart cities and such other institutions as 'new governance regimes' since they operate in parallel to the conventional urban governance system and are often granted exception to regular laws and regulations. It argues that new governance regimes are created to allow capital to bypass the social, economic and political realities of Indian cities and operate in a space removed from the routine pressures of the regulatory state and recalcitrant society. Such governance innovations attempt to supersede the local democratic and political processes that exist in Indian cities by locating themselves outside the legal and geographical boundaries of the city. Though new governance regimes operate through the suspension of certain laws, I argue that the extra-legality of these spaces is distinct from the informality that characterizes much of urban India. Instead, they operate above the logic of master plans and seek to create sanitized spaces that overcome the barriers posed by an active informal economy and a bureaucratized regulatory state.

This essay is organized into three main sections. The first section examines how global capital unfolds across new spaces and how this is resisted by existing social systems. It provides the necessary context for understanding how new urban governance regimes emerge in India. The second section discusses the nature and characteristics of such new urban governance regimes. It specifically examines the institutional architecture of SEZs, industrial townships, smart cities and charter cities. The third part discusses how we can conceptually characterize and make sense of the emergence of new governance regimes in the context of the spread of neoliberal urbanism across the globe.

## Global Capital and Local Politics

As global capital spreads to new spaces, existing economic and political divisions that were based on the sovereign state's national boundaries have become much weaker. David Harvey (2001) argued that capitalism operates by an inherent logic that aims to eliminate spatial barriers to the flow of capital or, as Karl Marx had put it, the 'annihilation of space through time'. As

Rosa Luxemburg argued, for the 'untrammelled accumulation' of capital, it needs to engage with non-capitalist strata and social organizations and obtain ascendancy over these territories and social organizations. Since the majority of natural resources and labour power are in pre-capitalist production, capital needs to access these territories and transform its social systems. Such a transformation has been conceptualized by David Harvey (2003) as 'accumulation by dispossession', whereby neoliberal policies cause the concentration of wealth in the hands of a few by dispossessing the larger section of the public of their assets and rights.

This process, Harvey argues, is currently being played out in the Global South as new territories are forcefully opened to facilitate accumulation due to declining growth rates and absence of avenues to absorb overproduction in capitalist economies. It has accentuated since the 1970s as a result of capitalism's crisis of over-accumulation, whereby the surplus arising out of capital reaches a point where reinvestment no longer produces returns and hence requires the moving of capital to new territories (Harvey 2003). Hence capitalism, which is 'addicted to geographical expansion', devises a 'spatial fix' that is achieved by restructuring investments geographically (Harvey 2001). Accumulation by dispossession is itself Harvey's reworking of Karl Marx's exposition of 'primitive accumulation' to argue that accumulation is a continuing process and not a one-time event. Primitive accumulation, according to Marx, is a process that led to the emergence of industrial capitalism when the primary producers like peasants and workers were separated from the means of production (Marx 1867).

The attempt of global economic forces to capture new territories in the developing world is, however, met with various forms of resistance from the existing social systems of these spaces. According to James Holston (2009), countries in the Global South are witnessing the emergence of an 'insurgent citizenship' challenging the upshots of the global urbanization process. Holston uses the example of Brazil to argue how insurgent citizenship confronts entrenched and differentiated forms of citizenships with alternative formulations of citizenship that make claims over property, urban infrastructure, social justice and demands to legalize the illegal. As urban residents make a claim to having a 'right to the city', they become active citizens who mobilize their demands through various means to challenge the practices of citizen inequality.

In India, the conditions of informal economy, non-modern social systems and insurgent political processes act as hindrances towards the unfolding of the process of global urban transformation. Rajesh Bhattacharya and Kalyan Sanyal (2011) have argued that unlike the traditional urban regeneration approach in the West, which overhauls the physical, social, economic and environmental character of the city, India follows a 'bypass' approach to urbanization by focusing on new towns in the peripheries of older metropolises. Bhattacharya and Sanyal use the concept of 'political society' popularized by Partha Chatterjee (2004; 2008) to argue that the informal workforce in existing cities creates an urban governmentality that limits the ability of planners to engage in Western-type gentrification. Hence, capital seeks to bypass the insurgent politics of existing cities and move to new towns in the periphery where the laws of public space and private property can be more strictly enforced.

A major sphere of the Indian economy, especially land, operates by a logic not fully in sync with purely capitalist systems. This is because a lot of land lies with small landholding peasants who do not always treat it as a pure financial asset (Levien 2011). Hence the state performs the function of a 'land broker' by acquiring land from farmers using the Land Acquisition Act and transferring it to private players. This works on a Lockean rationale where the state expropriates land from 'low-value users' and hands it to classes that can 'improve it'. The resistance to land acquisition increases due to the huge difference in the prices paid to farmers for the land and the value of the land once it is handed to large private companies. Hence, the unfolding of capital is severely contested on the grounds and is not sustainable without special legal instruments provided by the state.

In Indian cities, global capital is also confronted by a form of urban localism embedded in peculiarities of local municipal politics. Through 'vote bank' politics, as Solomon Benjamin (2008) argues, poor groups are able make claims to the state and access basic infrastructure and services. As the locally elected councillors are embedded in society, their agency is made use of by these groups to pressurize the administration to channel public investments. Further, as Arjun Appadurai (2001) argues, poorer groups also act strategically by building broader alliances with the help of NGOs to reconstitute citizenship in a manner that mediates globalizing forces to benefit the poor and results in a 'deep democracy'. Hence, the political agency exercised by people on the ground in various forms prevents global capital from gaining complete domination in India. It is the presence of such urban local politics and an informalized economy that requires the state to create new governance regimes that can overcome the barriers faced by global capital to remake Indian urban spaces.

## The Emergence of New Governance Regimes

The dominance of state-aided economic globalization is evident in the emergence of new governance regimes in the form of SEZs, industrial townships, smart cities and charter cities. As Saskia Sassen has argued, globalization has resulted in the 'denationalisation of sovereignty', whereby cities and other strategic regions replace the nation as the key spatial unit (Sassen 2000). Though globalization does not alter the territorial boundaries of the national state, it transforms the exclusive territoriality of the national state. As Neil Brenner (1999) further argues, globalization does not occur merely through the geographical extension of capitalism but is premised on the construction of large-scale territorial infrastructures and state institutions that enable the expansion of capital accumulation. The creation of new territorial infrastructures is hence part of the reterritorialization of states taking place with globalization.

With global economic forces altering the territoriality of the national state, new governance regimes take precedence. National states are also deeply involved in the implementation of the global economic system by producing the legal encasements necessary for the functioning of global economic transactions (Sassen 2000). The emergence of new governance regimes like SEZs, industrial townships and smart cities can be seen as new legal encasements necessary for the functioning of global economic transactions. These new governance regimes operate at a level separate from the national, regional and local state but are created with the help of state institutions. We will now look at the institutional architecture of some of the most prominent new governance regimes emerging in India.

## Special Economic Zones

Special Economic Zones (SEZ) are the most prevalent institutions in India that operate under a parallel legal–institutional framework. To attract foreign direct investment (FDI) and promote the export of goods and services, SEZs have been created as forms of extra-territorial enclaves with exemptions from regular tax laws, customs and excise duties and relaxations in labour laws.[2] Since one of the main objectives of SEZs is the 'generation of additional economic activity', it can be argued that SEZs are a mechanism of the state-led process of spatial reorganization in which the state acquires land for 'public purpose' and transfers it to a private developer (Dey 2012). India's Export and Import Policy of 2000–01 allowed SEZs to be set up by public, private or joint ventures, and this was provided a more robust legal structure by the SEZ Act in 2005.

Though India has experimented with the concept of Export Processing Zones (EPZs) since the 1960s, only with the SEZ Act of 2005 did it adopt a comprehensive legal regime for these zones to operate outside the sphere of the regular state. While EPZs were public sector-based operations, whose transactions required official attestation by the state, India's China-inspired SEZs operate on the basis of self-certification on tax-exempt transactions (Jenkins 2011). But unlike Chinese SEZs, Indian SEZs represent a privatized model of industrial development whereby private companies develop, maintain and govern economic zones on a for-profit basis (Levien 2011).

The SEZ Act provides that goods and services imported from and exported to SEZs be exempt from the payment of taxes, duties or cess under twenty-one different enactments specified in a schedule to the act. SEZs have hence been characterized as instruments of 'radical deregulation', which is a 'tax giveaway to the rich' (Jenkins 2011). The SEZ Act is also seen as a regime of labour governance that has been consciously structured to promote the non-implementation of labour laws by making the development commissioner rather than the labour commissioner responsible for the implementation of labour laws (Singh 2009). Only 50 per cent of the SEZ land needs to be used for any productive purpose, and the rest can be used for real estate projects that perform the task of reinvesting corporate profit for further capital growth (Sampat 2010). Hence, SEZs represent a new governance regime that is designed to allow global capital to operate outside the regular norms of state institutions.

## Industrial Townships

Along with SEZs, industrial townships are the key legal instruments by which corporate enterprises can exist in enclaves outside the regular legal framework of the state. Industrial townships emerge out of the history of industrial towns, which have existed for a long time, the classic case being the 100-plus-year-old Tatanagar, Jamshedpur. However, the governance of some of these industrial sites have come under major criticism (Sood 2015). Areas falling under industrial townships are the only ones that have been given an exception to the constitutional requirement of local self-government mandated after the passing of the 73rd and 74th Amendments to the Constitution (Idiculla 2016).

Article 243Q of the Constitution mandates the creation of elected municipal governments in all urban areas but provides an exception to the areas declared as 'Industrial Townships'. It empowers the state government to declare certain areas as an industrial township if the industrial establishment of that area provides or is capable of providing municipal services in the specific area. Interestingly, the proviso was a last-minute introduction into the 74th Constitutional Amendment Act and was not present in the previous versions of the bill. As K.C. Sivaramakrishnan (2015), one of the chief architects of the amendment, pointed out, this proviso was introduced only when the bill was being taken up for clause-by-clause consideration. Industrial townships have hence become the ideal legal instrument used by the state to allow commercial enclaves to operate without local democracy.

The industrial township exemption provision has been employed in varied ways by different states in India. In Karnataka, a provision in its Municipal Councils Act has allowed Electronics City in Bangalore, home to India's most prominent IT establishments, to operate under the Electronics City Industrial Township Authority (ELCITA).[3] ELCITA collects and retains the majority of the property tax from the tech companies that operate within it and hence works a unique regime of private governance (Idiculla 2016). States such as Andhra Pradesh,

Gujarat, Jharkhand, Karnataka, Kerala, Madhya Pradesh, Odisha, Rajasthan, Tamil Nadu, Uttar Pradesh and West Bengal have notified SEZs as 'industrial townships' under Article 243Q of the Constitution (Dey 2012). The guidelines for development of SEZs issued by the Government of India to the states provide the following: 'State Government should take appropriate steps to declare the SEZs as industrial townships under Article 243 Q of the Constitution with appropriate governing body giving suitable representation to the SEZ developer, units and SEZ residents.' Hence, SEZs and industrial townships are associated instruments that are used by the state to ensure that certain geographical enclaves function outside the regular legal regime of the state.

## Smart Cities

Smart cities also represent a new regime of capital-centric urbanization which champions technological solutions to urban problems and bypasses local democracy. Smart cities may be created either as built-from-scratch new cities or by retrofitting existing cities with new technologies. In India, the push for smart cities initially involved building brand-new cities. Smart cities were to be the nodes of larger industrial corridors like the Delhi–Mumbai Industrial Corridor, the Chennai–Bangalore Industrial Corridor and the Bangalore–Mumbai Economic Corridor (Idiculla 2014). The BJP manifesto for 2014 also promised the creation of '100 new cities; enabled with the latest in technology and infrastructure'.[4] However, with the launch of the Smart Cities Mission in June 2015, it became clear that the Indian government wasn't creating 100 new cities, but rather converting 100 existing cities into smart cities.[5]

In fact, the Smart Cities Mission is predominantly about retrofitting or redeveloping a tiny fraction of an existing city. The purpose of the mission is to 'drive economic growth and improve the quality of life of people by enabling local area development and harnessing technology'.[6] The entry requirements for foreign direct investment in real estate have also been substantially reduced to allow global economic players to play a larger role in the development of smart cities. Hence, the smart city initiative can be said to be an attempt to attract international investment by creating new urban centres—investment that circumvents the regulatory hurdles it otherwise faces (Idiculla 2014). This utopian imagination of the city, based on the rhetoric of 'speed', seeks to build new cities by avoiding 'bottlenecks' caused by politics through 'fast policy' (Datta 2015).

Apart from their narrow vision of urban development, what makes India's smart cities a new governance regime has to do with the manner in which local governments are undermined. The smart city mission guidelines state that the body which will implement the smart city projects is a special purpose vehicle (SPV), in the form of a company in which the private sector can also invest.[7] It will be these SPVs which will 'plan, appraise, approve, release funds, implement, manage, operate, monitor and evaluate the Smart City development projects'. The mission guidelines state that the SPVs will have 'operational independence and autonomy in decision making and mission implementation' and that this also 'encourages' local government to delegate its decision-making powers to the CEO of the SPV.[8] Hence, smart cities in India represent a new mode of decision-making that further disempowers urban local governments.

## New Governance Regimes and Neoliberalism

New governance regimes like SEZs, industrial townships and smart cities are various instruments that seek to bypass the politics of the local. A key feature of many of such governance regimes is the requirement for a 'single window' clearance system which provides for expedited approval of various permits needed from the government for setting up any project. The requirement of single-window clearance for projects is also a conditionality commonly imposed by international financial institutions while approving loans for projects.[9] While the legal form might differ, what these new institutional arrangements do is reduce the state's regulatory control over these areas in an attempt to attract international investment.

How do we explain the emergence of such new urban governance regimes in India? It is not enough to characterize this transformation merely as an instance of 'neoliberalism' or 'neoliberal urbanism' (Banerjee-Guha 2009). Neoliberalism, a term specifically associated with the polices followed by Ronald Raegan in the USA and Margaret Thatcher in the UK in the early 1980s, implies a laissez-faire society where the state performs a limited role and the free market determines the way the economy is organized. However, in the context of India, despite the economic reforms of the early 1990s, the state has not retreated in spending in social sectors in a similar manner (Sud 2006). Rather than a retreat of the state, as Kanchan Chandra (2015) argues, the patronage-based relationship between the state and the market has been relocated and transformed in post-liberalization India as the state plays the role of gatekeeper in newly liberalized sectors such as power, telecommunications and mining, and also the role of a supplier of inputs like land and natural resources.[10]

Hence, it is important to look at alternative ways of conceptualizing the post-liberalized state in India. One useful framework to understand such transformations is what Neil Brenner and Nik Theodore (2002) called 'actually existing neoliberalism'. This approach examines the contextually embedded manner in which neoliberal restructuring takes place instead of using the deterministic framework of 'neoliberal ideology' that assumes the operation of market forces in the same manner wherever it is unleashed. It is important to focus on the contextual nature of the operation of globalization especially in a country like India where multiple economic, social and political rationalities compete for ascendency. In the case of India, it is clear that the unfolding of economic reforms has not prevented the state from entrenching welfare rights through legislations like the National Rural Employment Guarantee Act, 2005 and the National Food Security Act, 2013, going against the trend followed in many other countries where International Monetary Fund (IMF)-inspired structural reforms were carried out.[11]

Given the nature of new governance regimes in India, it is also useful to examine Aihwa Ong's (2006) framing of 'neoliberalism as exception'. Neoliberalism here is seen as a technology of governing that is extraordinarily malleable, manifesting itself in different ways in different regimes. Through ethnographic case studies in East and South-East Asian countries, Ong explains how states, in order to compete in the global economy, make exceptions to their usual practices of governing and employ a variety of neoliberal strategies to re-engineer political spaces. Ong uses Foucault (1991) to examine how neoliberalism does not actually diminish state power but encourages a varied form of governmentality through which states manipulate populations. She further draws on the idea of exception from Carl Schmitt (1922) and Georgio Agamben (2005) to explain how new forms of state treat citizenship and sovereignty not as normative rights, which are defined territorially, but as privileges which are distributed unevenly (Karl 2007).

If one observes the changes in the state form after liberalization, the unfolding of special enclaves, such as SEZs, industrial townships and smart cities, strikes as a key aspect of state transformation. These new governance regimes operate as private enclaves at a level separate from the state but brought about by formal enactments by the state. Hence, the very instrument of law is used here to circumvent the operation of multiple laws, rules and regulations and create an enclave of exception. These new regimes prioritize a few cities and regions catering to niche sectors like information technology and seek to make them 'engines of growth' for the national economy. These new institutions provide the 'geographic scaffolding' (Brenner 1998) and 'legal encasements' (Sassen 2000) necessary for the smooth operation of the global economic system. Such new institutional architectures can be said to emerge out of the negotiations that economic globalization enters into with the existing social systems of the new spaces it seeks to capture.

The most brazen attempt at creating new governance regimes distinct from the existing democratic system are charter cities.[12] This idea, initiated by Nobel laureate Paul Romer, advocates developing countries to lease out a chunk of their land to developed countries to build new cities with distinct rules that promote economic growth (Romer 2010). To create a charter city, the developing country must enact a charter in the form of a founding legislation which defines the new rules that operate in the city. Inspired by the example of Hong Kong and Shenzhen, Romer believes that these cities with distinct rules will emerge as hubs of economic activities that attract investment and people. Charter cities essentially ask developing countries to make a Faustian bargain: give up your sovereignty and gain economic growth. While charter cities have still not emerged in India, it has its advocates in India, with an editorial of *Mint* opining that the idea of charter cities should be taken seriously by the Narendra Modi government.[13]

How do new governance regimes relate with the rest of urban India? India's cities are said to be characterized by informality since a high number of people, especially the urban poor, live in informal settlements and unplanned neighbourhoods, on the margins of legality, and strategically negotiate with the state to make their claims (Chatterjee 2004). In fact, informalities permeate the Indian urban space to such an extent that much of the city can be classified as unauthorized due to widespread violations in planning and building laws (Ghertner 2008). Hence, as Ananya Roy (2009) has argued, the very process of urban planning can be said to be characterized by informality in which the claims over land are not based on a prescribed set of regulations but on a contestation between published plans and territorial claims made on them. While much of Indian urban space is characterized by such informalized planning and legal regime, new urban governance regimes challenge the pre-eminence of urban informality. Though new governance regimes also work through the suspension of laws, the extra-legality of these spatial entities, I argue, is distinct from the informality that characterizes much of urban India. All forms of circumvention of plans cannot be seen as symptomatic of the state working through the idiom of informality through active deregulation. However, the institutional character and motivations of new governance regimes like SEZs, industrial townships and smart cities are fundamentally different from the informalities and illegalities that operate in urban India. These spaces operate above the logic of master plans and hence are not instances of 'planned illegality' (Bhan 2013) or informality where the planning regime works through deregulation. As this essay has demonstrated, new governance regimes are by law and institutional design exempted from the regular legal regime and hence do not operate through the daily contraventions of the law or the routine 'regularizations' and 'legalizations' of such contraventions.

## Conclusion

New governance regimes are created by the state under the influence of capital's need for enclaves in the developing world that operate at a level separate from the state and society. Unlike the capital-led urbanization in the global north, here global capital encounters an Indian social that does not quite march according to the tunes of capitalist modernity. Traditional forms of landholding in rural areas and a large informal economy in urban areas act as barriers to the unfolding of global capital. Globalization is hence essentially mediated by the local and has to evolve and transmute itself into new forms. And so, global capital transforms itself to new avatars to fit the conditions of the local. New governance regimes in the form of SEZs, industrial townships and smart cities are being created by such a process with the aim of overcoming the politics of the local.

Though new governance regimes seek to bypass the regular legal regime, their institutional character is different from informalities and illegalities that characterize much of urban India. These entities are, in fact, designed to overcome the informality of the regular urban space and create an enclave of exception. However, it is difficult to characterize these spaces as Agamben's (2005) 'state of exception'. While individual civil rights are suspended under the 'state of exception', fundamental rights and criminal laws are not suspended in India's new governance regimes. Since the exceptional nature of these spaces are more in terms of economic incentives and special governance systems, it needs to be seen as particular modes through which the state reinvents itself in the context of economic globalization.

As global market forces are met with the social and political realities of existing localities, they need to come up with innovations. These innovations take the form of new governance regimes like SEZs, industrial townships and smart cities. These new institutional arrangements are required because global market forces cannot often successfully transform the geographies of local economy in the manner envisioned. New governance regimes hence function as enclaves of exception that operate at a level detached from the official state and the social and political churnings that otherwise dominate the local sphere. Any triumphalist rendering of these governance innovations needs to be challenged for the threats they pose to urban local democracy.

## References

Agamben, Giorgio. *State of Exception*. University of Chicago Press, 2005.

Appadurai, Arjun. 'Deep Democracy: Urban Governmentality and the Horizon of Politics'. *Environment and Urbanization*, (2001): 13.2, pp. 23–43.

Banerjee-Guha, Swapna. 'Neoliberalising the Urban': New Geographies of Power and Injustice in Indian Cities.' *Economic and Political Weekly* (2009): 95–107.

Benjamin, Solomon. 'Occupancy Urbanism: Radicalizing Politics and Economy beyond Policy and Programs'. *International Journal of Urban and Regional Research* 32, no. 3 (2008): 719–29.

Bhan, Gautam. 'Planned Illegalities: Housing and the 'Failure' of Planning in Delhi: 1947-2010'. *Economic and Political Weekly* 15 (2013): 58–70.

Bhattacharya, Rajesh, and Kalyan Sanyal. 'Bypassing the Squalor: New Towns, Immaterial Labour and Exclusion in Post-Colonial Urbanisation'. *Economic & Political Weekly* (2011), 46 (31): 28–41.

Brenner, Neil. 'Global Cities, Glocal States: Global City Formation and State Territorial Restructuring in Contemporary Europe'. *Review of International Political Economy* 5, no. 1 (1998): 1–37.

Brenner, Neil, and Nik Theodore. 'Cities and the Geographies of 'Actually Existing Neoliberalism''. *Antipode* 34.3 (2002): 349–79.

Chandra, Kanchan. 'The new Indian state: The relocation of patronage in the post-liberalisation economy.' *Economic and Political Weekly* (2015): 46-58.

Chatterjee, Partha. *The Politics of the Governed: Reflections on Popular Politics in Most of the World*. Columbia University Press, 2004.

Datta, Ayona. 'New Urban Utopias of Postcolonial India: "Entrepreneurial Urbanization" in Dholera Smart City, Gujarat'. *Dialogues in Human Geography* 5, no. 1 (2015): 3–22.

Dey, Ishita. 'Emerging Spaces and Labour Relations in Neo-Liberal India: A Review Essay'. *Policies and Practices* 49 (2012).

Foucault, Michel, et al., eds. *The Foucault Effect: Studies in Governmentality*. University of Chicago Press, 1991.

Ghertner, D. Asher. 'Analysis of New Legal Discourse behind Delhi's Slum Demolitions'. *Economic and Political Weekly* (2008): 57–66.

Harvey, David. 'Globalization and the Spatial Fix'. *Geographische Revue* 2, no. 3 (2001): 23–31.

Harvey, David. *The New Imperialism*. Oxford University Press, 2003.

Holston, James. 'Insurgent Citizenship in an Era of Global Urban Peripheries'. *City & Society* 21, no. 2 (2009): 245–67.

Idiculla, Mathew. 'Crafting 'Smart Cities': India's New Urban Vision'. *openDemocracy*, (2014), August 22.

Idiculla, Mathew. 'New Regime of Private Governance: The Case of Electronics City in Peri-Urban Bangalore'. *Economic and Policy Weekly* 51, no. 17 (2016): 102–10.

Jenkins, Rob. 'The Politics of India's Special Economic Zones'. In S. Ruparelia, S. Reddy, J. Harriss and S. Corbridge (eds) *Understanding India's New Political Economy. A Great Transformation?*. Routledge, 2011: 49–65.

Kapur, Devesh, and W. E. B. B. Richard. 'Governance-related conditionalities of the international financial institutions'. No. 6. United Nations Conference on Trade and Development, 2000.

Karl, Rebecca E. 'Neoliberalism as Exception: Mutations in Citizenship and Sovereignty'. *The China Quarterly*, vol. 189 (2007): 188–90.

Khera, Reetika. *Democratic politics and legal rights: Employment guarantee and food security in India*. New Delhi: Institute of Economic Growth, University of Delhi, 2013.

Levien, Michael. 'Special Economic Zones and Accumulation by Dispossession in India'. *Journal of Agrarian Change* 11, no. 4 (2011): 454–83.

Luxemburg, Rosa. *The Accumulation of Capital*, trans. Schwarzchild (1951): London

Marx, Karl. *Capital: A Critique of Political Economy (I): The Process of Capitalist Production*, 1867.

Ong, Aiwha. *Neoliberalism as Exception: Mutations in Citizenship and Sovereignty*. Duke University Press, 2006.

Romer, Paul. 'Technologies, rules, and progress: The case for charter cities.' Center for Global Development, No. 2471. 2010.

Roy, Ananya. 'Why India Cannot Plan Its Cities: Informality, Insurgence and the Idiom of Urbanization'. *Planning Theory*, 8(1) (2009): 76–87.

Sampat, Preeti. 'Special Economic Zones in India: Reconfiguring Displacement in a Neoliberal Order?'. *City & Society* 22, no. 2 (2010): 166–82.

Sassen, Saskia. 'Territory and Territoriality in the Global Economy'. *International Sociology* 15, no. 2 (2000): 372–93.

Schmitt, Carl. *Political Theology: Four Chapters on the Concept of Sovereignty*. University of Chicago Press, 1985 (1922).

Shatkin, G. 'Planning Privatopolis: Representation and Contestation in the Development of Urban Integrated Mega Projects'. In Roy, A., and Ong, A. (eds) *Worlding Cities: Asian Experiments and the Art of Being Global*. John Wiley & Sons, 2011: 77–97.

Singh, Jaivir. 'Labour Law and Special Economic Zones in India'. Centre for the Study of Law and Governance Working Paper Series, Jawaharlal Nehru University, 2009.

Sivaramakrishnan, K.C. 'Who Rules the City?'. *Indian Express*, 10 February 2015.

Sood, Ashima. 'Industrial Townships and the Policy Facilitation of Corporate Urbanisation in India'. *Urban Studies* 52.8 (2015): 1359–378.

Sud, Nikita. 'The Indian State in a Liberalizing Landscape'. *Development and Change* 40.4 (2009): 645–65.

# Inclusive Urbanization[1]

## Romi Khosla

I used to love cities long before I began to study them. They nourished my early life and continued to trigger my dreams about the future during my student days. And then, as the future began to unfold, I found that cities felt rather different from my dreams. But still, the magical feeling of cities continued to be with me during my travels as a playground for my imagination, in which I would play the games of my ambitions. Now, as I look around me, I have a feeling that I must have been blind in those happy days. Now, it's time to join that magical imagination to my common sense, because either I have changed or the city has changed.

Why, I ask myself, am I unable to negotiate my way through that urban magical imagination any more? Have all those milestones of my hopes and wishes vanished? It now feels so messy. Has the charm of urban life taken a nosedive, or is it that we and the world around us have changed? The answer to these questions unfolded as I began to work professionally at the city, and see both its magical side and its darker side together as two sides of a coin. That darker underside, the tails of the coin, which had remained hidden from my view in those happy days, has now begun to show on its flip side.

## The Secret Ingredient Called Inflation

Even before I had qualified to become a professional architect and planner, cities had become the focus of my life's work. As my knowledge of them grew and as I began to study their histories, economies and their fates in the longer-duration social dimension, I began to see them differently. Their subliminal levels, their darker sides began to clarify. One saw that cities were used as silos where the elite stored their accumulating wealth in layers. All around me, the city was expanding, mushrooming and bursting at its seams. The city has become a container of real estate investments, and its advocates regard inflation as the best way for growing the value of their built investments. Wealth that has been accumulated as liquid wealth or black money has been placed into the city in a built form that keeps growing from its own dynamics, like a mushroom culture. The power elite oblige builders and help them acquire agricultural land by converting its planned land use from agriculture land use to urban land use by applying the legal legislation that is called 'Change of Land Use' to legalize its conversion from agricultural or orchard use.

Once that has been done, the mushroom effect called inflation simply enables that land to swell in value as flats and real estate gated communities. It's as if the new colonies act as yeast which investors 'cook' to rise like baked bread. This swelling rise in the urban volume of the city creates built spaces that need migration to service the flats and shopping malls, etc., and so the city authorities do everything to encourage it.

## Absorbing Dark Money

Real estate absorbs the swelling and accumulating wealth. It becomes the depository for darkly earned cash. It explains the darkest reasons for our cities becoming barren and punctuated with elite gated estates in its midst. However, our financial elite knows that by letting inflation thrive, they could harm the voters. Their adverse reactions had to be controlled somehow. The only way to do this was to continuously invent promises that would persuade the subaltern urban population to have faith in their future life, which our policies would eventually ensure would be better than the present. Inflation had to be tolerated and would be blamed on the previous regime. And so the city deepened its social divide. On one side sit the elite families in their luxury flats watching the same TV programmes with shared values and children in universities abroad, all alike and happy with the same happiness that comes from rising real estate values and rents, a sense of happiness which they share with urban Europeans and Americans. On the other side, listening to the promises being made, sit the poor unhappy families who remain, each of them, uniquely unhappy in their own particular way. Each of them, whose families are devastated in a different way. Each of them coping with their food shortages and bad health in their own particular way.

## Giving up on Happiness

Despite living in the twenty-first century, seven decades after Independence, our policies have not been framed to be able to generate enough happiness to share with everybody. Like accumulated wealth, the happiness of living in cities too is preserved and reserved for those who are afloat and taking a ride in a sort of inflated air balloon. They experience a happiness that wraps around the swelling wealth that forms the city. Below the hot air balloons, large areas of the city are covered with temporary shelters, where tens of thousands of our divided people continue to live in terrible conditions. Some terrible wrong is being perpetrated in our cities on our own people, and this wrong has been going on for decades. Freed from colonial rule, our successive governments have not been able to plan their cities without the ghettoization of the poor into what we, in independent India, call slums, squatter settlements, illegal colonies or shanty towns. It's a practice that comes down from colonial times, and our policymakers simply cannot help themselves and continue to replicate that practice. The British used to simply call such areas 'black towns' and disinfected them frequently, which is something our governments have not bothered to do.[2] So really, not much has changed. Inequality remains and the same persistent poverty lingers.

What has changed, however, is the surrounding neighbourhoods of these blighted areas. Instead of building spacious bungalows, our newly liberated ruling elite is busy building gated tower bubbles of high living that float above the stubborn slums. Like our colonial masters, successive post-Independence governments have regarded it as perfectly natural for overwhelming wealth and persistent poverty to live side by side.

## Cities Are the Core of Our Future Civilization

Our cities form the core of our entire modern civilization. They are the instruments that will forge our evolving society. We have to look after them and love them rather than exploit them as providers of wealth for the elites. Cities are places where modern identities are being invented. Places where our contemporary history is being written. Today, more than ever before, our cities have become mirrors of our times, where the richest of the rich and the poorest of the poor get pulled or pushed around searching for ways to improve and change their lives. If we continue to pump our urbanization landscape around mega cities and identify our already gigantic cities as sources for our future prosperity, our patterns of wealth distribution in the future will continue to reflect that elite urban landscape of gated communities and shopping malls. Wealth patterns can only be radically rearranged if the pattern of urban settlements gets rearranged. The future of our civilization could prosper beyond our expectations if the settlement patterns and urban governance of our habitat get radically decentralized. Without that happening, we will just watch the disintegration of our rural economy while its inhabitants migrate and come to the mega city to survive.

The poor who migrate from the villages into the growing cities are joined by other migrants from the middle-class privileged minority who also move into the city in thousands. Every day, millions of people across India pack their belongings and move from one place to another in search of better opportunities, safety or simply a fresh start. This constant movement of people, known as migration, is reshaping our cities, villages and the very fabric of Indian society. But what exactly is migration, and how does it impact the places people leave behind and the communities they join? Understanding migration is crucial because it affects everything from job markets to cultural diversity, making it one of the most significant demographic phenomena in modern India.[3]

## We Have to Find Hope

There is some hope that we can rectify this dreaded onslaught of neoliberalism and its renewed efforts to take over the lands of the city and convert the city into a wealth-accumulating machine rather than being a place where all the inhabitants can live happily. We have to find that hope. The city, we should recall, has always been the place for alternative views and philosophies, some of which nurture resistance to exploitation. It is the place where groups and individuals living in close proximity not only inspire each other but also lead each other into describing alternative just causes.

A choice awaits us. Our cities, as they function today, can be transformed into becoming the pivots for an entirely new national economy and they can continue to spin the thread of wealth accumulation that can be shared among each and every human settlement. With such a change, an entirely new pattern of urban-led wealth generation can be developed within an umbrella of decentralized self-employed micro-capitalist modes of development, which are spread across the city in the form of nodes, with employers running small workforces as an alternative to the mega-corporate centralized monopoly over the city's resources. The city can provide a hospitable environment for innumerable cellular economies that are powered by the self-employed and engaged producers who are spread across Indian cities and across our smaller towns. Such an economic transformation that encourages and sponsors microenterprises rather than large-scale mass employment industries alone can transform our cities.

## A New Urban Landscape

This proposal to reconstitute our urban landscape and our urban settlements across our entire subcontinent is inevitable because the urban crisis facing India is shared by the cities of our neighbouring countries. It is extremely serious and leads us to ponder the question: 'What will become of our cities now that we have encouraged the formation of mega-cities?'

It is not possible to change the entire system of wealth generation to a system that has a decentralized economic base without transforming our cities. Our urban paralysis cannot be solved by pleasing our loan creditors and stock markets with elite housing and better highways and flyovers for the exclusive benefit of private car owners.

Our TV anchors have become the authors of our contemporary history. With information being bombarded at such high-decibel levels, it is easy to overlook that the causes of urban poverty are syncretic and the lives of each of the poor relates to their own varied terrains of geography and culture and to the microeconomics of their particular ways of survival. It is not the telephone and the TV that need to reach them—it is the agents of change who will reconstitute the economy of each city in the country and revive the land use, the urban landscape and the productive capability of the inhabitants.

## Our Capabilities and Potentials

Our urban crisis is allied to our inability to search for a future from our own capabilities and geographies. We need to ignore the rules and utopias of the global community and stop treating the poor as patients in need of dole. They are the agents of change with huge potential and capabilities. We need not have the pretext of trying to become a global power by using false strengths and resolves to emulate models of economic progress and social development that come from nations grown rich through questionable means.

We must remember that no country can become modern without removing poverty. India has remained a remarkable exception in the modern search for freedom under the influence of Gandhi, who advocated balanced practices that avoid the violence of the wars and revolutions that grand strategies need before they promise utopias in the future. The answer to what will become of us now is therefore a very troubled one since, in the post-Gandhi period, we have increased our blind faith in the questionable trajectories of progress that had once industrialized the West, while forgetting that it took two world wars, civil wars and revolutions for the Western countries to industrialize.

## Asian Cities

As we step away from the global constraints, we will also need to recall that our new modern cities are just recent appendages to our urban civilization. While these modern cities have displaced the fabric of the earlier Asian urbanism, which was a component in our regional economy for many millennia, they are unstable in form and size in comparison with earlier Asian urban centres, such as Old Istanbul, Beijing, Vijayanagar and others. Around AD 1500, only about 1,25,000 people lived in Paris, and less than 1,00,000 lived in London. At the time, 1,25,000 lived in Paris and fewer than 1,00,000 in London. The largest cities in the world were in Asia and the Near East:[4]

|  | Population (circa 1500 AD) |
|---|---|
| Constantinople (Istanbul), Turkey | 7,00,000 |
| Beijing, China | 6,00,000 |
| Vijayanagar, India | 5,00,000 |
| Cairo, Egypt | 4,00,000 |
| Hangzhou, China | 2,50,000 |
| Tabriz, Iran | 2,50,000 |
| Gaur, India | 2,00,000 |

## The Colonial Capture of Our Urban Landscape

Today, we need to search for a clearer insight into decisions made long ago that continue to affect us to this day. The colonial economy of the nineteenth-century city changed the land use in each conquered country and dislodged the ecological and economic balance in the entire region. It traumatized the farmer, indigenous ruling elite and indigenous traders by dismantling their trading networks that were spread out and decentralized across the country. A new export-oriented, colonial, extractive economical system was wedged into the self-sufficient, naturally occurring one by redirecting the commodities of the then existing multi-nodal economy towards new colonial entrepot cities fitted out for exporting to the West. These decisions to tie the urban Indian production infrastructure to the Western world began many centuries ago and continue to this day, determining our identities and prospects. There is a need to relook at our inheritance and place the events of the present into a much wider canvas of history and speculate about 'how did we get here'.

## Alternative Subcontinental Urban Landscapes

We need to unpack alternative ways of seeing our future. We need another future than the one being forced on us by our policies that are selling a utopia taken from large multinational corporation reports. We need to uncover the roots of an alternative future that lie buried in our own urban history, and we need to dig them up and see how we can learn from them and consider safer and more just contemporary urban landscapes. In the process of unpacking alternative ways of seeing our own future, we need to discover our inherent capabilities and potentials to give ourselves forms of development and freedoms that are deeper and more complex than the smart ones being offered by neoliberal policymakers as solutions geared towards economic development.

The potential for a new future, one that will save our urban civilization, lies in the diversity of multiple, decentralized and alternative democratic forms of urbanism. This will inspire us to work in new directions for inter-city, inter-district, inter-*tehsil* and inter-panchayat regional trading and then give value to varying community identities and prosperities. Our rates of economic growth must remain heterogeneous and we must set in motion multiple ways of self-governing cities of much smaller size than the bloated dysfunctional ones that get captured as consumer markets by the global marketing companies. In this new future, development freedoms will be assembled and re-clustered together in micro-locations. We have no choice.

The micro or quantum existence of our lives has been broken by colonial rule and we must repair it by repairing our cultural, economic and social chassis by tightening it bolt by bolt to support that alternative future. Such a situation can only come about with the redistribution of the formations of urbanism and of urban wealth and resources that need to be generated by multiple small cities and production centres, instead of a few mega-cities.

Our urban policymakers have been duped into believing in a grand concept of India that is awaiting its destiny, which will be realized with a 'big bang/take-off'. These policymakers believe that centralized industrial corridors punctuated with lumps of smart macro cities and satellites can become the anvil for beating a new Indian modern identity into shape. The binders of the new urban landscape consist of five industrial corridors. Apart from the Delhi–Mumbai Industrial Corridor (DMIC), there's the Bengaluru–Mumbai Economic Corridor (BMEC), the Chennai–Bengaluru Industrial Corridor (CBIC), the Amritsar–Kolkata Industrial Corridor (AKIC) and the East Coast Industrial Corridor. They have all the illusory glamour of borrowed jewellery, and are intended to garland India.

By investing borrowed international loans into new city formation, the policymakers hope that the national income will rise and a smart supra-national urban identity will emerge to be proud of our smart cities. Experts have already, however, sounded the warning bells on this idea of smartness. 'We have to deal with the basics first,' Executive Director, Shivani Chaudhry, Housing and Land Rights Network, said in an interview with Citiscope. 'The fact is that a large part of our urban population is living in really dismal conditions, without basic services. Smart cities are not based on city-wide plans. They cater to a select population within a city. More than smart cities, we need smart solutions in an inclusive policy framework. Equity should be at the heart of urban planning.'

But since the beginning of the last century, despite the spectacular growth of urban populations, the poorest half of the world has received just 1 per cent of the total increase in global wealth. We have been simply complying with neoliberal corporate investor temptations and pressing the accelerator on increasing the extent of our urbanization at the price of increasing our debt to investors and lenders.

## Dangers of Debt Slavery

Very briefly, we should be warned about a potential decline of our cities and our modern urban civilization. India is facing unsurmountable migration into the cities, of people who come in search of illusory jobs and clean drinking water too. It is a crisis-laden, dangerous situation building up in a country with little hope of industrializing or increasing its national wealth. We cannot afford to retreat into a corner, afraid, uncertain, with a growing taste of bitterness in our mouths. If the prospects of industrial growth are declining and the possibilities of premature de-industrialization are real, such a model of growth will be accompanied by worse social upheaval, the tip of which is already beginning to surface because of the increase in unemployment.

There is an assumption that grand concept strategies and 'trickle down' will somehow solve the problems of Indian cities, which are dogged by increasing poverty, closely held concentrations of wealth, extensive regions under drought and high suicide rates among the extremely destitute.

As far as we can determine, there is a new Indian urban landscape being planned that consists of smart cities and export-directed industrial corridors binding the landmass and securing its people with centralized intel and identity papers. The migration figures predicted by the designers in the corridor project are explained in the Delhi–Mumbai Industrial Corridor (DMIC) plan. Smart cities will give urban India a supra-national loyalty, common currency, common language, common laws and rights, a common identity, a common patriotism and a common allegiance to the macro-economic model of prosperity.

## Recent Shifts in Thinking about Economics

Theorizing about urban-led economic growth, worldwide, has now become a multidisciplinary activity and proposition. Some embrace socio-economics, some anthropology, while others look through the lens of cultural studies. It is generally recognized universally that urbanization can be an extremely complex phenomenon. However, our policymakers have opted for the simpler big-bang model of urban investment. It is not the intention of this essay to review the models. Apart from the investment required in transport, there is additional real estate required to allow the cities to expand as well as the vast consumer market that draws retailers like honeybees.

However, despite the confusions surrounding the question 'What to do next', the last five decades have seen a shift in the epistemology of economics. Amartya Sen's *Development as Freedom* and Thomas Piketty's *Capital in the Twenty-First Century* are just two recent examples of books in which the debate about economic growth and wealth generation has recovered some of the ground that was lost to economics in the 1950s and 1960s, when the focus shifted away from political economy towards mathematical or scientific economics outside the imponderables of development history and political corruption. The return of economics after the 1960s into a hybrid discipline allied to the social sciences has placed it, once more, in the middle of the cleavage between the Left and the Right. In contradiction to these new trends of thinking pioneered by Sen, Piketty and Elinor Ostrom, the libertarian view was championed by economic theoreticians such as Friedrich Hayek and W.W. Rostow, who wrote *The Stages of Growth,* and Milton Friedman, who suggest linear theoretical approaches to economic development that relies on the private sector to deliver more simplified outcomes.

## An Alternative Urban Landscape

To enter the next era of history, we need to imagine our future urban landscape within a wider historical framework of global prospects and governance. The emerging Indian condition is one of extreme uncertainty. It is almost as if, in the coming era, the social and economic conditions of our civilization will begin to turn full circle, and we will be wearing, once more, a new life jacket thrown to us, this time by the neoliberal lifeguards. It has happened before, when the East India Company came and pulled us on to their boats as their slaves. In the twenty-first century, the corporates of today do not need the rule and soldiers of the Queen of England. They now have extraordinary inventions in artificial intelligence and manipulated social media to capture the space of our freedom, discussion and democracy. We have known, since gaining our freedom, that those friends that come to us bearing gifts have actually come to drive us into debt to the global institutional framework.[5]

As an independent country, we have continued to be dependent on external aid. In the early days, soon after the 'India will awake' speeches of 1947, came the Soviets with ample handouts to set up our steel industry and defence systems. Then came the Americans to help us feed our population with PL 480 funds and massive irrigation and river-damming projects. The British could do little for us as they had been bankrupted by the war. Giving us independence was a much easier option than trying to administer an awakened people.

However, the wider question before us concerns the condition of indebtedness as a form of continuity in financial captivity. We have taken our debt–donor dependence for granted as a way of life. The Second World War did not deconstruct the colonial empires of the Anglo-Saxons. Our dependence on colonial rulers simply shifted from Britain to Pax Americana and the Soviet Union, who simply occupied the space vacated by the retreating English colonial empire. The British had controlled our economy and our society by occupation and direct rule. The Second World War had, however, gutted the institutional frameworks of the colonial world and the neoliberal lobbies had begun to rise up in America, led by their economists advocating initiatives to start assembling a new network of institutions to control global affairs as well as the affairs of the struggling colonies.

It is within such a wider historical framework of our global prospects, which will be really governed by global institutions, that we need to imagine our future urban landscape. The boldest debt trap that has been primed to snap around our ankles has been devised in a way to transform our urban landscape, and indeed our urban economy and sociology into a haven for the private sector to accumulate wealth for its donors. An example of such a policy being enacted is the Delhi–Mumbai Industrial Corridor project. The Union cabinet has decided to divert $90 billion for the DMIC project. This will be one link in the chain of industrial corridors that will take our dependence on global financial institutions to a new level, never before seen in history. These will be implemented in collaboration with Japan and begin with the setting up of an industrial corridor along the Delhi– Mumbai stretch. This project is well under way and has been endorsed by the McKinsey Global Institute and documented by Scott Wilson. It intends to build several new cities, twenty-four industrial nodes, three ports, six airports and a 1500-km-long high-speed rail and road line. The project's footprint stretches across six states, and the population in the region is expected to grow from 231 million in 2009 and 314 million in 2019 to 518 million in 2039. This is the first formulation of the mega projects that McKinsey has predicted India will need in the coming decades. For the first time in history, the consolidated Indian census data shows that the majority of people may soon be living in cities.[6]

## Conclusion

I believe that all our cities together will become the prime instruments for defining our future identity. The question before us is whether our policymakers can give us the protection to expand our freedom in the coming decade, or will their projects lead us to become enslaved by debt?[7]

I conclude with three observations:

1. There has been an inability through measures framed by Central policies to redistribute the lopsided accumulation of wealth. Since Independence, it has never been demonstrated that there has been any success in redistributing incomes. According to the Inequality Lab Report of March 2024, the income and wealth inequality between 1922 and 2023 led to the rise of the Billionaire Raj.
2. We have lived through a notorious modern era, of the unipolar world order of the Anglosphere (Great Britain and the United States of America) that built our urban infrastructure during the colonial times as we know it. But this era is coming to an end, and new economic concepts of multipolarity are evolving to replace the notions and workings of the nineteenth and twentieth centuries. This colonial and post-colonial era will be remembered for the unprecedented human levels of suffering and how our policymakers were unable to help the poor during our entire post-Independence period up to now.
3. For the coming next era, for our survival as a civilization, we will need different concepts for both equality and

freedom. These concepts will be rooted in the micro-level instruments of quantum human habitation, where both democracy and productivity have to begin to flower all over again. At this micro or quantum level, the smallest possible discrete units of community will reconstitute the subcontinent and connect us again to the slow movement of our long-duration history.

## 1. Failure to Redistribute Wealth

In our cities, wealth has remained concentrated in a few hands. For three centuries, this failure has been real, and we are now faced with the enormity of this failure as the modern unipolar era comes to a close. To understand this failure, we should consider the influences of many more slow-motion events over a much longer duration time of slow history, beyond just a century or two. Our inquiry has to be set, instead, within a longer duration in which one can see how the current modern era set its trends by committing genocides among the indigenous people of the Americas.

The abstract theories of wealth presented by the early economists such as Adam Smith in his *The Wealth of Nations* were faulted from the start because the hidden intention behind these European Enlightenment theories was never to provide social justice. The true intention was always to safeguard accumulated wealth—individually or nationally. This was only to be expected in our era since the New World experience had shown the Anglo–Atlantic victors that real wealth could only be accumulated by spiriting it away from someone else.[8]

## 2. *The Empire of the Anglosphere Is Coming to an End*

Like so many city-centred empires in history, this unipolar Anglo–American urban empire, too, will come to an end soon as its distant territories break away from the coercive centrality. Some commentators already see that approaching end coming. The Social Science Research Council opines, 'The events of September 11 mark the end of a period in international relations, a period known as the unipolar moment, when the US was the sole superpower, and debate raged over what kind of world order and power structure would characterize and then emerge from this moment.'[9]

The digital revolution has already shifted the centralism of the empire into the hands of private players of our future digital age. As the empire begins to have less relevance, the questions about our own democratic polity will assume much larger proportions as we have begun to see. In the coming age of climate change and mass migrations away from drought-hit regions, the internal migrations will overcome the centralized democratic system, as they did in Syria. We need to learn from the observations of experts, as scholars of climate change, about the close link between the environmental disasters preceding the civil war in Syria and the terrible consequences that followed. With 4,70,000 casualties, 45 per cent of the Syrian population has been displaced.[10]

Just as cross-border issues are making Atlantic democracies vulnerable, we too should expect our internal migrations to result in the same situation. We need to redefine the boundaries of our territorial state and its democracy as we enter an age of weakening state power, growing private ownership of digital capacities and existentialist global environmental threats.

## 3. *The Coming Era*

Looking towards the future, I think about what may happen to the subcontinent and, more specifically, to its urban landscape when the unipolar empire begins to give way to multipolarity. In the coming era, we will have a choice of living in two possible urban landscapes (for me, the instrumentality of the urban landscape as the lever of both democracy and freedom is crucial). One, that beckons us from the past and is dotted with imperial–corporate Google–Amazon smart cities; and the other which I insist is the only alternative: the Natural City.

Clearly, cities will continue to be the drivers of change in the coming era. However, our nineteenth-century metro-centred mega cities are nearing extinction. The choice of living in the coming era is therefore going to be between living in an urban landscape that forms part of a crazed centralized scheme that makes us cling to corridors with smart corporate cities, which will drag us to places where our darkening hearts can prosper; or to choose to live in a decentralized multinodal urban landscape that can enable us to evolve and deliver freedom and democracy using new democratic 'quantum units' for generating and sharing wealth, which counter the centralized control over digital technology.

Thus, these new concepts of localized quantum-level democracy can prepare us for the coming era to change our ways of seeing as well as shake off our blind faith in nineteenth-century Newtonian linear progress, arithmetic equality, growth, development and our obsession with Atlanticism. The instrument of the future era in the subcontinent is the new Natural City. Our metro cities inherited from colonial times, as well as many other cities in the country, have reached a critical condition of instability and unsustainability that far exceeds their holding capacities. We have therefore proposed a new generation of cities referred to as Natural Cities that are based on the premise of:

- Self-sufficiency in food, energy, water and waste management
- Self-governance through decentralized democratic systems

The most basic module of governance, production and wealth generation proposed in this decentralized democracy of the coming era will avoid centrality and instead will be located as urban nodes spread across the geography of the subcontinent.

When we begin to realign the compass needles of our national and regional ambitions in the direction of our long-duration connections towards the east–west axis of the Indian Ocean, away from our obsession with the north–south axis of the Atlantic Ocean, a new era will begin for the Indian subcontinent. Such a change in the compass directions of our attention is inevitable in the long term. The point, however, is to begin it in the short run, which will enable the democratic and productive capabilities of our subcontinent to connect to the engines of its long-duration prosperity and identity along that east–west axis.

# The Urban Commons Outlook

## A Vision for Transformative and Inclusive Indian Cities

*Seema Mundoli and Harini Nagendra*

We live in a world of rankings—a variety of indices provide an idea of the development status of countries across the globe. When we think of India in the context of rankings, the mention of its population size is inevitable: the country is today ranked first among the countries of the world in terms of population size. More recently, it is also seen as an influential emerging economy in the Global South.[1] But on indices that reflect the quality of life and status of environment, India does not fare too well. The quality of life and of environment, especially in Indian cities, is a cause of increasing concern. India is in the medium human development category,[2] and air pollution is at extremely hazardous levels.[3] And with India on the cusp of urbanization, amid the uncertainties of climate change,[4] ensuring a good quality of life for urban citizens will pose a formidable challenge in the coming decades.

According to the UN World Urbanization Prospects 2018, India, which has 31 per cent population living in cities, will add

416 million urban dwellers by 2050—taking the urban population to 52 per cent.[5] Along with this demographic growth, cities will also witness an increase in spatial extent, a process we can see is already under way, resulting in the creation of the peri-urban interface (PUI).[6] In addition to the environmental challenges already faced by our cities, the projected spatial and demographic growth will only exacerbate degradation. This is more so in the PUI, which represents a transition zone between the rural and urban, and is experiencing unplanned development, high levels of inequity and high levels of environmental degradation of urban ecosystems.[7]

Urban ecosystems support biodiversity and provide essential urban ecological functions, such as groundwater recharge, flood control and mitigating pollution.[8] They are also accessed by residents for recreation and are a space to unwind. The role of urban greenery in reducing stress and contributing to the health of urban residents is increasingly being recognized.[9] But urban ecosystems are also common pool resources (henceforth, urban commons) on which people depend for livelihood and subsistence. In the increasingly unequal cities of today, urban commons are especially critical as they provide safety nets and contribute to the resilience of the poorer urban population.[10]

However, urban ecosystems are not seen as the commons in our city planning or development. Even urban residents are often unaware that these ecosystems are in fact the commons. The imagination of our cities of the future is limited to urban ecosystems. Such visions—for example, the Smart Cities Mission in India—perceive urban ecosystems as one-dimensional spaces of recreation and entertainment, failing to understand that they are multi-use commons.[11]

In this essay, we outline the different kinds of urban ecosystems that constitute the commons in our cities and explain why these ecosystems can be characterized as the commons. We highlight how urbanization and visions for cities are contributing to alienation from and enclosure of the commons, with examples from cities across India. We argue for a different vision for urban ecosystems in our India cities, that prioritizes not just the ecology but inclusiveness in access.

The examples we present are largely from our own research in Bengaluru, as well as ongoing research in other cities in Karnataka (Belagavi, Davanagere, Hubballi–Dharwad, Mangaluru, Shivamogga, Tumakuru)[12], as well as in Kolkata[13] and New Delhi[14]. Additionally, we draw on research of other scholars working on urban commons in other parts of India. In conclusion, we outline the major gaps in knowledge and action on the urban commons in India, which demand focus if we are to meet the environmental and equity challenges posed by India's rapid urbanization.

## Urban Commons in India

Common pool resources have most often been referred to in the rural context in India. The role of common pool resources in supporting livelihood and subsistence across a range of agro-climatic landscapes[15] continues to be of relevance for rural communities across the country. But urban ecosystems in our cities are also commons, a fact that is less understood.

The ecosystems that comprise the urban commons in India's cities can be found across a spatial spectrum, from the city centre to the PUI, and are of different kinds. They could be blue spaces, such as a well, small ponds or tanks, a lake or a river with the associated wetlands. Thus, the man-made lakes in the city of Bengaluru, the East Kolkata Wetlands in Kolkata and the Yamuna River in New Delhi all constitute urban commons.[16] Coastal commons are another category of urban commons found in cities, where the ocean and the interface between the sea and the shore becomes a site that supports the livelihood and subsistence of local communities. Coastal commons comprise different sites: the sea, the shore, the estuaries and the mangroves.[17] Many green spaces in cities, including trees along a busy road, neighbourhood parks, urban forests and wooded groves are also urban commons. The other ecological spaces that constitute the commons include cemeteries and remnant grazing lands, the latter more commonly found in the PUI of cities.[18]

But how can we characterize urban ecosystems as commons in our Indian cities? After all, most of these green and blue spaces are land that is under the jurisdiction of one government department or the other, such as the local municipality, or the revenue, forest, irrigation or fisheries departments. For example, lakes in Bengaluru come under the jurisdiction of different departments such as the Forest Department, the Bruhat Bengaluru Mahanagara Palike or the Bengaluru Development Authority. What makes these ecosystems urban commons is how they are used by local communities, for tangible or intangible benefits, in spite of being state-owned[19] or even privately held. This can be termed as a process of 'commonizing' or 'commoning'.[20]

Water bodies in cities are part of the commons because of the multiple ways in which water, and the surroundings of these water bodies, are used for subsistence and livelihood. Water extracted from a well, pond or tank situated in a city slum is used by residents collectively for household use—for washing vessels and clothes. Lakes and rivers, along with their associated wetlands, support a range of livelihoods and subsistence uses— of agriculturists, grazers, *dhobies* and fishers. In Bengaluru, the area around the man-made lakes are used by grazers for washing and watering their livestock and for grazing. Fodder grass is also collected from around the lakes, and alligator weed (*Alternanthera philoxeroides*), which the grazers say is a nutritive plant for the livestock, is collected from the water's surface.[21] Grazing is also carried out around water bodies in the other cities in Karnataka and in the East Kolkata Wetlands.

The wetlands of the lakes in Bengaluru are used for cultivation of paddy, millets and a variety of vegetables that are grown for home consumption and for sale in the market. Flowers for sale and fodder grass grown and sold for stall feeding livestock are also common around lakes.[22] While paddy cultivation in Bengaluru has reduced considerably owing to the degraded state of many lakes,[23] in the smaller cities in Karnataka, such as Davanagere and Shivamogga, paddy cultivation is still being done in the vicinity of the lakes. Plots of land on the banks of the Yamuna are also used for the cultivation of flowers, vegetables and melons—grown by the poor struggling to earn an income and braving the seasonal submergence of their plots during the monsoons.[24] The East Kolkata Wetlands serve as the kidneys for Kolkata, recycling the city's wastewater and sewage. These sewage-fed wetlands also support agriculture and aquaculture. Cultivation of paddy and vegetables, and fish farms are an important source of livelihood, as well as of food, especially for the poor.[25] In Bengaluru's lakes, tender-based fishing is carried out, supporting both the tender holders, who are often locals, and the workers they employ. But migrants, including children, who live in temporary hutments and blue plastic tents adjacent to lakes, also fish in these lakes. Though such fishing is illegal in leased lakes, it is often tolerated by the tender holders themselves.[26] We found fishing to be a common practice in water bodies in the cities of Belagavi, Davanagere, Shivamogga and Tumakuru. Water bodies support other livelihoods and subsistence use. Dhobies continue to earn a living by washing clothes using the water from the lakes. Especially critical for migrants who come to the city in search of work fleeing drought in their villages, the urban waterbodies support daily household needs.[27]

In Mumbai, the seashore is an important urban coastal commons. Here, salt panning is a livelihood source for the Agari community, who are traditional salt workers.[28] Chennai and Mumbai have grown from tiny fishing villages into the metropolises of today. For the fishers, the sea and the shore are critical commons, and fishing is also carried out in the rivers, creeks and rivulets crisscrossing the cities and emptying into the sea. Supporting activities, such as parking boats, drying, weaving and repairing nets and drying fish, also take place on the coastal commons.[29]

Urban greenery along roads and in parks, groves and forests are the commons from which a variety of raw materials are extracted by different groups of city dwellers. Fuelwood from fallen dried branches are collected for use in cooking and heating water. Wooded groves in Bengaluru, locally known as *gunda thopes*, are also accessed for wood and for grazing.[30] In the National Capital Region, the Mangarbani grove and its surroundings are common lands used for grazing, fuelwood and fodder collection.[31] Migrants and adivasis in India's financial capital, Mumbai, forage for wood, flowers, fruits, medicinal plants and other minor forest produce in the forest patches of Aarey Milk Colony and Sanjay Gandhi National Park.[32] Even neighbourhood parks and cemeteries with tree cover are commons that provide multiple raw materials.[33]

Urban foraging is a common but very inadequately documented practice in Indian cities. In cities in Karnataka, a plant known locally as *onagane soppu* (*Alternanthera sessilis*) is collected from lakebeds by the women. Rich in medicinal and nutritive value, it contributes to the family diet at no extra cost. Foraging also includes collecting fruits such as mango (*Mangifera indica*), jamun (*Syzygium cumini*) and tamarind (*Tamarindus indica*), which grow on common lands in cities. Parts of trees and plants are also collected for medicine: a first resort for minor ailments for urban residents and a cheap source of medicine for the poor.[34]

'Commoning' or 'commonizing' is not only done by extracting tangible resources from urban ecosystems. Urban ecosystems are also commons because of the cultural linkages people have forged, sometimes over generations. Urban commons are thus also cultural commons, characterized thus because their use and protection are undertaken as a result of the social and cultural interactions[35] between the commons and urban residents. Thus, trees, for example, the peepal (*Ficus religiosa*) or the neem (*Azadirachta indica*), serve as a source of food, fuelwood, fodder and medicines, but are also considered sacred and worshipped. While wooded groves in Bengaluru have small shrines where prayers are offered, the Mangarbani grove itself is considered sacred. Stone idols and snake shrines consecrated at the foot of trees in groves and lake bunds are worshipped along lakes in Karnataka.[36] Rituals are performed at the lake during times of overflow. Idol immersion during festivals and worship on auspicious days are carried out along the seashore and in inland water bodies. Rituals around death anniversaries are also carried out in lakes in cities and at the ghats of rivers that run through cities. Special prayers are held by those whose livelihoods are linked to the water bodies, such as agriculturists, fishers, grazers and dhobies seeking protection and prosperity.[37] Even tree-covered cemeteries, such as the Lakshmipuram cemetery in the heart of Bengaluru city, are transformed during the festival of Shivaratri, when a huge crowd gathers to offer food and prayers at the graves of deceased family members.[38] This is but a microcosm of the relationships that people retain and nurture with the urban commons.

## Loss of the Commons and Alienation of Users

We still know little about the different types of commons in cities, as well as about their many uses, both tangible and cultural. But we are increasingly witnessing a loss of these commons, both in terms of physical access and erosion of cultural links. The causes are many and complex.

Urbanization in India, with its spatial and demographic growth, requires one important asset: land. Common lands have often been the first casualty of expanding cities, resulting in their conversion, degradation and encroachment. Our study of the commons in East Bengaluru taluk, including ponds, lakes, wooded groves, cemeteries and grazing lands, presents a grim picture. The majority of these commons were either converted or degraded. Around 77 per cent of ponds, 68 per cent of groves and 82 per cent of grazing lands were lost, with much of the remaining commons found in a degraded state. Many commons were converted to public property, such as schools, community centres, toilets, libraries, bus stops and roads. But conversions were also carried out for creating residential layouts for the middle and upper classes, housing for the economically weaker sections and for private industry.[39] Degradation was the result of unplanned urbanization, especially in the PUI, where the expansion of the city was not followed by adequate provision of infrastructure, such as sanitation facilities or solid waste disposal.[40] These conversions and degradations were visible in other cities in Karnataka as well, where our research is currently in progress, as well as across the country.[41] Conversion of the commons along the coasts of Mumbai and Chennai, along the banks of the Yamuna in Delhi,[42] to construct public infrastructure like roads, and then the diversion of these projects towards private residences and resorts have also resulted in a loss of the commons. The East Kolkata Wetlands are being reclaimed for the construction of urban infrastructure, and that has reduced the inflow of sewage as well as the recycling capacity of the wetlands with adverse effects on users of the commons. In our interviews with farmers and fishers, they expressed concerns about the lack of sewage water, which has impacted their ability to fish and farm.[43] The Mangarbani grove in Delhi is similarly threatened by expansion in the National Capital Region,[44] while mega projects, such as the construction of a metro shed, threaten the Aarey Milk Colony in Mumbai.[45]

One of the characteristics of common pool resources is that it is difficult to enclose the commons to exclude users from accessing them. This is very true in the case of forests, irrigation systems and seas that have traditionally been the main kinds of commons studied.[46] However, exclusion of the urban commons is taking place at an alarming rate through different mechanisms.[47] Urban lakes and parks are kept open only during specified times of the day; at other times, security personnel prevent users from entering these fenced spaces. Another, more subtle way of alienating traditional users from the urban commons is by prioritizing recreational use. For example, the surroundings of lakes in cities in Karnataka are landscaped by the creation of paved pathways, jogging tracks and gazebos, and by putting in exercise and play equipment.[48] Citizen groups in cities have played an important role in protecting the commons, but their actions have advertently or inadvertently also resulted in the alienation of other groups.[49]

Perceptions about how cities should be have also been the cause of enclosure of the commons. Some communing activities around urban ecosystems are frowned upon by certain groups of urban residents, and even by the state. These include urban foraging, grazing and fishing, which are seen as being not aesthetic and going against the visions people might hold of world-class cities. This results in beautification drives that not only exclude users but also result in their displacement: as their presence and use of commons is considered an eyesore, such as the removal of slums for the beautification of the Sabarmati riverfront in Ahmedabad[50] or the Yamuna in Delhi.[51] The stink from the fishing activities in the coastal commons of Mumbai and Chennai is intolerable for the elite who live in the posh residences along the shore, and there have been calls to have the fishing stopped and fishing community removed.[52] Then there is the vocabulary handed down from British times that continues to influence perceptions. Under the British, what were actually the commons were classified as government land under the revenue department.[53] These common lands even today are perceived as lands lying unused and empty—wastelands for the taking—for building public infrastructure or meant to be handed over to private entities.[54]

Privatization of the commons is another worrying trend that contributes to alienation. In the case of Bengaluru, a public–private partnership (PPP) was initiated for the management of lakes. In a study[55] it was shown that the lakes under PPPs had reduced in livelihood and subsistence activities by traditional users when compared to non-PPP lakes. Entry into the PPP lakes was also restricted via ticketing, further alienating not just traditional users of the commons but also other urban residents who might not be able to afford to pay to access these green spaces. Commodification of the commons by their privatization is increasingly being adopted[56] and is a worrying trend. The resulting alienation and segregation of urban spaces has implications for equity in our already highly unequal cities.

Another cause for concern is the recent visions for cities that are being adopted, for example, that of smart cities. Smart cities in India have been criticized for being more of a business model than anything else,[57] but the state has gone ahead with the plan to set up 100 smart cities across the country. The Smart Cities Mission documents outline the development of green and open spaces, but much of the development emphasizes the creation of recreational spaces. For example, the riverfront development of the Tunga River in Shivamogga involves the conversion of a stretch along the river with the aim of attracting tourism.[58] However, the river is a commons, with communities depending on fishing for a livelihood and slum dwellers accessing water for household use. This preference for investing in developing aesthetically pleasing infrastructure repeats itself across other smart cities in India, along river fronts, and around waterbodies and green spaces. There is no acknowledgement of the multi-use nature of these urban ecosystems or the dangers of alienating traditional users from these commons.[59] Further, the model for funding smart city projects being promoted is through PPPs. The PPP model applied in Bengaluru's lakes should serve as a warning of the resulting alienation of users, especially the urban poor, from a critical source of livelihood and subsistence.[60]

Culture has an important role to play, as it is the cultural and social interactions with the commons that make them what they are. But with urbanization, the physical conversions and changing perceptions have resulted in eroded cultural links that gave the commons their character and protection. The collective responsibility that was built around the cultural links to the commons is thus lost.[61]

## Governance of the Urban Commons: Alternative Vision

Our planet is not just urbanizing, cities are also facing the additional impacts from climate change. According to a 2018 report of the Intergovernmental Panel on Climate Change, heat stress and flooding of coastal cities due to a rise in temperatures will be of particular concern in the coming years. Cities in India, for example, Kolkata, are at risk from heatwaves, and this, in the absence of adaptation measures, could have an extremely adverse impact on the health of urban populations, especially the poor.[62]

In this scenario, what kind of visions for urban development will tackle the impacts of urbanization compounded by the effects of climate change? What role can the urban commons play in transforming Indian cities both from the perspective of ecological sustainability and inclusiveness? What are the enabling institutions and policies that will have to be leveraged?

Our urban plans need be designed using the ecological landscape of cities as the base. Plans and utopian visions, such as that of smart cities, give little importance to the individual ecological landscape or the historical role of urban ecosystems as the commons. A mapping of the commons, the different kinds, of various users and stakeholders, and the multiple uses needs to be carried out to begin with. The fishing community in Chennai, faced with the loss of their coastal commons, prepared detailed maps outlining the community's link with the coastal commons. The maps challenged the view that the seashore was a 'wasteland' that lay empty and unused. The outcome of the mapping was not just limited to making the commons visible, but the participative and inclusive nature of the mapping process ensured that the voices of groups, otherwise invisible, such as women and children from the community, were also heard. Mapping using traditional knowledge can be a powerful tool in reclaiming and protecting the commons, as was shown by the fisherfolk in Chennai. But such community mapping exercises also need to be recognized by the state and not be overridden by other legislations.[63]

The urban commons can play an important role in the mitigation of climate change impacts, especially in addressing micro-climate issues such as urban heat island effects.[64] For this we need to maintain the integrity of our urban commons, ensuring that they are not converted and are also maintained. With cities in India seen as engines of economic development and employment generation, the pressure to convert land use is immense,[65] and in the trade-off, the commons are lost. One way of preventing this is to make protection and maintenance of the commons itself a source of employment generation and development. A. Basole et al.[66] have proposed a National Urban Employment Guarantee Scheme to provide urban residents with a legal right to employment, via works aimed at restoring, maintaining and monitoring the urban commons. The jobs under this scheme will be for the manual workforce, as well as in the form of apprenticeships for educated youth to help them acquire work experience and skills that will prepare them for employment opportunities. The scheme, in addition to employment generation, will provide spillover economic, ecological, health and environmental benefits through the protection of the urban commons.

Finally, we argue for a commons outlook in the governance[67] of urban ecosystems that can translate to more realistic visions and plans for Indian cities. This can be done by leveraging existing institutional mechanisms and designing enabling policies. The 74th Constitution Amendment Act, 1992, allows for the urban local bodies to function in a democratic and inclusive manner, allowing for wards in cities to be consulted in decision-making. For example, in the case of the proposed employment guarantee scheme, it will be at the ward level that the prioritization of works on the commons will be done. The state needs to continue to play a role by providing resources and stepping in to intervene where issues of inclusivity may arise, where specific communities are being sidelined in the process of accessing resources in the ward, including the commons. The collective responsibility of citizens at the ward level, along with the cultural and social links, can go a long way in protecting the commons for the future. The role of urban local governance is seen as important in mitigating impacts of climate change,[68] and the nested legal (de jure) and traditional (de facto) institutional mechanisms need to be leveraged for the governance of the commons.

## Conclusion

We still know very little about how ecological spaces in cities and towns are used as the commons, what kind of cultural and historical relations people have forged with the commons and the threats to these spaces as urbanization in the country progresses.[69] But what we do know is that India is moving towards an urban future, in a time of unprecedented climate change. Our urban visions and plans, and implementation plans, need to reflect how we can move together towards creating sustainable and inclusive cities. The urban commons, in their use and collective governance, hold the potential to transform our cities and the lived experience of all city dwellers in India.[70]

# Whose Town Is It Anyway?

## Urban Inequality in the Face of Climate Change

*Vishnu M.J., Kavya Michael and Tanvi Deshpande*

Urbanization in India can be divided into two distinctive periods, which coincide with the introduction of neoliberal policies and reforms since the mid-1980s. As the impact of liberalization reached a larger section of the country's population, urban settlements of all sizes increased in population, from internal growth and spatial expansion of cities and from migration, particularly for larger cities.

India's overall development trajectory over the past two decades has also been increasingly shaped by its cities. However, the urban experience in Indian cities is increasingly being shaped through the emerging development paradigm dominated by neoliberal structures of market-oriented governance and enhanced privatization. Like in other parts of the world, the entrenched structures have only managed to exacerbate inequality (see Ahmed, 2011; Shrivastava and Kothari, 2012; Vakulabharanam and Motiram, 2012; Michael and Vakulabharanam, 2016; Chattopadhyay, 2017[1]).

Even for an untrained visitor, the stark difference within Indian cities is evident. Posh enclaves seek to cut themselves off from the rest of the masses, while the urban poor try to get shelter and go about their daily lives in unplanned and often informal settlements (see Michael et al., 2019[2]). When it is present, government service delivery usually only reaches the elite (Basu, 2019; Ghertner, 2011[3]), while political leadership uses clientelist practices to underprovide essential services to the majority (or slums [Auerbach, 2016; 2019[4]]).

A study of the ten largest Indian cities[5] showed that the scheduled caste (SC)/scheduled tribes (STs) and religious minorities were most likely to live in informal settlements, where they have lesser access to services such as water, sanitation and adequate housing. Another study[6] of exclusions among groups in urban India showed that only 14 per cent of households in squatter settlements had access to drinking water for their exclusive use as compared to 47 per cent of all urban households in the country. That is, only about half of all urban households in the country had access to individual connections.

## Gandhi and Ambedkarite Visions of Urbanity

Gandhi's vision of India since *Hind Swaraj* centred on self-reliant villages that upheld the traditional values and customs of Indian society. As widely documented, for him, this represented a direct contradiction to cities which he viewed as corrupted and removed from traditional ways of living.[7] In contrast, Ambedkar, as he famously pointed out in his speech introducing the Draft Constitution, viewed the Indian village 'as a sink of localism, a den of ignorance, narrow-mindedness and communalism'.[8] Economic opportunities and freedom the cities offered could enable the liberation of Dalits from a stigmatized existence, oppressed livelihood and living conditions. The urban space also offered anonymity where economic production could overpower caste differences.[9] These trains of thought were also in line with other global thinkers such as Hobsbawm[10] (1973) and Rostow[11] (1960), both of whom felt that urbanization was a largely democratizing process.

However, have neoliberalization and urbanization lived up to the dreams of Ambedkar and Phule? Have caste structures been diluted or are they gradually fusing into class structures in our cities? Having faced prejudice and discrimination all his life, Ambedkar might not be too surprised to hear that inequality continues to widen its reach in Indian cities faster than ever. While urban scholars in India have extensively dealt with emerging patterns of socio-economic inequality from a broad class- and income-based analysis,[12] the research on lived urban experience for Dalits and other stigmatized social groups in the country has been lesser.[13]

One of the striking features of contemporary urbanization in India is an accelerated pace of distress-driven rural–urban migration, reinforcing the spatial manifestation of socio-economic patterns of vulnerability and marginalization found in rural areas. Historically, the migration of backward castes to the cities has been viewed as a mechanism to counteract oppressive sociocultural practices in villages, but there is very little research on how they have been integrated into the urban economy and their actual lived experiences. Most of these migrants are temporary or footloose migrants circulating between rural and urban areas. The National Sample Survey (NSS) data on temporary migration shows that temporary migration is a strategy pursued by those who are relatively poor, have little or no land, are low-skilled/semi-skilled and lower caste (see Keshri and Bhagat, 2012[14]). These workers are often integrated into the urban economy through the urban informal sector under extremely exploitative conditions with limited access to multiple forms of citizenship rights, such as employment security, access to social protection schemes and adequate housing and tenure rights, among others. Srivastava and Kothari[15] (2012) reiterate that while the Indian economy has embraced the principles of a modern capitalist economy, it still retains resilient feudal characteristics. They further argue that distinctions on the basis of caste and gender enable a convenient basis for exploitation and appropriation of surplus by capital.

While informal settlements are universally considered to be one of the starkest manifestations of urban poverty and inequality, the caste composition of informal settlement dwellers is often overlooked. According to the 2011 census, the population of Dalits across urban areas saw an increase of 40 per cent between the decennial census accounts of 2000 and 2011.[16] Using the NSS data, Zacharias and Vakulabharanam[17] (2011) show that urban SCs are at the bottom of the urban wealth ladder, with urban STs having a marginally higher median wealth, followed by OBCs and non-Hindus. In this context, it can be argued that Indian cities often replicate or mimic the socio-spatial patterns of inequality prevalent in its villages. As Abraham and Barak[18] argue, the caste system in India is not just a remnant of the past but is equally constitutive of contemporary India. Here we draw upon a few case studies conducted in informal settlements of Bengaluru to see how factors such as caste and gender intersect with the modes of production in the urban economy and define livelihood and living conditions.

## Gender

Along with social stratification along the lines of religion, caste and class, the Indian city is also gendered. The patriarchal nature of Indian urbanization can be first seen in the composition of the population itself. Urban India's sex ratio stands at 929, lower than rural India's at 949.[19] Of the ten largest cities in the country, all of them economic powerhouses for their regions, only Kolkata and Pune had sex ratios higher than its parent state.[20]

At the same time, when they are present in the city, women's lived experience in cities differ from those of men, right from their ability to access public spaces to their access to sanitation. Women's restricted access to the city begins from their ability to find work. Data from the 2011 census shows that only 17 per cent of women in Indian cities were part of the workforce, as opposed to 61 per cent of men.[21] Although the census figures are surely an inadequate reflection of productive labour undertaken by women,[22] figures such as this also show that women need to be integrated more into both formal and informal workspaces.

Another aspect of the gendered city comes into play here, with women having much lower mobility than men. Again, data from the 2011 census is deeply illustrative. Women workers tend to travel more by foot and by (formal or informal) public transport as compared to men, who overwhelmingly constitute the majority of motorists. Walking (45 per cent) and buses (22 per cent) covered two-thirds of women commuters (for men, the corresponding figure is 40 per cent), while only 10 per cent of women commuted by two-wheelers, as opposed to 24 per cent of men. As has been pointed out by other scholars, working women tend to save more for their families as opposed to men and therefore, take cheaper modes such as (formal and informal) public transport, or even choose walking at the cost of increasing their commute time.[23] Such choices also tend to restrict women's access to employment alongside patriarchal norms.

This essay uses the case-study approach to try and understand some of the processes that are ongoing in the Indian city, which have been described earlier. While the above sections used socio-economic data to highlight several overarching trends, they are unable to provide glimpses into how vulnerabilities of religion, caste, class and gender intersect in the daily lives of our urban residents or how the state could decisively intervene.

The cases described below are from the authors' own fieldwork in Bengaluru between 2015 and 2017 and was done as part of the ASSAR (Adaptation at Scale in Semi-Arid Regions) project, funded by the Canadian International Development Research Centre (IDRC) (see Michael, Deshpande et al., 2019[24]). Information provided in this chapter was collected using qualitative methods (e.g. transect walks, semi-structured interviews, participation observations and focus group discussions) and quantitative methods (household level survey using random sampling). The cases are meant to be illustrative; while they are specifically rooted in their local contexts, they also represent commonalities of the lived experience for most across urban India.

## A Case of Footloose Migrants in Rachenahalli, Bengaluru

This settlement is located in north-eastern Bengaluru, adjacent to a tech park near Rachenahalli Lake. The settlement is ten years old and initially housed construction workers building the Manyata Tech Park. The houses and land are privately owned, and the residents pay a monthly rent to the landlord. The dwellers are migrants from north-eastern Karnataka from places such as Yadgir, Gulbarga, Bijapur, Bellary, Raichur, Manuve, Haveri and Koppala. Most residents here migrated due to agrarian distress caused by increasingly persistent drought.

The primary source of livelihood in the settlement is non-agricultural wage labour. After the construction of the tech park was complete, further construction work was no longer available. Hence, they are forced to travel all over the city to find a source of livelihood. They revealed that they are often not paid their due wages. However, they lack the political and economic capital required to enforce legal action against contractors and are rendered helpless. Most residents in the settlement are uneducated, and yet they realize the importance of education. Unfortunately, they are unable to send their children to school since there is no government school nearby and they cannot afford private education.

Observations during field visits revealed that, most housing in the settlement is semi-*pucca*. Walls are made of bricks or metal sheets, and tarpaulin sheets are the most common roofing material. There are strict terms and conditions imposed on the residents by the landlord; a delay in paying rent could result in forced evacuation from the houses. Due to its location next to the lake, some parts of the settlement are low-lying; these areas get submerged during heavy rains. This combination of living in potentially hazardous environments with uncertainty of tenure and work means that residents here must make trade-offs between focusing on their health and education or immediate survival.

Like most Bengalureans, the residents here also depend on groundwater; they receive water from a borewell in the settlement, but only for a limited period of two hours daily. Therefore, non-essential tasks, such as washing clothes, etc., are done at the lake, into which all nearby residents dump their liquid waste. Due to the high incidence of pollution in the lake, it has become an excellent breeding ground for mosquitoes, whose population has increased. There are no toilets near or in the settlement, and the dwellers are forced to resort to open defecation. This poses security concerns for the women of the settlement (Focus Group Discussion, Women's group, Rachenahalli Settlement, July 2016).

The lack of street lighting in the settlement also poses serious security concerns post dusk, especially for women. There is no electricity connection in the settlement. Even for the simple necessity of charging their phones, the residents are forced to use nearby shops, and they must pay for this service on a daily basis. Firewood is the fuel in use, since most residents do not possess the tenure rights documents required for obtaining an LPG subsidy.

The residents depend on a nearby government hospital in Yelahanka for medical assistance. Due to the land being privately owned, the settlement and its residents are not formally recognized for government support.

## A Case of Historic Marginalization: Muneshwara Settlement, Bengaluru

This thirty-year-old notified settlement is located adjacent to a railway track near JP Park in Mathikere, in north-west Bengaluru. The earliest residents in the settlement were from Raichur district in Karnataka and had migrated to the city due to agricultural distress. Our (primary) data collected during field work showed that the majority of residents belonged to marginalized castes and minority groups. Sixty per cent of residents fell under the category of SCs, 20 per cent under OBC, 10 per cent under ST and 10 per cent were Muslim.

Despite being recognized by the Karnataka Slum Board, they do not have reliable access to basic services that notified settlements are supposed to receive. The predominant livelihood among the men is wage labour, like construction work, and some are engaged as lorry drivers. The nature of their jobs is highly insecure as they are unable to secure long work contracts from contractors.

Located at a lower elevation than its surrounding areas, the settlement often gets flooded during heavy rains. However, there are no formal drainage facilities provided by the state. Although public stand posts are present in the settlement to provide water, there are no public sanitation facilities. Residents, therefore, have to resort to open defecation in areas around the settlement or along the railway track. While this poses serious health concerns, especially in the event of flooding, for the women of the settlement, it also poses safety and security concerns. The settlement dwellers are unable to avail of the benefits of the public distribution system due to the lack of proper identity cards in Bangalore (see Michael et al., 2019).

## Lack of Recognition and Its Impact on Justice

I.M. Young[25] notes that if social differences exist, and are attached to both privilege and oppression, social justice requires an examination of those differences to undermine their effect on distributive injustice. Lack of recognition, demonstrated by various forms of insults, degradation and devaluation, at both the individual and cultural levels, inflicts damage on oppressed communities as well as on the image of those communities in the larger cultural and political realms. Nancy Fraser's[26] central argument in this respect is that justice requires attention to both distribution and recognition, where only the combination of economic and cultural justice can guarantee that form of 'participatory equality', which is to be understood as the morally supreme principle of liberal societies. According to her, a lack of recognition is manifested in three forms: cultural domination, non-recognition or being rendered invisible, and being routinely stereotyped or maligned in public or cultural representations. Those groups who are subject to misrepresentation find that this serves to make them less credible knowledge claimants. They are less likely to be believed because their claims differ sharply from claims consistent with the dominant interpretations in society; their ability to make knowledge claims is stifled by the lack of available rhetorical space or interpretive domain.[27]

In most of these informal settlements, we observed how the historical and structural nature of vulnerability manifests itself. As one of the residents at a focus group discussion in a settlement observed, 'We are exposed to the same challenges faced by our parents. Nothing has changed for us' (Respondent A, Focus Group Discussion, Muneshwara Settlement, July 2016).

This statement and the mountain of evidence from publicly available data show that Ambedkar's vision of cities as emancipatory spaces remains woefully under-realized. As Roy[28] notes, urban labour markets have only managed to reinforce caste hierarchies rather than remove them. Some scholars have even pointed out that informal settlements reflect the union of Gandhi and Ambedkar, albeit in a thoroughly disenchanting and dystopian manner.[29]

Most of the residents in the settlements we visited were landless agricultural labourers belonging to backward castes. While most of them had moved to the city in the hope of decent livelihood options, it was often the case that the social structures of exclusion prevalent in the villages also played out in the city. The strong link between caste and economic status can be understood as a function of exclusion from productive resources, such as land and education, and of discrimination in the labour market. In the city, members of marginalized castes often lack the bargaining or political power to get access to decent livelihood options and living spaces with access to basic services.

The prominent occupations in these settlements were construction and waste-picking. 'Back in the village, we had no land; we had no money. Here we earn enough to survive,' (Respondent B, Focus Group Discussion, Hebbal Settlement, June 2016). Another waste-picker from the Hebbal settlement observed, 'We know this is filthy and lowly work. But anything that allows poor people to earn well for themselves and their family as long as it doesn't qualify as a crime is not too bad' (Respondent C, Semi-structured Interview, Hebbal Settlement, June 2016). These statements throw a great deal of light on how the urban poor and vulnerable see themselves and the city. These statements also reflect how misrecognition (both internal and external) have come together to create severe inequalities in opportunity for the majority of urban residents.

## Migration and the City

While natural population growth has surely contributed to the boom in urban population, the cases above also illustrate a key point on Indian urbanization—that migration also continues to contribute significantly to the same. Deshingkar and Start[30] estimated that there might be up to 100 million temporary migrants in India as of 2003—current estimates are unavailable but would undoubtedly be manifold. Many of these migrants work in seasonal industries, such as construction, brick-making, small and artisan mining, and assorted low-skill services in urban areas.[31]

While migration used to most often involve working men temporarily moving to the city in search of jobs and livelihood options during fallow agricultural periods (thus resulting in the lower sex ratios in urban areas), it is seen now that more and more rural families are either moving permanently to urban areas or engaging in footloose circular migration, moving between their homes and urban areas in search of livelihood opportunities.[32]

Rao and Vakulabharanam[33] also argue that this phenomenon shows the social reproduction crisis that was inherent in earlier migration patterns. They find that for young men, moving to the city meant that they left behind their traditional support systems (held up by women) of social reproduction. The absence of reproductive labour support in urban areas further disenfranchised these migrants, reducing their quality of life. For the women in rural areas, too, this has often meant that they continue to take up both productive (farming, household labour or any other available work) and reproductive labour (taking care of both children and the elderly) (Rao and Vakulabharanam, 2018).

## Policy Recommendations

Even seven decades after Independence, the social bonds that Dr Ambedkar and others wished to create through the Constitution have not been fully actualized, remaining in practice subservient to earlier clientelism.[34] The growth in inequality after liberalization efforts began and the oncoming climate emergency show that the current paradigm is woefully inadequate. How can the Indian state and citizens then begin to work together to overcome these challenges?

The first step should be to reiterate the role of the state and the efforts it would undertake. The provision of water and electricity to its citizens by the Delhi government in 2015 was seen as a novel step in this regard.[35] The same government, in 2019, also offered free public transport to women across its metro rail and bus systems. But should these initiatives be viewed as 'freebies' or should these be regarded as the state doing its minimum duty, especially when it keeps to current public finance wisdom as Delhi had done?[36]

Access to water and sanitation is a fundamental right under Article 21 according to the Supreme Court.[37] For decades, even though the Indian state had acknowledged the necessity of providing water and sanitation to its residents, its lack of capacity along with existing clientelism meant that the state was not successful, and citizens largely had to fend for themselves. To compound matters, the link between land tenure and access to services ensured that the worst-off of our society do not get the services that they are entitled to. Therefore, the urban poor end up literally paying more money per litre of (usually poor-quality) water than an affluent urban resident.[38]

The Delhi government's 2015 intervention showed two things. One, which was already known to practitioners, that a smart fiscal strategy can help the state increase its revenue, which can be used for the universal provision of fundamental goods, such as water, education, health and mobility, and not be a strain on the public exchequer.[39] The permeation of neoliberalization as an ideology ensured that the provision of public goods was seen as a wastage of resources while elites lobbied for the free provision of club goods (expressways, SEZs, etc.) from the government. Several similar experiments around the world—free public transport for citizens in Estonia[40] and Luxembourg[41], and for women in states such as Punjab, Tamil Nadu, Karnataka—showed that the provision of public goods also aided in generating positive externalities for society as a whole.[42] In the case of housing, water, sanitation and health, academics and practitioners have been pushing for universal basic services because of the outsize negative impact that the lack of these goods have on citizens, especially on vulnerable groups.[43] Several studies have documented the importance of providing universal healthcare coverage—given how crippling debts incurred due to health conditions can burden poorer households for years on end—and education—again for the same reason, pushing families and individuals into lifelong debt.[44]

Secondly, and more importantly, the (relative) prominence of these interventions in the public imaginary show that the language around the debate itself has changed, where the state's role to provide has been tied with the citizen's duty to ask and avail of their rights. The emerging citizen movements around the globe demanding their rights—such as the Extinction Rebellion, school strikes for climate, the farmers' movement in India rejecting the corporatization of Indian agriculture, Hong Kong and Parisian uprisings—show that a new vocabulary of citizen–state relationship is being created, which categorically rejects existing paradigms. As David Harvey[45] has pointed out, these reflect a change towards a collective demanding their rights, away from the idea of (neoliberal and libertarian) individual rights. These new approaches by civil society are also intricately tied with a global realization that the current state of late capitalism will indeed have to be replaced with a more just and equitable approach. Will they be successful before it's too late?

# Notes

## Introduction: The Hollow Promise of Neoliberal Urbanization

1. Mohan, Shriya, 'Migrants Walk back to Their Villages', *BusinessLine*, 22 May 2020, https://www.thehindubusinessline.com/blink/cover/lonliness-of-the-long-distance-walker/article31647895.ece.
2. 'Coronavirus Lockdown | Activists Say over 300 Deaths Related to Lockdown Troubles', *The Hindu*, 2 May 2020. https://www.thehindu.com/news/national/activists-say-over-300-deaths-related-to-lockdown-troubles/article31491525.ece.
3. Ibid.
4. BQ Desk, 'Coronavirus Lockdown: Kerala Has 69% of India's Government-Run Relief Camps for Migrant Workers', NDTV Profit, 9 April 2020, https://www.ndtvprofit.com/coronavirus-outbreak/coronavirus-lockdown-kerala-has-69-of-indias-government-run-relief-camps-for-migrant-workers.
5. unemploymentinindia.cmie.com.
6. Censusindia.gov.in, 2024, https://censusindia.gov.in/nada/index.php/catalog/42617/download/46288/Census%20of%20India%202011-Rural%20Urban%20Distribution%20of%20Population.pdf.

7   'Transit Oriented Development for Indian Smart Cities', Niua.org, 2014, https://niua.org/tod/todfisc/book.php?book=1&section=2.
8   'Washington Consensus', Wikipedia, Wikimedia Foundation, 25 November 2018, https://en.wikipedia.org/wiki/Washington_Consensus.
9   Ursula Hews, *Socialist Register,* p. 65, 2019.
10  Ibid.
11  Ibid.
12  Jamie Peck, Nik Theodore and Neil Brenner, 'Neoliberal Urbanism: Models, Moments, Mutations', *The SAIS Review of International Affairs* 29 (1): 49–66, https://www.jstor.org/stable/27000166.
13  'Communist Party of India (Marxist)', cpim.org 2016, https://cpim.org/changes-socio-economic-conditions-working-class/.
14  Auguste Tano Kouamé, 'Gearing up for India's Rapid Urban Transformation', World Bank, 30 January 2024, https://www.worldbank.org/en/news/opinion/2024/01/30/gearing-up-for-india-s-rapid-urban-transformation.
15  Tikender Panwar, 'Oxfam India: Impose 1% Surcharge on Richest 10% Indians to Reduce Inequality,' Bridge India, 19 January 2022, https://bridgeindia.org.uk/oxfam-india-report-to-reduce-inequality/.
16  Oxfam, 'India: Extreme Inequality in Numbers', Oxfam International, 2024, https://www.oxfam.org/en/india-extreme-inequality-numbers.
17  Nitin Kumar Bharti, Lucas Chancel, Thomas Piketty and Anmol Somanchi, 'Income and Wealth Inequality in India, 1922–2023: The Rise of the Billionaire Raj,' https://wid.world/wp-content/uploads/2024/03/WorldInequalityLab_WP2024_09_Income-and-Wealth-Inequality-in-India-1922-2023_Final.pdf.

18 Pratap Bhanu Mehta, 'Ordinances by States to Change Labour Laws Are a Travesty,' *Indian Express*, 12 May 2020, https://indianexpress.com/article/opinion/columns/industrial-relations-code-india-labour-law-amendment-pratap-bhanu-mehta-6405265/.
19 'State of Working India 2023', Azim Premji University, 19 September 2023, https://azimpremjiuniversity.edu.in/the-indian-economy/state-of-working-india-2023.
20 'Share of Government Health Expenditure in Total Health Expenditure Increases from 28.6 Per Cent in FY14 to 40.6 Per Cent in FY19', n.d. pib.gov.in, https://pib.gov.in/PressReleasePage.aspx?PRID=1894902#:~:text=In%20keeping%20with%20this%20objective,1.6%20per%20cent%20in%20FY21.
21 Amit Sengupta, 'Universal Health Care in India Making It Public, Making It a Reality', https://nhsrcindia.org/sites/default/files/2021-04/Universal%20Health%20Care%20in%20India%20A%20Sengupata%20May-2013.pdf.
22 Ibid.
23 'India's Healthcare Crisis: Profit over Care and the Urgent Need for Reform | Nivarana', Nivarana.org., 2024, https://nivarana.org/article/indias-healthcare-crisis-profit-over-care-and-the-urgent-need-for-reform.
24 'India Water Purifier Market - Industry Analysis and Forecast (2022-2029)', n.d. Maximize Market Research, https://www.maximizemarketresearch.com/market-report/india-water-purifier-market/20066/.
25 'New Urban Agenda', https://habitat3.org/wp-content/uploads/NUA-English.pdf.
26 S. Jamuna, 'Challenges in Managing Slums in India', ResearchGate 11 (1): 635–44, https://www.researchgate.net/publication/377895187_Challenges_in_managing_slums_in_India.

27  Shiny Varghese, 'Urban design is a civic responsibility: Raj Rewal', *Indian Express*, 14 May 2020, https://indianexpress.com/article/lifestyle/art-and-culture/urban-design-is-a-civic-responsibility-architect-urban-designer-raj-rewal-6408388/.
28  S. Jamuna, 'Challenges in Managing Slums in India', ResearchGate.
29  Sanjeev Routray, Review of *Displacement, Revolution, and the New Urban Condition: Theories and Case Studies*—Ipsita Chatterjee (Pacific Affairs, University of British Columbia, 2016), https://www.jstor.org/stable/44874361.
30  Rose Deller, 'Book Review: Capital City: Gentrification and the Real Estate State by Samuel Stein - LSE Review of Books', LSE Review of Books - the Latest Social Science Books Reviewed by Academics and Experts, 27 September 2019, https://blogs.lse.ac.uk/lsereviewofbooks/2019/09/27/book-review-capital-city-gentrification-and-the-real-estate-state-by-samuel-stein/.
31  D. Asher Ghertner, 'India's Urban Revolution: Geographies of Displacement Beyond Gentrification', Environment and Planning A: *Economy and Space* 46 (7): 1554–71, https://doi.org/10.1068/a46288.
32  Tikender Panwar, 'Neither Work nor Housing nor Food: People's Dispatch', Peoples Dispatch, 12 April 2020, https://peoplesdispatch.org/2020/04/12/neither-work-nor-housing-nor-food/.
33  https://www.researchgate.net/publication/30457156_Urban_Housing_and_Exclusion
34  'Understanding Homelessness in Delhi', Indo-Global Social Service Society, October 2018, https://igsss.org/wp-content/uploads/2022/06/Understanding-Homelessness-in-Delhi.pdf

35 'Interrogating Governance and Financial Implications of "Smart Cities" – Part I Report – Environment Support Group', Esgindia.org, 17 November 2020, https://esgindia.org/new/campaigns/interrogating-governance-and-financial-implications-of-smart-cities-part-i-report/.
36 'CHAPTER-IV Devolution of Functions and Institutional Mechanism for Empowerment of Urban Local Bodies 4.1 Actual Status of Devolution of Functions to ULBs', n.d. https://cag.gov.in/uploads/download_audit_report/2022/Chapter-IV-06239c581d1cd26.54306180.pdf.
37 Harsh Mittal and Arpit Shah, 'Discursive Politics and Policy (Im)Mobility: Metro-TOD Policies in India', Environment and Planning C: Politics and Space, July, 239965442110292. https://doi.org/10.1177/23996544211029295.
38 'Looking Back at 25 Years: A Review of 74th Constitutional Amendment Act a National Level Roundtable', n.d., https://igsss.org/wp-content/uploads/2022/06/A-Review-of-74th-Constitutional-Amendment-Act.pdf.
39 'National Consultation On Urban Governance- Key Finding From 21 States', praja.org/praja_docs/praja_downloads/National Consultation On Urban Governance-Key Finding From 21 States_HINDI.pdf.
40 Tikender Singh Panwar, 'Give India's Cities Their Due', *Deccan Herald*, 12 January 2024, https://www.deccanherald.com/opinion/himalayas-municipalities-funds-cities-finance-commission-property-tax-gst-2845956.
41 Lalitha Kamath and Yacoub Zachariah, n.d., 'Impact of JNNURM and UIDSSMT/ IHSDP Programmes on Infrastructure and Governance Outcomes in Cities/ Towns in India', accessed 24 October 2025, https://tiss.edu/uploads/files/TISS_Working_Paper-7-Lalitha_Kamath.pdf.

42  Science, Health and Medical Journals, Full Text Articles and Books, Sciencedirect.com, 2025, https://www.sciencedirect.com/science/article/am/pii/S0264275118300593.
43  Ibid.
44  'Cisco CEO Pegs Internet of Things as $19 Trillion Market', Bloomberg.com, 8 January 2014, https://www.bloomberg.com/news/articles/2014-01-08/cisco-ceo-pegs-internet-of-things-as-19-trillion-market.
45  Sarwant Singh, 'Smart Cities: A $1.5 Trillion Market Opportunity, *Forbes*, 19 June 2014, http://www.forbes.com/sites/sarwantsingh/2014/06/19/smart-cities-a-1-5-trillion-market-opportunity/#7ca400c87ef9.
46  Yeo Shinjoung, Dissertation, n.d. 'Behind the Search Box: The Political Economy of a Global Internet Industry', Core View Metadata, Citation and Similar Papers at Core.ac.uk, Provided by Illinois Digital Environment for Access to Learning and Scholarship Repository, https://core.ac.uk/download/pdf/158301852.pdf.
47  James Blackman, 'The Top 10 Smart City Suppliers', *RCR Wireless News*, 29 September 2017, https://www.rcrwireless.com/20170929/fundamentals/top-10-smart-city-suppliers-tag99.
48  'Convergence: Smart Cities Mission, Government of India', n.d. 164.100.161.224, http://164.100.161.224/content/innerpage/convergence-sp.php.
49  Neeraj Jain, 'The Smart City Obsession: A Critique', Lokayat and Socialist Party, India, 2015.
50  Ibid.
51  Annexure V in the Smart City Guidelines issued by the Government of India, http://smartcities.gov.in/writereaddata/SmartCityGuidelines.pdf.
52  Alberto Vanolo, 'Whose Smart City?', OpenDemocracy, 8 April 2014, https://www.opendemocracy.net/opensecurity/alberto-vanolo/whose-smart-city.

53 Ibid.
54 Chris Williams, 'How Will We Reach an Ecological Civilization and Who Will Build It?', Truthout, 31 October 2015, http://www.truth-out.org/opinion/item/33439-how-will-we-reach-an-ecological-civilization-and-who-will-build-it.
55 Risha Chitlangia, 'Parliamentary Panel Tells Centre to Identify Reasons for "Slow Pace" of Its Smart Cities Mission', ThePrint, 12 February 2024, https://theprint.in/india/governance/parliamentary-panel-tells-centre-to-identify-reasons-for-slow-pace-of-its-smart-cities-mission/1963475/.
56 Tikender Panwar, 'Where Are the Smart Cities, Mr Modi?', NewsClick', 1 January 2019, https://www.newsclick.in/where-are-smart-cities-mr-modi.
57 P. Raman, 'An Unceremonious End to Modi's Smart Cities Mission', The Wire, 1 April 2025, https://m.thewire.in/article/business/an-unceremonious-end-to-modis-smart-cities-mission.
58 PMF IAS, Smart Cities Mission: Successes & Challenges, 25 April 2025, https://www.pmfias.com/smart-cities-mission/.
59 Drishti IAS, AMRUT (Atal Mission for Rejuvenation and Urban Transformation) Scheme, 4 June 2024, https://www.drishtiias.com/daily-updates/daily-news-analysis/amrut-atal-mission-for-rejuvenation-and-urban-transformation-scheme.
60 Amit Kapoor, 'Municipal Fiscal Reforms Crucial for Addressing Urban Governance Challenges: Moving beyond Dependence' – Institute for Competitiveness, Competitiveness.in., 20 December 2024, https://www.competitiveness.in/municipal-fiscal-reforms-crucial-for-addressing-urban-governance-challengesmoving-beyond-dependence/.

61 'The Curious Case of Indian Smart Cities', Centre for Financial Accountability, 27 September 2019, https://www.cenfa.org/the-curious-case-of-indian-smart-cities/.
62 Lucie Krahulcova, 'Techno Solutionism—Very Few Things Actually Need to Be an App', Digital Rights Watch, 24 March 2021, https://digitalrightswatch.org.au/2021/03/25/technosolutionism/.
63 Steven Poole, 'The Truth about Smart Cities: "In the End, They Will Destroy Democracy"', *Guardian*, 17 December 2014, http://www.theguardian.com/cities/2014/dec/17/truth-smart-city-destroy-democracy-urban-thinkers-buzzphrase.
64 Subin Dennis, 'Housing Cooperatives Are Building a Workers' City in Solapur', *National Herald*, 26 August 2018, https://www.nationalheraldindia.com/poverty/housing-cooperatives-are-building-a-workers-city.
65 Francesca Bria, 'Madrid Democratic-Open Source City', 2015.

## Right to the City: Unleashing India's Untapped Capital

1 Rukmini S., 'Urban voters, Muslim voters – Lok Sabha mysteries solved', Indian Census 2011, Rural Urban Distribution of Population, *The Hindu*, 2011, https://www.thehindu.com/opinion/blogs/blog-datadelve/article6383006.ece; last accessed on 3 December 2022 at 13:37 hours.
2 https://censusindia.gov.in/census.website/
3 *World Urbanization Prospects 2014*, United Nations Department of Economic and Social Affairs.
4 Ibid.
5 National Sample Survey Organisation, 2007–08.
6 Erica-Irene A. Daes, 'Working Paper on the Concept of "Indigenous People"', prepared for the Working Group

on Indigenous Populations, UN, Doc. E/CN.4/Sub.2/ AC.4/1996/2.
7   P. Hall and R. Taylor, 'Political Science and the Three New Institutionalisms', 44 (5), *Political Studies*.
8   UNESCO (2000): 'Status and Trends', International Consultative Forum on Education for All, EFA Forum.
9   '2011 Census of India', Wikipedia, Wikimedia Foundation, 21 April 2019, https://en.wikipedia.org/wiki/2011_Census_of_India.
10  National Family Health Survey (NFHS-4), 2015–16, International Institute for Population Sciences (IIPS) and ICF. 2017, Mumbai.
11  Indian Census, 2011.
12  Ibid.
13  Ibid.
14  The Constitution lays down certain Directive Principles of State Policy, which though not justiciable, are 'fundamental in governance of the country', and it is the duty of the state to apply these principles in making laws. These lay down that the state shall strive to promote the welfare of people by securing and protecting as effectively as it may, a social order, in which justice—social, economic and political—shall form in all institutions of national life.
15  Article 21 of the Constitution of India: Protection of life and personal liberty – No person shall be deprived of his life or personal liberty except according to procedure established by law.
16  P. Bhagwati, *Francis Coralie Mullin v UT of Delhi*, 1981 AIR 746, 1981 SCR (2) 516.
17  Registrar General of India (2011), 'Housing Tables', Census 2011, New Delhi: RGI.
18  '2011 Socio Economic and Caste Census', Wikipedia, Wikimedia Foundation, 23 August 2025.

19  Sunil Kumar (2001), *Rental Housing Markets and the Poor in Urban India*, London: Asia Research Centre.
20  Indian Census, 2011.
21  Saugato Dutta and Vikram Pathania, 'For whom does the phone (not) ring? Discrimination in the rental housing market in Delhi, India', Helsinki, Finland United Nations University World Institute for Development Economics Research May 2016.
22  The Gujarat (Prohibition of Transfer of Immovable Property and Provisions) in Disturbed Areas Act, 1991 was amended in 2009. The main purpose of the 2009 amendment was to clarify the scope of the Act and address concerns about the arbitrary declaration of areas as 'disturbed'. The amendments have been criticized and remain ineffective, particularly due to concerns about their impact on community relations and potential for discrimination. https://www.indiacode.nic.in/bitstream/123456789/4609/1/disturbedareasact.pdf.
23  Sameera Khan, 'Negotiating the Mohalla: Exclusion, Identity and Muslim Women in Mumbai', *Economic and Political Weekly*, vol. 42, no. 17, 2007.
24  Mayank Austen Soofi, 'Life in an illegal colony', LiveMint, 26 November 2016, https://www.livemint.com/Leisure/yJi2UuW8ZcW92Ta34n3mBI/Life-in-an-illegal-colony.html; last accessed on 3 March 2020.
25  S. Muralidhar, 'Ajay Maken & Ors. vs Union Of India & Ors. on 18 March, 2019', indiankanoon.org, https://indiankanoon.org/doc/159570569/.
26  Ibid.
27  Mathew Idiculla, 'A Right to the Indian City? Legal and Political Claims over Housing and Urban Space in India', Volume 16, *Socio-Legal Review*, https://77c86aee-837e-44bb-89c9-565f7c248f89.filesusr.com/ugd/d56aa6_ea3e1f059d6d49e1ac159a0ce4ff65f1.pdf?index=true; last accessed on 7 December 2022 at 14:51 hours.

28  The Government of India implemented one of the major components of JNNURM, namely Basic Services to Urban Poor (BSUP) for a select sixty-five JNNURM cities. The Government of India considered that provision of basic services to the poor, including affordable housing and basic amenities, was itself a major goal under JNNURM and also a key reform.

29  The IHSDP was introduced to cover the provision of affordable housing and basic services in slums in small and medium towns. The sharing pattern of funds between the Centre and State/ULB/Parastatal/beneficiary is 80:20. The cost ceiling for dwelling units (DU) under the scheme has been kept at Rs 1,00,000 per DU.

30  The ISHUP scheme was implemented on a pilot basis during the 11th Plan Period to create an enabling and a supportive environment for expanding credit flow to the housing sector and increasing home ownership in the country under the policy 'Affordable Housing for All' envisaged in the National Urban Housing and Habitat Policy, 2007.

31  Report to the People 2012–13, Government of the United Progressive Alliance.

32  Ibid.

33  In pursuance of the vision of a 'Slum-free India', Rajiv Awas Yojana was launched in June 2011.

34  Report to the People 2012–13, Government of the United Progressive Alliance.

35  Ibid.

36  'Key Indicators of Urban Slums in India', pib.gov.in, 2025, https://www.pib.gov.in/newsite/PrintRelease.aspx?relid=102108.

37  Jane Borges, 'There is a caste system based on water in Mumbai, say urbanists', *Mid-Day*, 21 April 2019, https://www.mid-day.com/articles/there-is-a-caste-system-

based-on-water-in-mumbai-say-urbanists/20782175; last accessed on 1 April 2020.

38 'Supreme Court Stays Demolition of 200 Jhuggis at Delhi's Sarojini Nagar', The Leaflet, NewsClick, 26 April 2022, https://www.newsclick.in/supreme-court-stays-demolition-200-jhuggis-delhi-sarojini-nagar.

39 Memorandum for the Expenditure Finance Committee 2012, Ministry of Housing & Urban Poverty Alleviation, Government of India.

40 Policy on In-Situ Slum Redevelopment/Rehabilitation on PPP Mode in Delhi to be adopted in DDA, https://dda.gov.in/sites/default/files/Housing%20Department/DDA%20In-Situ%20Rehabilitation%20Policy%20under%20PMAY07122021.pdf#:~:text=Delhi%20Development%20Authority%20is%20executing%20an%20In%2Dsitu%20Re%2D%20development%20Project%20at%20Kathputli%20Colony.&text=DDA%20will%20also%20undertake%20in%2Dsitu%20redevelopment/rehabilitation%20of,agreed%20terms%20with%20the%20land%20owning%20agencies.

41 File no. EM3(44)2001/Vol.2/, Delhi Development Authority, 26.08.2008.

42 Pradhan Mantri Awas Yojana-Urban (PMAY-U), (previously known as PM-Rajiv Awas Yojana [PM-RAY]), a flagship programme of the Union government, addresses urban housing shortage among the EWS/Low Income Group and Medium Income Group categories including the slum dwellers by ensuring a pucca house to all eligible urban households.

43 List of 675 JJ Clusters, https://delhishelterboard.in/main/wp-content/uploads/2015/12/675_JJ_Cluster_List.pdf.

44 Hernando de Soto, *The Mystery of Capital: Why Capitalism Triumphs in the West and Fails Everywhere Else* (New York, Basic Books, 2000).

45 Caroline Boin, 'Slum Dwellers Need Rights Not Projects', *Economic Times*, 22 June 2007, https://m.economictimes.com/slum-dwellers-need-rights-not-projects/articleshow/2142774.cms.
46 Guidebook on Housing Department, https://dda.gov.in/sites/default/files/inline-files/guidebook_on_housing_department_0.pdf.
47 Report of the Committee on Slum Statistics/Census, https://nbo.gov.in/pdf/REPORT_OF_SLUM_COMMITTEE.pdf.
48 Arjun Sengupta Committee Report, National Commission for Enterprises in Unorganised Sector.
49 Population of Delhi, StatisticsTimes.com, n.d., https://statisticstimes.com/demographics/india/delhi-population.php.
50 Reportage, 'How the Jahangirpuri Demolition Destroyed Lives of India's Poorest Women', The Wire, 29 April 2022, available at https://thewire.in/women/how-the-jahangirpuri-demolition-destroyed-lives-of-indias-poorest-women; 'SC Hearings on "Bulldozer Justice": What Has Happened so Far?', *Supreme Court Observer*, 9 October 2024, https://www.scobserver.in/journal/sc-hearings-on-bulldozer-justice-what-has-happened-so-far/.
51 'Street Vendors and the Law', *India Legal*, 21 December 2021, https://indialegallive.com/cover-story-articles/il-feature-news/delhi-high-courtstreet-vendors-act-delhi-government/.
52 PM SVANidhi Yojana Guidelines, https://pmsvanidhi.mohua.gov.in, last accessed on 7 December 2022.
53 PM SVANidhi Yojana Dashboard, https://pmsvanidhi.mohua.gov.in, last accessed on 7 December 2022.
54 Ibid.
55 Prerna Prabhakar, 'Why PMAY-U fails to address India's intrinsic housing problems', *Economic Times,* 2 November

2021, https://government.economictimes.indiatimes.com/news/governance/why-pmay-u-fails-to-address-indias-intrinsic-housing-problems/87481136.

56   Nine Years of PMAY-U 2015–2024, Ministry of Housing and Urban Affairs, available at https://pmay-urban.gov.in/pmay/pmayu-9-years.

57   Union Budget 2020–21, Ministry of Housing and Urban Affairs, available at https://www.indiabudget.gov.in/doc/eb/sbe57.pdf.

58   Ministry of Housing and Urban Affairs, 'Fact Check: PM Modi Is Lying About the Houses Built Under PMAY', NewsClick, 6 February 2019, https://www.newsclick.in/fact-check-modi-lying-about-houses-built-under-pmay; 'Fact check: Did the UPA construct only 25 lakh houses in their last 4 years?', NewsLaundry, 15 November 2018, https://www.newslaundry.com/2018/11/15/fact-check-upa-modi-awas-yojana.

59   Ibid.

60   Ashish Batra, 'After a Decade of Its Launch, Only 18 out of 100 Cities Have Completed Smart Cities Mission Projects—but There Are Some Positive Takeaways', *Down to Earth,* 29 April 2025, https://www.downtoearth.org.in/governance/after-a-decade-of-its-launch-only-18-out-of-100-cities-have-completed-smart-cities-mission-projects-but-there-are-some-positive-takeaways.

61   Starred Q. No 134, Ministry of Housing and Urban Affairs answered in Lok Sabha on 12.02.2019.

62   'Without Conceptual And Structural Clarity, Smart Cities Will Remain A Dull Plan', *The Secretariat,* 29 March 2024, https://thesecretariat.in/article/without-conceptual-and-structural-clarity-smart-cities-will-remain-a-dull-plan.

63   Mohan Guruswamy, 'What has led to failure of Swachh Bharat Abhiyan?', *Deccan Chronicle,* 15 February 2022, available at https://www.deccanchronicle.com/opinion/

columnists/140222/mohan-guruswamy-what-has-led-to-failure-of-swachh-bharat-abhiyan.html.
64   Press India Bureau, Release Id: 1814401, 7 April 2022, available at https://pib.gov.in/PressReleaseIframePage.aspx?PRID=1814401.
65   Ministry of Housing and Urban Affairs, available at https://pmay-urban.gov.in/.
66   Meenakshi Shina, 'Special purpose vehicles for smart cities: A question on governance', *Ideas for India*, 5 July 2019, available at https://www.ideasforindia.in/topics/urbanisation/special-purpose-vehicles-for-smart-cities-a-question-on-governance.html.
67   Ibid.

Demolition City: Planning Violations and the Erosion of Housing Rights

1   A. Kumar, S. Vidyarthi and P. Prakash, *City Planning in India, 1947–2017* (1st ed.), (Routledge India), https://doi.org/10.4324/9781003055969.
2   Abhay Pethe et al. 'Re-thinking urban planning in India: Learning from the wedge between the de jure and de facto development in Mumbai', *Cities* 39 (2014): 120–32.
3   Judge Isher Ahluwalia and R. Kanburand, 'Planning for urban development in India', ICRIER Paper, Indian Council for Research on International Economic Relations (ICRIER), New Delhi (2011).
4   Urban informality refers to self-organized, spontaneous settlements like slums and bazaars, existing outside formal planning, characterized by marginalization and resilience, crucial for survival in rapidly urbanizing areas, especially in the Global South.
5   People's settlements are self-organized communities, like slums and squatter areas, that develop informally due to

inadequate formal housing, reflecting residents' resilience and resourcefulness in urban environments.

6   The term 'basti' originates from the Hindi and Urdu languages, derived from the Sanskrit word 'vasti' (वस्ति), which means a settlement, habitation or dwelling place. Over time, basti has come to specifically refer to densely populated, informal urban settlements, often associated with inadequate housing and infrastructure. The term 'slum' is avoided as it carries pejorative connotations, stigmatizing residents and neglecting their resilience and community cohesion.

7   G. Bhan, *In the public's interest: Evictions, citizenship, and inequality in contemporary Delhi* (Geographies of Justice and Social Transformation), (Athens, GA: University of Georgia Press), xiv, 290.

8   D. Asher Ghertner, 'Green evictions: Environmental discourses of a "slum-free" Delhi', in *Global Political Ecology*, Routledge, 2010, 159–80.

9   L. Weinstein, 'Demolition and Dispossession: Toward an Understanding of State Violence in Millennial Mumbai', *St. Comp. Int. Dev.* 48, 285–307 (2013), https://doi.org/10.1007/s12116-013-9136-9.

10  Mahadevia Darshini and Harini Narayanan, 'Shanghaing Mumbai: Politics of evictions and resistance in slum settlements' in Mahadevia Darshini (ed.), *Inside the transforming urban Asia: Processes, policies and public actions* (2008): 549–89.

11  'Slum Numbers Show Cities Don't Help Dalits Shed Caste', *Indian Express*, 29 November 2020, https://indianexpress.com/article/opinion/columns/slum-numbers-show-cities-dont-help-dalits-shed-caste-7072206/.

12  Smart Cities Mission (SCM), launched on 25 June 2015, is an initiative by the Indian government aimed at promoting sustainable and inclusive urban development through the adoption of smart technologies and infrastructure improvements in selected cities. Refer

for more details: https://smartcities.gov.in/about-the-mission

13. Pradhan Mantri Awas Yojana - Urban (PMAY-U), launched on 25 June 2015, is an Indian government initiative aimed at ensuring affordable housing for all urban poor by 2022 through various subsidy and support schemes. Refer for more details: https://pmay-urban.gov.in/about.

14. Swachh Bharat Mission - Urban (SBM-U), launched on 2 October 2014, is an Indian government initiative aimed at achieving a clean and open defecation-free urban India by improving sanitation facilities and promoting hygiene practices. Refer for more details: https://sbmurban.org/storage/app/media/pdf/swachh-bharat-2.pdf.

15. 'The Curious Case of Indian Smart Cities', Centre for Financial Accountability, 27 September 2019, https://www.cenfa.org/the-curious-case-of-indian-smart-cities/.

16. Shivani Chaudhry, 'The Human Rights Dimensions of India's Smart Cities Mission – Urbanet', 16 August 2018, https://www.urbanet.info/india-smart-cities-human-rights/.

17. 'Forced Evictions in India in 2018: An Unabating National Crisis', Housing and Land Rights Network, New Delhi, 2019, https://hlrn.org.in/documents/Forced_Evictions_2018.pdf.

18. 'India's Cities Need to Be Sustainable, Not Smart', *Indian Express,* 30 June 2021, https://indianexpress.com/article/opinion/india-smart-city-mission-7383242/.

19. Report of the Public Hearing on The Forced Evictions across India and G20 Events, May 2003, https://wgonifis.net/wp-content/uploads/2023/07/g-20-public-hearing-6.pdf.

20. '40% of Indore under Knee-Deep Water; 3000 People Evacuated', *Hindustan Times,* 5 August 2015, https://www.hindustantimes.com/indore/40-of-indore-

under-knee-deep-water-3000-people-evacuated/story-aK2JjMRadIkw1z9k5pQUbO.html.
21  It was first featured in 2006: https://www.hindustantimes.com/india/cp-shekhar-nagar-residents-evacuated/story-OAAJSRjD4qJVlum7Tu9gcN.html#:~:text=%E2%80%9COnly%2040%20families%20have%20been%20temporarily%20shifted,was%20a%20common%20sight%20to%20see%20residents.
22  'Forceful Eviction of a Dalit Community in Indore', *Round Table India*, 27 October 2015, https://www.roundtableindia.co.in/forceful-eviction-of-a-dalit-community-in-indore/.
23  The Matang community is a Dalit community primarily found in the Indian states of Maharashtra and Gujarat. Historically marginalized, the Matangs have traditionally been engaged in occupations such as leatherwork and scavenging.
24  Round Table India – for an Informed Ambedkar Age, 23 October 2025, http://roundtableindia.co.in/index.php?option=com_content&view=article&id=8387:forceful-eviction-of-a-dalit-community-in-indore&catid=122&Itemid=138.
25  Forceful Eviction of a Dalit Community in Indore', *Round Table India*, 27 October 2015, https://www.roundtableindia.co.in/forceful-eviction-of-a-dalit-community-in-indore/.
26  The Madhya Pradesh Nagariya Kshetron Ke Bhoomihin Vyakti Pattadhriti Adhikaron Ka Pradan Kiya Jana, Act 15 of 1984, n.d., accessed 24 October 2025, https://prsindia.org/files/bills_acts/acts_states/madhya-pradesh/1984/1984MP15.pdf.
27  Forceful Eviction of a Dalit Community in Indore', *Round Table India*, 27 October 2015, https://www.roundtableindia.co.in/forceful-eviction-of-a-dalit-community-in-indore/.

28  'Slum Free City Plan for Indore Metropolitan Area Revised Draft Final Report Volume -I -Report and Appendices', 2013, http://mohua.gov.in/upload/uploadfiles/files/52Ind_MP_sfcp_Vol_I-min.pdf.
29  Ibid.
30  Ibid.
31  'Smart City Blues, IMDb, 14 November 2018, https://www.imdb.com/title/tt9310072/.
32  Shantha Sukanya, 'Demolitions, Evictions and Toilets for Show: How Indore Won Swachh Bharats Top Rank', The Wire, 2 October 2017, https://m.thewire.in/article/politics/indore-swachh-bharat-abhiyan/amp.
33  'Examining the "Slum" in the Narratives of Urban Planning Processes Study and Capacity Building Based in Indore', n.d., https://yuvaindia.org/wp-content/uploads/2023/04/Yuva_Indore_2021.pdf.
34  'Indore's Housing Agenda and the Curious Case of Tenability and Viability', Medium, 7 July 2018, https://medium.com/@yuvaonline/indores-housing-agenda-and-the-curious-case-of-tenability-and-viability-1ed3e6f530d6.
35  https://indiaenvironmentportal.org.in/in-court/order-of-the-national-green-tribunal-regarding-pollution-and-encroachment-of-saraswati-river-west-bengal-20012025/.
36  Bagish Jha, 'NGT Directs to Develop Green Belt on Khan, Saraswati Rivers like Sabarmati River Front', *Times of India*, 28 August 2014, https://timesofindia.indiatimes.com/city/indore/ngt-directs-to-develop-green-belt-on-khan-saraswati-rivers-like-sabarmati-river-front/articleshow/41108106.cms.
37  'Indore: IMC Razes CP Shekhar Nagar, Relocates Dwellers, *Hindustan Times*, 11 October 2015, https://www.hindustantimes.com/indore/indore-imc-

razes-cp-shekhar-nagar-relocates-dwellers/story-JB2snpxbVknvf6uBrVGnQK.html.
38 'Housing for All? Over 9,000 Homes Already Demolished in 2015', Press Release, Housing and Land Rights Network, New Delhi, 20 August 2015, https://www.hlrn.org.in/documents/HLRN_Press_Release_Forced_Evictions_20_August_2015.pdf.
39 W.P. No.5281/2015, 11/08/2015, https://mphc.gov.in/upload/indore/MPHCIND/2015/WP/5281/WP_5281_2015_Order_11-Aug-2015.pdf.
40 'Indore: IMC Razes CP Shekhar Nagar, Relocates Dwellers, *Hindustan Times*, 11 October 2015.
41 W.P. No.5281/2015, 25.8.2015, https://mphc.gov.in/upload/indore/MPHCIND/2015/WP/5281/WP_5281_2015_Order_25-Aug-2015.pdf.
42 'MP High Court Orders Action against Cops Who Beat up Lawyer in Pandarinath, *Hindustan Times*, 22 September 2015, https://www.hindustantimes.com/indore/mp-high-court-orders-action-against-cops-who-beat-up-lawyer-in-pandarinath/story-NAwDN4g3ZknZ4WiSQtFahP.html.
43 CP Shekhar Nagar through received rights under the Madhya Pradesh Nagariya Kshetro Ke Bhoomihin Vyakti (Pattadhriti Adhikaron Ka Pradan Kiya Jana) Adhiniyam, 1984.
44 'Indore: IMC Razes CP Shekhar Nagar, Relocates Dwellers, *Hindustan Times*, 11 October 2015.
45 http://yuvaindia.org/wp-content/uploads/2017/03/Human-Rights-Assessment-of-Housing-Schemes-in-Indore.pdf.
46 Local term for 'multistorey' dwelling units.
47 'Indore's Housing Agenda and the Curious Case of Tenability and Viability', Medium, 7 July 2018, https://medium.com/@yuvaonline/indores-housing-agenda-

and-the-curious-case-of-tenability-and-viability-1ed3e6f530d6.
48. 'Smartcities', Ministry of Housing and Urban Affairs, Smartcities.gov.in, 2020, https://smartcities.gov.in/.
49. 'Water Systems in Indore – An integrated approach', Indore Municipal Corporation, Indore, http://icrier.org/Urbanisation/events/23-2-15/Indore%20Presentation%20-%2023.02.15.pdf.
50. http://smartcities.gov.in/upload/uploadfiles/files/04_RiverFront_INDORE_Final.pdf.
51. W.P. No.5281/2015, 25.8.2015, https://mphc.gov.in/upload/indore/MPHCIND/2015/WP/5281/WP_5281_2015_Order_25-Aug-2015.pdf.
52. Forceful Eviction of a Dalit Community in Indore', *Round Table India*, 27 October 2015.
53. 'Indore's Housing Agenda and the Curious Case of Tenability and Viability', Medium, 7 July 2018.
54. 'IMC Plans Another Footbridge on Kanh', *Times of India*, 14 December 2018, http://timesofindia.indiatimes.com/articleshow/67083218.cms?utm_source=contentofinterest&utm_medium=text&utm_campaign=cppst.
55. 'India's Unrelenting Forced-eviction Crisis', hlrn.org, 9 April 2019, https://hlrn.org/activitydetails.php?title=India%E2%80%99s-Unrelenting-Forced-eviction-Crisis&id=pmtoZw.
56. 'Forced Evictions in India: 2022 & 2023', Housing and Land Rights Network, New Delhi, 2024, https://hlrn.org.in/documents/Forced_Evictions_2022_2023.pdf.
57. 'Introduction and History', Indore Municipal Corporation, https://imcindore.mp.gov.in/about.
58. 'Swachh Survekshan – 2017: Sanitation Rankings of Cities/Towns State/UT-wise', Press Information Bureau, Government of India, Ministry of Housing & Urban

Affairs, 4 May 2017, https://www.pib.gov.in/newsite/PrintRelease.aspx?relid=161527.

59  'Indore Bags Cleanest City Tag for 8th Year in Row; President Murmu Presents 78 Swachh Survekshan Awards', Newsonair.gov.in, 2025, https://www.newsonair.gov.in/president-murmu-to-confer-swachh-survekshan-2024-25-awards-in-new-delhi/.

60  'From Demolitions to Toilets for Show: How Indore Won Swachh Bharat Top Rank', *Business Standard*, 3 October 2017, https://www.business-standard.com/article/economy-policy/from-demolitions-to-toilets-for-show-how-indore-won-swachh-bharat-top-rank-117100300141_1.html.

61  Gaothans refer to traditional village settlements within the city.

62  Notable amongst them are Mumbai Urban Transport Project (MUTP), Mumbai Urban Infrastructure Project (MUIP), Mahatma Gandhi Pathkranti Yojana (MGPY), Brihan Mumbai Storm Water Drainage (BRIMSTOWD), Mithi River Development Project (MRDP), Bandra–Worli Sea Link, Eastern Express Freeway, the Metro and Mono Rail.

63  https://www.mmrcl.com/sites/default/files/R%26R-policy.pdf.

64  'India: Urban Resettlement', World Bank Group, 24 July 2012, https://www.worldbank.org/en/news/feature/2012/07/24/india-urban-resettlement.

65  Ipshita Karmakar, 'Rehabilitation of Project-Affected People along Tansa Pipeline in Mumbai', Rethinking the Future, 12 March 2019, https://www.re-thinkingthefuture.com/article/rehabilitation-of-project-affected-people-along-tansa-pipeline-in-mumbai/.

66  Order dated 16 February 2018 passed by the Bombay High Court in the case in Janhit Manchh & ors.

v. MCGM & ors., PIL No. 140/2026, before, available at https://www.casemine.com/judgement/in/5dc075d13321bc77c508b4d4.

67 'A Struggle for the Right to the City: The Case of Mahul', Ashank Desai Centre for Policy Studies, IIT Bombay, 10 May 2019, http://www.cps.iitb.ac.in/a-struggle-for-the-right-to-the-city-the-case-of-mahul/.

68 'Mahul Residents' Crucial Uphill Battle against the "Toxic Hell". Part One', Groundxero.in, 25 May 2019, https://www.groundxero.in/2019/05/25/mahul-residents-crucial-uphill-battle-against-the-toxic-hell-part-one/.

69 Shubham Kothari, 'Evicted for the Protection of Tansa Water Pipeline; Affected People Still Await Rehabilitation in Mumbai', Land Conflict Watch, 15 March 2023, https://www.landconflictwatch.org/conflicts/evicted-for-the-protection-of-tansa-water-pipeline-affected-people-still-await-rehabilitation-in-mumbai#.

70 https://ecf.com/sites/ecf.com/files/Suresh_F._Cycling_Infrastructure_vs_Critical_Mass_in_Developing_Countries_Like_India.pdf.

71 Ipshita Karmakar, 'Rehabilitation of Project-Affected People along Tansa Pipeline in Mumbai', Rethinking the Future, 12 March 2019.

72 Ibid.

73 http://www.indiaenvironmentportal.org.in/files/industry%20pollution%20Ambapada%20Mahul%20NGT.pdf.

74 'Mumbai: 5,500 Families to Be Moved to Kurla from Toxic Mahul, *Times of India*, 12 November 2018, https://timesofindia.indiatimes.com/city/mumbai/mumbai-5500-families-to-be-moved-to-kurla-from-toxic-mahul/articleshow/66598280.cms.

75 'Mahul Residents' Crucial Uphill Battle and the Mumbai Real Estate. Part Two', Groundxero.in, 28 May 2019,

https://www.groundxero.in/2019/05/28/mahul-residents-crucial-uphill-battle-and-the-mumbai-real-estate-part-two/.

76. 'Mahul Residents' Crucial Uphill Battle against the "Toxic Hell". Part One', Groundxero.in, 25 May 2019.
77. 1750/2018 c/w. 165/13/16/2019 (MHRC), PIL No. 140/2006 (Bombay HC), https://bombayhighcourt.nic.in/generatenewauth.php?bhcpar=cGF0aD0uL3dyaXRlcmVhZGRhdGEvZGF0YS9vcmlnaW5hW5hbC8yMDE4LyZmbmFtZT1XUDg3NDE4MDgwODE4LnBkZiZzbWZsYWc9TiZyan VkZGF0ZT0mdXBsb2FkZHQ9MjEvMDgvMjAxOCZzcGFzc3c9Bocm FzZT0yMjA2MjAyMDE2MDEvb bmNpdGF0aW9uPSZzbWNpdGF0aW9uPSZkaWdjXJ0ZmxnPVkmaW50ZXJmYWNlPQ==.
78. Ibid.
79. The Commissioner, Municipal Corporation of Greater Mumbai & Anr. versus Vishwanath Pandurang Dede & Ors, https://api.sci.gov.in/supremecourt/2019/17829/17829_2019_4_3_14573_Order_24-May-2019.pdf
80. 'Mahul Residents' Crucial Uphill Battle against the "Toxic Hell". Part One', Groundxero.in, 25 May 2019.
81. 'Victory for Mahul Residents: SC Disposes of BMC's Petition, Directs Payment of Rent', SabrangIndia, 26 July 2019, https://sabrangindia.in/victory-mahul-residents-sc-disposes-bmcs-petition-directs-payment-rent/.
82. https://bombayhighcourt.nic.in/generatenewauth.php?bhcpar=cGF0aD0uL3dyaXRlcmVhZGRhdGEvZGF0YS9qdWRnZW1lbnRzLzIwMTkvJmZuYW1lPU9TV1A4NzQxOC5wZGYmc21mbGFnPnP U4mcmp1ZGRhdGU9JnVwbG9hZGR0PTIzLzA5LzIwMTkmc3Bhc3N3aHJhc2U9U9MjIwNjI1MjAxODEwJm5jaXRhdGlvbj0mc21jaXRhdGlvbj0mZGlnY2VydGZsZz1OJmludGVyZmFjZT0=.

83 Anita Dhole, 'Help Us Leave #MumbaisToxicHell', Change.org, 8 December 2018, https://www.change.org/p/devendra-fadnavis-get-us-out-of-mumbaistoxichell-mahul?use_react=false.

84 Chaitanya Marpakwar, 'From Mahul's Toxic Hell, 1,600 Families to Move into Kurla', *Times of India*, 20 March 2022, https://timesofindia.indiatimes.com/from-mahuls-toxic-hell-1600-families-to-move-into-kurla/articleshow/90331046.cms.

85 Sabah Virani, 'Rehabilitated from Malad to Mahul, Residents Remain Stuck in a Highly Polluted Area', Citizen Matters, 14 November 2022, https://citizenmatters.in/slum-rehabiliation-malad-to-mahul-mumbai/.

86 Manjula Lal, 'A Little Bit of Magic in Delhi's Kathputli Colony', Newslaundry, 25 February 2019, https://www.newslaundry.com/2019/02/25/a-little-bit-of-magic-in-delhis-kathputli-colony.

87 With the help of the Asian Heritage Foundation, Kathputli artists found work through the Sangeet Natak Academy, a performing arts council established by the Indian government in Delhi. In the 1980s, the artists in Kathputli gained international recognition through performances at the Festival of India in the UK in 1982 and in the United States in 1985.

88 Regina F. Bendix and Galit Hasan-Rokem, *A Companion to Folklore* (John Wiley & Sons, 2012), 244.

89 Sunayana Wadhawan, 'In the Concrete Jungle', Norient, 2017, https://norient.com/sunayana-wadhawan/concrete-jungle.

90 'Transient and Differentiated Resettlement: The Case of Kathputli Colony, Delhi', India Housing Report, 27 April 2021, https://indiahousingreport.in/outputs/opinion/transient-and-differentiated-resettlement-the-case-of-kathputli-colony-delhi/.

91 Master Plan for Delhi-2021, Delhi Development Authority, https://dda.gov.in/sites/default/files/inline-files/Master_Plan_for_Delhi_2021_text_report.pdf.

92 The Slum Rehabilitation Authority (SRA) in Mumbai, which had acquired the status of a planning authority by way of an amendment to the Maharashtra Town and Country Planning Act in 1991, had always been criticized for its overemphasis on the private sector and the incentivization of providing housing to the poor.

93 Subhadra Banda, Yashas Vaidya and David Adler, 'The Case of Kathputli Colony: Mapping Delhi's First In-Situ Slum Rehabilitation Project', Centre for Policy Research, https://www.cprindia.org/system/tdf/working_papers/The%20Case%20of%20Kathputli%20Colony_CPRWorkingPaper%20(2)_1.pdf?file=1&type=node&id=3558&force=1.

94 Ibid.

95 'Climate Change, Corporate Accountability, Indigenous Struggles for Land, Mining Scams and Urban Displacement, Kathputli Colony: The Illusion of Rehabilitation', Ritimo, 18 December 2014, https://www.ritimo.org/Kathputli-Colony-The-Illusion-of-Rehabilitation#:~:text=The%20Master%20Plan,was%20given%20to%20Raheja%20Builders.

96 Aravind Unni, the lead author, was also the court commissioner appointed by Hon. Delhi High Court following the evictions. He thereby was witness to the eviction process.

97 'Forced Evictions in India in 2017: An Alarming National Crisis', Housing and Land Rights Network, https://www.hlrn.org.in/documents/Forced_Evictions_2017.pdf.

98 Police, residents clash as DDA begins demolition at Kathputli Colony', the *Tribune*, 31 October 2017, https://www.tribuneindia.com/news/archive/delhi/police-

residents-clash-as-dda-begins-demolition-at-kathputli-colony-489872/.
99 'Tensions Flare as DDA Begins Demolition of Kathputli Colony', *New Indian Express*, 31 October 2017, https://www.newindianexpress.com/pti-news/2017/Oct/30/tensions-flare-as-dda-begins-demolition-of-kathputli-colony-1687324.html.
100 'Kathputli Colony's Fear of Displacement', Uneven Earth – Where the Ecological Meets the Political, 25 April 2017, https://unevenearth.org/2017/04/kathputli-colonys-fear-of-displacement/; Somya Lakhani, 'Another eviction drive 10 km away sparks fear, anger at Kathputli Colony', *Indian Express*, 4 November 2017, https://indianexpress.com/article/cities/delhi/another-eviction-drive-10-km-away-sparks-fear-anger-at-kathputli-colony-4914582/; 'Murder of Democracy in Kathputli Colony, Houses Demolished, People Beaten Up, Annie Raja Injured', Countercurrents, 30 October 2017, https://countercurrents.org/2017/10/murder-of-democracy-in-kathputli-colony-houses-demolished-people-beaten-up-annie-raja-injured/; 'Delhi: Kathputli Colony facing threats of evictions and police action', Sanhati, 31 October 2014, https://sanhati.com/articles/11665/; Aranya Shankar, 'Tempers flare as DDA, police try to relocate Kathputli Colony locals', *Indian Express*, 27 December 2016, https://indianexpress.com/article/india/delhi-tempers-flare-as-dda-police-try-to-relocate-kathputli-colony-locals-4436162/.
101 Ankit Jha, 'Kathputli, Artist's Colony Demolished In Delhi: Thousands Rendered Homeless, Death Of Democracy!', architexturez, 31 October 2017, https://architexturez.net/pst/az-cf-185255-1509774726.
102 Centre for Holistic Development – Chd & Anr Versus Delhi Development Authority & Ors, https://delhihighcourt.nic.in/app/showlogo/208614_2017.pdf/2017.

103 'Delhi HC Rebukes DDA Counsel, Appoints Court Commissioners to Oversee Kathputli Colony Demolition, Rehabilitaton', SLIC, 2020, https://slic.org.in/publication/delhi-hc-rebukes-dda-counsel-appoints-court-commissioners-to-oversee-kathputli-colony-demolition-rehabilitaton.

104 'Delhi HC Stays Kathputli Colony Demolition for 10 Days', ETRealty.com, 1 November 2017, https://realty.economictimes.indiatimes.com/news/regulatory/delhi-hc-stays-kathputli-colony-demolition-for-10-days/61383293.

105 Centre for Holistic Development – Chd & Anr Versus Delhi Development Authority & Ors, https://delhihighcourt.nic.in/app/showlogo/200203_2017.pdf/2017.

106 'Delhi High Court Allows Demolition of Slums in Kathputli Colony', ndtv.com, 2 November 2017, https://www.ndtv.com/delhi-news/delhi-high-court-allows-demolition-of-slums-in-kathputli-colony-1770021.

107 Centre for Holistic Development – Chd & Anr Versus Delhi Development Authority & Ors, https://delhihighcourt.nic.in/app/showlogo/208614_2017.pdf/2017.

108 The issue was once again brought before the courts, following which the High Court constituted a committee to examine the cases of demolition and report them to senior officials of the DDA. However, the committee's efforts were largely ineffective, as the DDA continued its demolition drives by deploying large numbers of personnel and using coercive, house-to-house tactics. Reference: https://delhihighcourt.nic.in/app/showlogo/211121_2017.pdf/2017.

109 'Kathputli Colony: Slum Dwellers to Get Flats Soon', *Times of India*, 15 October 2023, https://timesofindia.indiatimes.com/city/delhi/kathputli-colony-slum-dwellers-to-get-flats-soon/articleshow/104436171.cms.

110 https://realtynxt.com/residential-news/2019-10-21/delhi-about-2800-kathputli-colony-residents-soon-to-shift-in-flats-by-december.

111 'Delhi HC Stays Kathputli Colony Demolition for 10 Days', ETRealty.com, 1 November 2017, https://realty.economictimes.indiatimes.com/news/regulatory/delhi-hc-stays-kathputli-colony-demolition-for-10-days/61383293.

## Urbanization, Migration and Reclassification: A Special Focus on West Bengal and the City of Siliguri

1 Handbook of Urban Statistics 2019, Ministry of Housing and Urban Affairs, Government of India, https://mohua.gov.in/pdf/5c80e2225a124Handbook%20of%20Urban%20Statistics%202019.pdf, 31.

2 A statutory town is one that is created by a statute of either a state government or even the Central government.

3 Jeffrey S. Rothstein, *The Steady but Uneven Decline in Manufacturing Job Quality* (Oxford University Press EBooks, 18 August 2022), 452–68, https://doi.org/10.1093/oxfordhb/9780198749790.013.21.

4 Balhasan Ali and Rachna Singh, 'Fertility Decline: A Success Story or Cause for Concern?', *New Indian Express*, 2 January 2025, https://www.newindianexpress.com/opinions/2025/Jan/02/fertility-decline-a-success-story-or-cause-for-concern.

5 https://cag.gov.in/uploads/download_audit_report/2016/Chapter_1_Introduction_15.pdf.

6 Ibid.

7 V.S. Jariwala, 'Urbanisation and its Trends in India –A Case of Gujarat', *Artha-Vikas Journal of Economic Development*, SSRN, Vol. 51, Issue 2, 20 Nov 2017, 72–85, https://papers.ssrn.com/sol3/Delivery.cfm/SSRN_

ID3072887_code517654.pdf?abstractid=3072887&mirid=1#:~:text=Urbanisation%20and%20the%20Development%20Process,attractions%20of%20the%20urban%20life.

8. https://dspace.spab.ac.in/xmlui/handle/123456789/888#:~:text=The%20whole%20country%20underwent%20a%20huge%20urban,has%20the%20maximum%20number%20(135%20Census%20towns).

9. Ibid.

10. Operation Barga was a landmark land reform programme launched in West Bengal in 1978. It was a movement to officially record the names and rights of sharecroppers, known as *bargadars*, who previously worked without legal protection on land owned by others.

11. Ambar Kumar Ghosh and Anasua Basu Ray Chaudhury, 'The Role of India's Northeast in the Regional Cooperation Architecture', Observer Research Foundation, 30 June 2021, https://www.orfonline.org/research/the-role-of-india-s-northeast-in-the-regional-cooperation-architecture.

12. Suhrid Sankar Chattopadhyay, 'A twist in the politics of the Darjeeling hills', *Frontline*, 8 November 2020, https://frontline.thehindu.com/politics/a-twist-in-the-hills/article32997536.ece#:~:text=The%20dramatic%20development%20will%20lead,a%20separate%20state%20of%20Gorkhaland.&text=Responding%20to%20Gurung's%20offer%20of,&%20prosperity%20of%20our%20motherland.%E2%80%9D.

13. Paromita Ghosh, 'Knowing The City, Siliguri', Centre for Koch (Rajbanshi) Studies and Development, 28 June 2021, https://kochrajbanshicentre.org/2021/06/28/knowing-the-city-siliguri/.

14. Ibid.

15 'Siliguri, India Metro Area Population (1950–2025)', MacroTrends, https://www.macrotrends.net/global-metrics/cities/21405/siliguri/population.

16 Ibid.

17 Economy and Communication of Siliguri, https://ir.nbu.ac.in/bitstreams/02c5f5b9-d48e-4eb8-a542-f59ed6b68760/download#:~:text=15%20Optics%20and%20watches%20478,economic%20study%2C%20SJDA%2C%202008.&text=for%20its%20woollen%20garments%20that,their%20positions%20in%20Siliguri's%20economy.

18 https://ir.nbu.ac.in/bitstreams/02c5f5b9-d48e-4eb8-a542-f59ed6b68760/download#:~:text=15%20Optics%20and%20watches%20478,economic%20study%2C%20SJDA%2C%202008.&text=for%20its%20woollen%20garments%20that,their%20positions%20in%20Siliguri's%20economy.

## On Homelessness

1 Indu Prakash Singh, *CityMakers: Tribulations and Triumphs: A Saga of Heroic Struggle of the Homeless Residents of India* (New Delhi: Mukul Prakashan, 2016, 2017 and 2021, ebook), i–xl and 1–608.

2 Jeremy Childs, 'Supreme Court Allows Politicians to Criminalize Homelessness', *Rolling Stone*, 28 June 2024, https://www.rollingstone.com/politics/politics-features/supreme-court-arguments-homeless-criminalization-case-1235007576/.

3 Indu Prakash Singh, *CityMakers: Tribulations and Triumphs: A Saga of Heroic Struggle of the Homeless Residents of India*, 27–39.

4 National Policy for The Urban Homeless (NPUH), CSOs of India, 2021, https://igsss.org/wp-content/

uploads/2021/09/National-policy-for-Urban-Homelessness.pdf.
5   Indu Prakash Singh, op. cit., 'India vs. non-India', 496–99.
6   From 'A Brief Background Note for Rajasthan Homeless Policy 2021', 8–9, a draft, 2021.

Conceptual Limitations: Analysing the Approach to Housing Projects for the Urban Poor

1   M. Hindmann, O. Lu-Hill, S. Murphy et al., *Dow Sustainability Fellowship 2015: Addressing Slum Redevelopment Issues in India*, Dow Sustainability Fellowship, International Institute at University of Michigan, 8.
2   *Economic Times*, 31 January 2017, http://economictimes.indiatimes.com/news/economy/policy/economic-survey-tells-you-8-interesting-facts-about-india/articleshow/56892398.cms.
3   M. Hindmann, O. Lu-Hill, S. Murphy et al., *Dow Sustainability Fellowship 2015: Addressing Slum Redevelopment Issues in India*, 20–22.
4   J. Jami, 'The Dilemma of Classification of Income Levels in Social Research', the *NEHU Journal*, Vol. XVI, No. 1, January–June 2018, 19–30, 20.
5   S. Kanwar, 'How the PM's Affordable Housing Scheme went from Promising to Dysfunctional: The Pradhanmantri Awas Yojna was once a decentralised scheme expected to solve India's 'housing shortage', but since a majority of the urban slum households did not own land they were automatically excluded from availing its benefits', Analysis, Urban subsection of e-edition of 14 May 2019, sourced at https://thewire.in/urban/housing-urban-policy-scheme.
6   M. Hindmann, O. Lu-Hill, S. Murphy et al., *Dow Sustainability Fellowship 2015: Addressing Slum Redevelopment Issues in India*, 15.

7   United Nations (2003), *Global Report on Human Settlements: The Challenge of Slums,* United Nations, Web 2015 cited in *Dow Sustainability Fellowship 2015: Addressing Slum Redevelopment Issues in India,* M. Hindmann, O. Lu-Hill, S. Murphy et al., Dow Sustainability Fellowship, International Institute at University of Michigan, 11.
8   Ibid., 12.
9   S. Gandhi and M. Munshi, 'Housing Paradox: Despite a severe shortage 12% of houses in Indian cities lie vacant', Scroll.in, 11 May 2017, https://scroll.in/article/836589/housing-paradox-despite-a-severe-shortage-12-of-houses-in-indian-cities-are-lying-vacant.
10  Min. of Housing & Urban Affairs, Govt. of India, from the homepage reporting figures achieved between 2015 and 2023, https://pmaymis.gov.in/.
11  DC Correspondent, 'Builders put under the scanner for misleading PMAY adverts', *Asian Age,* 16 May 2017, https://www.asianage.com/metros/mumbai/160517/builders-put-under-scanner-for-misleading-pmay-adverts.html.
12  A. Dutta, 'Affordable Housing: Here's why the once-booming sector is reeling under big challenges', *Business Today* (print edition), 30 April 2023, https://www.businesstoday.in/magazine/deep-dive/story/affordable-housing-heres-why-the-once-booming-sector-is-reeling-under-big-challenges-377851-2023-04-18.
13  S. Gandhi and M. Munshi, 'Housing Paradox: Despite a severe shortage 12% of houses in Indian cities lie vacant', Scroll.in.
14  Ibid.
15  Government of India, Jawaharlal Nehru National Urban Renewal Mission: Overview, http://mohua.gov.in/upload/uploadfiles/files/1Mission%20Overview%20English(1).pdf.
16  Ibid., 5–6.

17 Ibid., 6.
18 Ibid., 12.
19 Ibid., 6.
20 Ibid., 9.
21 Ibid., 13.
22 MoUD, Government of India; Smart Cities: Mission Statement & Guidelines, June 2015. http://smartcities.gov.in/upload/uploadfiles/files/SmartCityGuidelines(1).pdf, 6.
23 McKinsey Global Institute (2018), *Smart Cities: Digital Solutions for a More Livable Future,* McKinsey & Co., 8–9.
24 Ibid., 7.
25 Ibid., 1. Citing Adam Smith, the report talks of a system where the separate actions of different actors acting out of 'self-interest' would generate unpredictable benefits for society, 'an invisible hand' as it were.
26 Ibid., p. vi. The report states that while the public sector was the 'natural owner' of 70 per cent of the applications examined, 60 per cent of the initial investment required to implement the full range of applications could come from private investments. Thus, the report assumes that contrary to the present fact of a large proportion of public investment in applications controlling urban governance, private investment would suddenly come. It further talks of the opportunities to generate revenue on these public investments without explaining who is to extract that revenue and how it is to be used.
27 MoUD, Government of India; Smart Cities: Mission Statement & Guidelines, June 2015, http://smartcities.gov.in/upload/uploadfiles/files/SmartCityGuidelines(1).pdf, 10.
28 Ibid., 21.
29 Ibid., 8.
30 The Leela Sky Vilas, Navin Minar, Raheja Developers, 2018–2021, https://www.rahejanavinminar.in.

31 R. Chitlangia, 'Five Years on Kathputli Colony Residents in Delhi wait for promised homes', *Hindustan Times*, Delhi News, 3 January 2022, e-edition, https://www.hindustantimes.com/cities/delhi-news/five-years-on-katputli-colony-residents-in-delhi-wait-for-promised-homes-101641147870605.html.

32 Ibid. An article published in *Times of India* on 15 October 2023 claimed that the resettlement of displaced beneficiaries would begin in December 2023 (https://timesofindia.indiatimes.com/city/delhi/kathputli-colony-slum-dwellers-to-get-flats-soon/articleshow/104436171.cms) though no reports to that effect could be traced. A video published by Raheja Developers on 6 December 2023 showed the Navin Minar scheduled to start possession in 2022 as still having reached only its sixteenth floor plate of construction, which is only about one-third of its final intended height of 190 m. (https://www.youtube.com/watch?v=H7NuD6AGAP8). Recent Google Earth images of the site continue to show the site as having numerous cranes and equipment not consistent with a project ready for handover.

33 Delhi Development Authority, Master Plan for Delhi 2041 (MPD-2041), published in Gazette of India Extraordinary, Part-II, Section 3, Sub-section (ii), 1–6.

34 MoUD, Government of India; Smart Cities: Mission Statement & Guidelines, June 2015, http://smartcities.gov.in/upload/uploadfiles/files/SmartCityGuidelines(1).pdf.

35 Ibid., 8.

36 M. Menon and K. Kohli, 'East Kidwai Nagar Should Serve as a Warning, not a Model for Delhi's Redevelopment: The NBCC "model" project is hardly the totem of sustainability and responsibility. It has been fined for non-compliance of environmental laws, and official planning documents expose its shaky claims of urban design and

economic viability', Government, Urban, 28 Sept 2018, online edition, English, The Wire, https://thewire.in/urban/east-kidwai-nagar-should-serve-as-a-warning-not-model-for-delhis-redevelopment.

37  Ibid.
38  Ibid.
39  Delhi High Court, N. Chawla, Aman Lekhi & Ors. Vs. Union of India & Ors. on 11 February 2021, https://indiankanoon.org/doc/7896315/?type=print.
40  M. Menon and K. Kohli, 'East Kidwai Nagar Should Serve as a Warning, not a Model for Delhi's Redevelopment'.
41  R. Banka, Delhi High Court restrains NBCC from handing over commercial space in East Kidwai Nagar, *Hindustan Times*, 22 August 2018, https://www.hindustantimes.com/delhi-news/delhi-high-court-restrains-nbcc-from-handing-over-commercial-space-in-east-kidwai-nagar/story-kfgiE1u2Iihw269g54PNON.html.
42  Ibid. The article cites how the court asked Prof. Geetam Tiwari (IIT, Delhi) to prepare a detailed report on the impact on traffic while the New Delhi Municipal Corporation (NDMC) and Delhi Jal Board (DJB) were asked to file detailed affidavits pertaining to the manner of ensuring adequate supply for the large demand for the large residential project.
43  Chapman Taylor, *East Kidwai Nagar,* Projects, official website, https://www.chapmantaylor.com/projects/kidwai-nagar-east.
44  UN Habitat; Slum Almanac 2015/2016: Tracking improvement in the Lives of Slum Dwellers, https://unhabitat.org/slum-almanac-2015-2016/, 3.
45  C. Eames (ed.); Architecture of Democracy: Introduction; Architectural Design, August 1968, http://communityplanning.net/JohnTurnerArchive/pdfs/ADAug1968Intro.pdf.

46 J. Turner and R. Fichter, *Freedom to Build: Dweller Control of the Housing Process*, Chapter 7: Housing as a Verb (New York: Collier Macmillan, 1972), 151, http://communityplanning.net/JohnTurnerArchive/pdfs/FreedomtoBuildCh7.pdf.
47 Ibid., Chapter 6: Re-education of the Professional, 125.
48 Ibid., 128.
49 Ibid., Chapter 7: Housing as a Verb, 148–75.
50 Ibid., 152.
51 H. Sarkis, 'It's Elementary (Not): On the Architecture of Alejandro Aravena', January 2016, https://www.archdaily.com/780947/its-elementary-not-on-the-architecture-of-alejandro-aravena?ad_medium=mobile-widget&ad_name=recommendation.
52 A.B. Lall, *MLDL Chennai*, https://www.ashokblallarchitects.com/MLDL-CHENNAI.
53 Ministry of Rural Development, Govt of India with Indian Institute of Technology, Delhi, Centre for Scientific & Industrial Research-India, Central Building Research Institute and the United Nations Development Program, 1 April 2016, *Pahal: Prakriti, Hunar, Lokvidya*, http://pmayg.nic.in/netiay/Pahal.pdf.

New Governance Regimes and Urban Development

1 NITI Aayog and Asian Development Bank (ADB), 'Cities as engines of growth: TA 9508: Strengthening the states for broad based urban development', 2022, https://documents1.worldbank.org/curated/en/921651468149669044/pdf/577120NWP0Box31UBLIC10gc1wp10121web.pdf.
2 Special Economic Zones Act, 2005 and FAQ's - Special Economic Zones in India, Ministry of Commerce & Industry, Department of Commerce, https://sezindia.gov.in/index.php/FAQ.

3   Industrial Townships are provided under Chapter XVI-A (Sections 364(A) to 364(Q)), of the Karnataka Municipalities Act, 1964, amended in 2003.
4   BJP Manifesto 2014, https://www.bjp.org/bjp-manifesto-2014.
5   https://smartcities.gov.in/about-the-mission.
6   https://unhabitat.org/sites/default/files/2023/09/smart_cities_mission_web_version_low_version.pdf.
7   Smart Cities Mission Statement & Guidelines, Ministry of Urban Development, Government of India, June 2015, https://smartcities.gov.in/themes/habikon/files/SmartCityGuidelines.pdf, Annexure 5: Structure and Functions of SPV.
8   Ibid.
9   Devesh Kapur and W.E.B.B. Richard, Governance-related conditionalities of the international financial institutions. No. 6. United Nations Conference on Trade and Development, 2000.
10  Kanchan Chandra, 'The new Indian state: The relocation of patronage in the post-liberalisation economy', *Economic and Political Weekly* (2015): 46–58.
11  Reetika Khera, 'Democratic politics and legal rights: Employment guarantee and food security in India', New Delhi: Institute of Economic Growth, University of Delhi, 2013.
12  Paul Romer, 'Technologies, rules, and progress: The case for charter cities', Center for Global Development, No. 2471. 2010.
13  'Charter cities', Editorial, *The Mint*, 18 July 2016, available at: https://www.livemint.com/Opinion/hvCTPRUKVmXcnPWzZH0D8I/Charter-cities.html.

## Inclusive Urbanization

1   Earlier versions of this article appeared in the *Economic and Political Weekly*, 7 January 2017 and 14 April 2018.

2   'Fort St. George, constructed to safeguard British trading interests, soon became the political and economic centre for the British in southern India. Black Town was strategically positioned just outside the fort's walls and became home to Indian artisans, merchants and workers essential to the British economy. The area accommodated a large Tamil-speaking population, alongside other communities, including Armenians, Gujaratis and Marwari merchants. Due to its diverse demographic, Black Town served as a melting pot of languages and cultures, a characteristic that shaped its vibrant marketplace and unique heritage.' (*Navrang India*, 12 November 2024.)

3   'Understanding Migration in India: Concepts, Types, and Census Insights', CSR Education, 22 June 2024, https://csr.education/development-in-india/migration-india-concepts-types-census-insights.

4   Tertius Chandler, *Four Thousand Years of Urban Growth: A Historical Census* (St. David's University Press, UK, 1987).

5   A 2010 McKinsey report estimates that India would need $1.2 trillion by 2030, a far cry from current spending estimates. India's annual per capita spending on cities stands at a measly $50: www.mckinsey.com/mgi/overview/in-the-news/opinion-on-funding-indias-urban-infrastructure.

6   'Cabinet note moved on $90 billion DMIC project', *The Hindu*, 20 August 2011, https://www.thehindu.com/business/cabinet-note-moved-on-90-billion-dmic-project/article2376647.ece.

7   Deepanshu Mohan, 'In 9 Charts: India's Growing Debt Problem Has "Crisis-Like Symptoms"', The Wire, 27 December 2023, https://thewire.in/economy/in-9-charts-indias-growing-debt-problem-has-crisis-like-symptoms.

8   Romi Khosla, 'India's Urban Landscape', *Economic and Political Weekly*, 2017.

9   Steve Smith, 'The End of the Unipolar Moment: September 11 and the Future of World Order', Items, 1 November 2001, https://items.ssrc.org/after-september-11/the-end-of-the-unipolar-moment-september-11-and-the-future-of-world-order/.
10  'There is evidence that the 2007–2010 drought contributed to the conflict in Syria. It was the worst drought in the instrumental record, causing widespread crop failure and a mass migration of farming families to urban centers . . . We conclude that human influences on the climate system are implicated in the current Syrian conflict.' Rabie Nasser, 'Confronting Fragmentation', Syrian Centre for Policy Research, *Guardian*, 11 February 2016.

## The Urban Commons Outlook: A Vision for Transformative and Inclusive Indian Cities

1   United Nations, *World Economic Situation and Prospects, 2019*.
2   UNDP, *Human Development Indices and Indicators: 2018 Statistical Update*, 'Briefing Note for Countries on the 2018 Statistical Update: India', United Nations Development Programme.
3   World Health Organisation, *2014 Air Pollution Ranking*, http://aqicn.org/faq/2015-05-16/world-health-organization-2014-air-pollution-ranking/.
4   O. Hoegh-Guldberg, D. Jacob, M. Taylor et al., 'Impacts of 1.5°C Global Warming on Natural and Human Systems', in *Global Warming of 1.5°C*, an IPCC special report released in 2018 on the impacts of global warming of 1.5°C above pre-industrial levels and related global greenhouse gas emission pathways, in the context of strengthening the global response to the threat of climate change, sustainable development and efforts to eradicate poverty.

5   United Nations (2018) *World Urbanization Prospects: The 2018 Revision, Key Facts*. Economic and Social Affairs, United Nations.
6   World Bank (2013) *Urbanization beyond municipal boundaries: Nurturing metropolitan economies and connecting peri-urban areas in India*, The World Bank, Washington DC, USA.
7   C. Mallik, 'Urbanisation and the peripheries of large cities in India: The dynamics of land use and rural work', *Indian Journal of Agricultural Economics* 64(3):421–430, 2009.
8   H. Nagendra, *Nature in the City: Bengaluru in the Past, Present and Future* (New Delhi: Oxford University Press, 2016).
9   H. Nagendra and S. Mundoli, *Cities and Canopies: Trees in Indian Cities* (New Delhi: Penguin India, 2019).
10  V. Narain and S. Vij, 'Where have all our commons gone?' *Geoforum* 68: 21–24, 2015; S. Mundoli, H. Unnikrishnan and H. Nagendra, 'Urban commons of the Global South: Using multiple frames to illuminate complexity', book chapter, *Routledge Handbook of the Study of Commons*, 2019.
11  S. Mundoli, H. Unnikrishnan and H. Nagendra, 'The "sustainable" in smart cities: Ignoring the importance of urban ecosystems', *Decision* (Journal of the Indian Institute of Management-Calcutta) 44(2): 103–120, 2017a; Mundoli et al. 2019.
12  S. Mundoli, V.M. Hariprasad, Preeti Venkatraman and H. Nagendra, 'Urban visions that risk urban social and ecological sustainability: Smart cities in India', in *Urban Sustainability in India*, eds H. Nagendra and S. Mundoli (Orient Blackswan). (Accepted).
13  S. Mundoli, A. Sanfui and H. Nagendra, 'Pestilential or productive? Tracking two centuries of environmental change and current perceptions about ecosystem services of the East Kolkata Wetlands', *Urbanisation* 8(2): 1–21, 2023.
14  H. Nagendra and S. Mundoli, *Shades of Blue: Connecting the Drops in India's Cities* (Penguin Viking, 2023).

15 A. Menon and G.A. Vadivelu, 'Common-property resources in different agro-climatic landscapes in India', *Conservation and Society* 4(1): 132–54, 2006.
16 A. Baviskar, 'What the eye does not see: The Yamuna in the imagination of Delhi', *Economic and Political Weekly* 46(50):45–53; Nagendra 2016.
17 D. Parthasarathy, 'Hunters, gatherers and foragers in a metropolis: Commonising the private and public in Mumbai', *Economic and Political Weekly* 46(50): 54–63.
18 S. Mundoli, H. Unnikrishnan and H. Nagendra, 'Nurturing urban commons for sustainable urbanisation in India', *Journal of the India International Centre* (2017b) 43(3-4): 258–70.
19 Mundoli et al. 2019.
20 Parthasarathy 2011.
21 R. D'Souza and H. Nagendra, 'Changes in public commons as a consequence of urbanization: The Agara lake in Bangalore', *India Environmental Management* (2011) 47: 840–850; H. Unnikrishnan and H. Nagendra, 'Privatizing the commons: Impact on ecosystem services in Bengaluru's lakes', *Urban Ecosystem* (2014) 18(2): 613–32; S. Mundoli, B. Manjunatha and H. Nagendra, 'Effects of urbanization on the use of lakes as commons in the peri-urban interface of Bengaluru', *International Journal of Urban Sustainable Development* (2015) 7(1): 89–108.
22 Mundoli et al. 2015; H. Unnikrishnan, S. Mundoli and H. Nagendra, 'Down the drain: The tragedy of the disappearing urban commons of Bengaluru', *SAWAS* (2016) 5(3): 7–11.
23 Mundoli et al. 2015.
24 Baviskar 2011; A. Sharan, 'A river and the riverfront: Delhi's Yamuna as an in-between pace', *City, Culture and Society* (2016) 7(4): 267–73.
25 J. Mukherjee, 'Sustainable flows between Kolkata and its peri-urban interface: Challenges and opportunities', in:

*Untamed Urbanisms*, A. Allen, A. Lampis and M. Swilling (eds.), (London and New York: Routledge, 2016), 33–49.
26 Mundoli et al. 2015.
27 Nagendra 2016; Unnikrishnan et al. 2016.
28 Parthasarathy 2011.
29 Parthasarathy 2011; M. Kumar, K. Saravanan and N. Jayaraman, 'Mapping the coastal commons: Fisherfolk and the politics of coastal urbanisation in Chennai', *Economic and Political Weekly* XLIX (2014) (48): 46–53.
30 S. Mundoli, B. Manjunatha and H. Nagendra, 'Commons that provide: The importance of Bengaluru's wooded groves for urban resilience', *International Journal of Urban Sustainable Development*, (2017c) Special Issue 9(2): 184–206; Nagendra and Mundoli 2019.
31 A. Baviskar, 'Urban jungles: Wilderness, parks and their publics in Delhi', *Economic and Political Weekly* (2018) 53(2): 46–54.
32 Parthasarathy 2011; A. Sen and H. Nagendra, 'Mumbai's blinkered vision of development: Sacrificing ecology for infrastructure', *Economic and Political Weekly* (2019) LIV(9): 20–23.
33 Nagendra 2016.
34 Mundoli et al. 2017a; Nagendra and Mundoli 2019.
35 I.D. Rotherham ed., *Cultural severance and the environment: The ending of traditional and customary practice on commons and landscapes managed in common* (Springer, Dordrecht, 2013).
36 Nagendra 2016; Baviskar 2018; Nagendra and Mundoli 2019.
37 Mundoli et al. 2017a.
38 Nagendra 2016.
39 Mundoli et al. 2017b, 2017c.
40 Ibid.
41 Narain and Vij 2015.

42  Baviskar 2011; Sharan 2016.
43  Mundoli et al. 2023.
44  Baviskar 2018.
45  Sen and Nagendra 2019.
46  E. Ostrom, *Governing the Commons: The Evolution of Institutions for Collective Action* (Cambridge University Press, 1990).
47  Putting up physical barriers is one way. Lakes and wooded groves in Bengaluru are fenced, preventing access to traditional users such as grazers and fodder collectors.
48  In such spaces, traditional uses such as grazing or foraging are often prohibited.
49  Nagendra 2016; Mundoli et al. 2017a.
50  A. Joshi and N. Maheshwari, 'The Sabarmati riverfront development project: The issue of resettlement and rehabilitation', *Socio-Legal Review* (2016) 18.
51  A. Follmann, 'Urban mega-projects for a "world-class" riverfront: The interplay of informality, flexibility and exceptionality along the Yamuna in Delhi', *India, Habitat International* (2015) 45(3): 213–22.
52  Parthasarathy 2011; Kumar et al. 2014.
53  E. De Hoop and S. Arora, 'Material meanings: "Waste" as a performative category of land in colonial India', *Journal of Historical Geography* (2017) 55: 82–92.
54  Kumar et al. 2014.
55  Unnikrishnan and Nagendra 2014.
56  Baviskar 2011; Parthasarathy 2011; Kumar et al. 2014.
57  A. Datta, 'New urban utopias of postcolonial India: "Entrepreneurial urbanization" in Dholera smart city, Gujarat', *Dialogues in Human Geography* (2015) 5 (1): 3–22.
58  Mundoli et al. (Accepted)
59  Mundoli et al. 2017a; Mundoli et al. (Accepted).
60  Unnikrishnan et al. 2014; Mundoli et al. 2017a.
61  Rotherham 2013; Kumar et al. 2014; Mundoli et al. 2015.

62  Hoegh-Guldberg et al. 2018.
63  Kumar et al. 2014.
64  Hoegh-Guldberg et al. 2018.
65  M. Sharma, V. Kumar and S. Kumar, 'A systematic review of urban sprawl and land use/land cover change studies in India', *Sustainable Environment* (2021) 10(1): 233–269.
66  A. Basole, M. Idiculla, R. Narayanan, H. Nagendra and S. Mundoli, 'Strengthening Towns through Sustainable Employment: A Job Guarantee Programme for Urban India', State of Working India 2019, Azim Premji University Centre for Sustainable Employment (2019).
67  H.B. Weston and D. Bollier, *Green governance: Ecological survival, human rights and the law of the commons* (New York: Cambridge University Press, 2013); Mundoli et al. 2019.
68  Hoegh-Guldberg et al. 2018.
69  Mundoli et al. 2019.
70  We would like to acknowledge Azim Premji University for supporting our research. We would like to thank Ayushi Chauhan and Madhureema Auddy whose field work in the Yamuna in Delhi and East Kolkata Wetlands, respectively, provided useful insights for this essay. We also acknowledge Hariprasad V.M. and Preeti Venkatram for their field work in the smart cities of Karnataka.

## Whose Town Is It Anyway? Urban Inequality in the Face of Climate Change

1  W. Ahmed, 'Neoliberal utopia and urban realities in Delhi', *ACME: An International Journal for Critical Geographies*, (2011) 10(2), 163–88; A. Shrivastava and A. Kothari, *Churning the earth: The making of global India*, (UK: Penguin, 2012); V Vakulabharanam and S. Motiram, 'Understanding poverty and inequality in urban India since reforms: Bringing

quantitative and qualitative approaches together', *Economic and Political Weekly*, (2012) 48(47–48), 44; K. Michael and V. Vakulabharanam, 'Class and climate change in post-reform India', *Climate and Development*, (2016) 8(3), 224–33, doi:10. 1080/17565529.2015.1034235; S. Chattopadhyay, 'Neoliberal urban transformations in Indian cities: Paradoxes and predicaments', *Progress in Development Studies*, (2017) 17(4), 307–21.

2   K. Michael, T. Deshpande and G. Ziervogel, 'Examining vulnerability in a dynamic urban setting: The case of Bangalore's interstate migrant waste pickers' *Climate and Development*, (2019) 11(8), 667–78.

3   I. Basu, 'Elite discourse coalitions and the governance of "smart spaces": Politics, power and privilege in India's Smart Cities Mission', *Political Geography*, (2019) 68, 77–85; D.A. Ghertner, 'Gentrifying the state, gentrifying participation: Elite governance programs in Delhi', *International Journal of Urban and Regional Research*, (2011) 35(3), 504–32.

4   A.M. Auerbach, 'Clients and Communities: The Political Economy of Party Network Organization and Development in India's Urban Slums', *World Politics* (2016) 68(1), 111–48, https://doi.org/10.1017/s004388711500043x; A. Auerbach, 'Conclusion'. In *Demanding Development: The Politics of Public Goods Provision in India's Urban Slums*, Cambridge Studies in Comparative Politics (Cambridge: Cambridge University Press, 2019), 222–35, https://doi.org/10.1017/9781108649377.008.

5   P. Sidhwani, 'Spatial inequalities in big Indian cities', *Economic & Political Weekly*, (2015) 50(22), 55–62.

6   G. Anand, K. Wankhade, R.K. Raman, A. Deb and M.J. Vishnu, 'Tracing Exclusions in Urban Water Supply and Sanitation', *India Exclusion Report 2015*, (2016) 67.

7   M.K. Gandhi, *Hind Swaraj, or, Indian Home Rule*, 1939, Navajivan Publishing House.

8   *Constituent Assembly Debates* Volumes I- XII. (1999) Lok Sabha Secretariat, New Delhi.
9   V.M. Dandekar and N. Rath, 'Poverty in India-I: Dimensions and Trends', *Economic and Political Weekly*, (1971) 25–48; M.S. Andrea, and A. D'Souza, *The Urban Poor* (1980).
10  E.J. Hobsbawm, 'Peasants and Politics', *The Journal of Peasant Studies*, (1973). 1(1), 3–22.
11  W.W. Rostow, *The stages of growth: A non-communist manifesto* (Cambridge: Cambridge University Press, 1960), 4–16.
12  L. Fernandes, 'The politics of forgetting: Class politics, state power and the restructuring of urban space in India', in *Globalisation and the Politics of Forgetting* (Routledge, 2018), 121–36; M. Ranganathan, 'Caste, racialization, and the making of environmental unfreedoms in urban India', in *Rethinking Difference in India Through Racialization* (Routledge, 2022) 43–63.
13  S. Ahmad, 'Housing inequality in socially disadvantaged communities: Evidence from urban India, 2009', *Environment and Urbanization ASIA*, (2012) 3(1), 237–49.
14  K. Keshri and R.B. Bhagat, 'Temporary and seasonal migration: Regional pattern, characteristics and associated factors', *Economic and Political Weekly*, (2012) 81–88.
15  A. Shrivastava and A. Kothari, *Churning the Earth: The making of global India* (UK: Penguin, 2012).
16  R.H. Raghavendra, 'Literacy and health status of scheduled castes in India', *Contemporary Voice of Dalit*, (2020) 12(1), 97–110.
17  A. Zacharias and V. Vakulabharanam, 'Caste stratification and wealth inequality in India', *World Development*, (2011) 39(10), 1820–33.
18  J.K. Abraham and J. Misrahi-Barak, 'Introduction: Dalit literatures in India: In, out and beyond', in *Dalit Literatures in India* (Routledge India, 2015), 17–30.

19 Census of India, *Rural-urban distribution of population*, New Delhi: Government of India (2011).
20 Ibid.
21 Reproductive labour undertaken by women has obviously been not taken into account by the census.
22 S.C. Naidu and S. Rao, 'Reproductive work and female labor force participation in rural India', Political Economy Research Institute: Working Paper Series 458, April 2018.
23 S. Shah, K. Viswanath, S. Vyas and S. Gadepalli, 'Women and transport in Indian cities' *New Delhi, India: ITDP India*, (2017) 10.
24 K. Michael, T. Deshpande and G. Ziervogel, 'Examining vulnerability in a dynamic urban setting: The case of Bangalore's interstate migrant waste pickers', *Climate and Development*, (2019) 11(8), 667–78; T. Deshpande, K. Michael and K. Bhaskara, 'Barriers and enablers of local adaptive measures: A case study of Bengaluru's informal settlement dwellers', *Local Environment*, (2019) 24(3), 167–79.
25 Iris Marion Young, *Justice and the Politics of Difference* (Princeton, NJ: Princeton University Press, 1990).
26 Nancy Fraser, 'Justice Interruptus: Critical Reflections on the "Postsocialist" Condition' (New York and London: Routledge, 1997); Nancy Fraser, 'Rethinking Recognition', *New Left Review* (2000) 3: 107–20.
27 Jane McConkey, 'Knowledge and Acknowledgement: "Epistemic Injustice" as a Problem of Recognition', *Politics* (2004) 24 (3): 198–205, https://doi.org/10.1111/j.1467-9256.2004.00220.x.
28 A. Roy, 'Class Politics in the (Re) Making of Space: Displacing the Urban Poor in Kolkata, India', *Human Geography*, (2016) 9(3), 43–62.
29 Matias Echanove and Rahul Srivastava, 'Where Gandhi meets Ambedkar', *The Hindu*, 18 March 2018, https://

www.thehindu.com/society/where-gandhi-meets-ambedkar/article23279456.

30 P. Deshingkar and D. Start, 'Seasonal Migration For Livelihoods: Coping, Accumulation and Exclusion', Working Paper No 220. Overseas Development Institute, London (2003).

31 I. Agnihotri and I. Mazumdar, 'Dusty trails and unsettled lives: Women's labour migration in rural India', *Indian Journal of Gender Studies*, (2009) 16(3), 375–99; K. Lahiri-Dutt, 'Digging to survive: Women's livelihoods in South Asia's small mines and quarries', *South Asian Survey*, (2008) 15(2), 217–44.

32 J. Breman, 'The pandemic in India and its impact on footloose labour', *The Indian Journal of Labour Economics*, (2020) 63(4), 901–19.

33 S. Rao and V. Vakulabharanam, 'Migration, Crises, and Social Transformation in India Since the 1990s', *Handbook of Migration Crises* (2018).

34 Malini Ranganathan, 'Caste, racialization, and the making of environmental unfreedoms in urban India,' in *Rethinking Difference in India through Racialization* (Routledge, 2022), 43–63.

35 'First Session of Delhi Assembly Takes Off', *Al Jazeera*, 1 January 2014, https://www.aljazeera.com/news/2014/1/1/first-session-of-delhi-assembly-takes-off.

36 Kaushal Shroff, 'The Mathematics behind the AAP's Subsidies for Electricity and Water', *The Caravan*, 7 February 2020, https://caravanmagazine.in/government/delhi-elections-2020-aap-bjp-budget-campaign.

37 J. Kothari, 'The right to water: A constitutional perspective', in workshop entitled 'Water, Law and the Commons' organized in Delhi, (2006) Vol. 8, 2006–09; C. Ramachandraiah, 'Drinking water as a fundamental right', *Economic and Political Weekly*, (2001) 619–21; V. Narain,

'Water as a fundamental right: A perspective from India', *Vt. L. Rev.*, (2009) 34, 917; National Human Rights Commission, Right to Water (2021), link to report: https://nhrc.nic.in/sites/default/files/Right%20to%20water.pdf (last accessed on 16 June 2024); India Constitution Article 21 ('Protection of life and personal liberty'), link to document: https://www.mea.gov.in/Images/pdf1/Part3.pdf (last accessed on 16 June 2024).

38  K. Sharma, 'Waiting for water: The experiences of poor communities in Bombay', *The Society for the Promotion of Area Resource Centres (SPARC)* (1999), link to article: https://www.ucl.ac.uk/dpu-projects/drivers_urb_change/urb_infrastructure/pdf_public_private_services/W_SPARC_Kalpana_waiting_water.pdf (last accessed on 14 June 2024); N. Subramanian, 'Water is more expensive for the poor than the rich', *India Development Review* (IDR) (2019), link to article: https://idronline.org/water-is-more-expensive-for-the-poor-than-the-rich/ (last accessed on 14 June 2024); A global perspective is provided by J. Deck and S. Roy, 'Poorer people pay more for clean water', *Global Citizen* (2019), link to article: https://www.globalcitizen.org/en/content/world-water-development-report/ (last accessed on 14 June 2024); UNESCO, *The United Nations World Development Report 2019: Leaving no one behind*. United Nations. ISBN: 978-92-3-100309-7 (2019).

39  Kaushal Shroff, 'The Mathematics behind the AAP's Subsidies for Electricity and Water', *The Caravan*, 7 February 2020.

40  'Free Public Transport in Estonia', *The Economist*, 9 May 2019, https://www.economist.com/europe/2019/05/09/free-public-transport-in-estonia.

41  Steve Rose, 'All Aboard! Can Luxembourg's Free Public Transport Help Save the World?', the *Guardian*, 20 September 2023, sec. World news, https://www.

theguardian.com/world/2023/sep/20/all-aboard-can-luxembourgs-free-public-transport-help-save-the-world.

42. Satviki Sanjay, 'Free Bus Rides Offer Indian Women New Option for Work, and Play', Bloomberg, 7 November 2023, https://www.bloomberg.com/news/articles/2023-11-06/india-inside-shakti-the-free-bus-ride-program-for-women-in-karnataka-delhi.

43. A. Coote, P. Kasliwal and A. Percy, 'Universal basic services: Theory and practice - a literature review', (2019), https://discovery.ucl.ac.uk/id/eprint/10080177/1/ubs_report_online.pdf.

44. I. Gough, 'Universal basic services: A theoretical and moral framework', *The Political Quarterly*, (2019) 90(3), 534–42.

45. D. Harvey, 'Neoliberalism and the City', *Studies in Social Justice*, (2007) 1(1), 2–13; D. Harvey, 'The right to the city', *The New Left Review* (2008) 53, available at: http://newleftreview.org/II/53/david-harvey-the-right-to-the-city (accessed 20 June 2024).

# About the Contributors

**Ajay Maken** is a senior politician from the Indian National Congress. He currently serves as a member of Parliament in the Rajya Sabha, treasurer of the All India Congress Committee (AICC) and a member of the Congress Working Committee. Over the course of his distinguished political career, he has held several key ministerial positions, including Union Minister for Housing and Urban Poverty Alleviation (2012–13), Union Minister of State (Independent Charge) for Sports and Youth Affairs (2011–12), Union Minister of State for Home Affairs (2009–11) and Union Minister of State for Urban Development (2006–07). He has been elected thrice to the Parliament of India and three times to the Delhi Legislative Assembly.

**Aravind Unni** is an urban practitioner, researcher and activist working at the intersection of informality, livelihoods and urban planning in Indian cities. Trained as an architect from Jamia Millia Islamia and UC Berkeley, he is currently pursuing a PhD at the Tata Institute of Social Sciences, Mumbai, on street vendors and the politics of urban informality. With over fifteen years of experience, he works with national and international agencies to advance people-centred urban climate action and inclusive planning. His work and writings focus on informality, social protection and climate justice for marginalized urban communities.

**Evita Das** is an urban researcher and practitioner based in New Delhi, focusing on land, housing and caste dynamics in Indian cities. Her work seeks to make sense of a glorified yet unjust past and present through a critical lens shaped by caste. Actively engaged in movements and membership-based forums such as the Pakistan–India Peoples' Forum for Peace and Democracy and those working with natural resource-based communities, she is associated with the People's Commission and Public Inquiry Committees examining post-pandemic shifts with ground-based groups. Her writings, published in *The Hindu*, Scroll.in, The Wire, NewsClick and News Laundry, explore questions of caste, labour and urban life, and more recently, bring a critical caste lens to fisheries research.

**Asok Bhattacharya** is an Indian politician and the former mayor of the Siliguri Municipal Corporation in the state of West Bengal. He is a member of the Communist Party of India (Marxist) (CPI(M)). He is a prominent leader of the CPI(M) in the northern region of West Bengal. He was the Minister of Urban Development and Municipal Affairs in the Government of West Bengal for three consecutive terms (1996–2011). In May 2015, Asok Bhattacharya became the mayor of Siliguri Municipal Corporation after the Left Front won the municipal election in Siliguri and completed his term of five years. He was born in 1949 in Siliguri. He completed his graduation from the University of North Bengal in Siliguri.

**Indu Prakash Singh**, with over forty years of work experience in the development sector, is a human rights defender, socio-spiritual activist, poet, author, feminist, TEDx speaker (IIM Ahmedabad) and a PRA practitioner and facilitator. He is currently a consultant with a large number of national and international development organizations. Dr Indu has been bestowed with numerous awards. He is a petitioner in the Supreme Court of India on homeless matter WP (C) 572 of 2003. He has been working with the homeless in Delhi and around the country, whom he calls CityMakers, since 1999. The author of seven books, he has also edited over fifty publications.

**Kanishka Prasad** has been a practising architect since 2002 and has worked in organizations in Delhi, Mumbai and London before starting an individual practice focused on a search for traditional materials and techniques, and adapting them to modernist design languages. He has taught at various schools of architecture inculcating techniques of experimentation and research to architectural pedagogy. His recently concluded PhD research at JNU, New Delhi, focused on a study of labour processes and the dynamics of labour engagement in construction, and analysed the role of town planning in mediating the space of labour in the sector.

**Vertika Chaturvedi** has been in the practice of architecture since 2009 and has worked on projects with a focus on landscape and urban design development. She has worked to develop landscape design features, signages and wayfinding strategies for large-scale residential townships. She has also conducted design research, including natural heritage mapping in Gurgaon for INTACH, the infrastructure audit of healthcare centres in Nepal for the World Bank, and on design norms for senior living and assisted living facilities. She has engaged with teaching for BArch being focused on initiating students into architectural exploration and design research in their first year.

**Mathew Idiculla** is a legal and policy consultant and a PhD candidate at the Faculty of Law and Justice, UNSW Sydney.

His research interests are on issues concerning cities, local governance, federalism and constitutionalism. He has engaged with the field of urban law and governance for over thirteen years in multiple ways: academic research, teaching, legal consultancy, policy engagement, public advocacy and scholarly and popular writing. He has served as a visiting faculty member at Azim Premji University and the National Law School of India University and has contributed to the formulation of urban laws and policies of Karnataka and Kerala.

**Romi Khosla** is internationally known as an architect and consultant on urban planning. With a double graduation from Cambridge University (Economics) and the Architectural Association in London, he returned to India in 1972 to establish his Design Studios. Since then, he has designed and built over a hundred buildings, some of which have been awarded with national and international honours. In 2014, his Volvo–Eicher Headquarters building was given the international LEED platinum award. As a master planner, he has been a principal consultant to UNDP, UNESCO, WTO and UNOPS, and has worked on conflict resolution missions in the Middle East, Balkans and Cyprus, and on master plan missions in Tibet, China and Central Asia. He has been a jury member of the Aga Khan Awards in Geneva and for the city of Izmir in Turkey. As an earth walker for decades, he has travelled on foot to research ancient Buddhist sites in the deeper Himalayas, the findings of which were published in a book.

**Seema Mundoli** is a faculty at Azim Premji University, Bengaluru, where she teaches in the undergraduate and postgraduate programmes. Her research focuses on the role of nature in cities, urban sustainability and climate change communication. Her research has been published in peer-reviewed journals and appeared in the popular press. Her publications include the co-authored books (with Harini Nagendra) *Cities and Canopies: Trees in Indian Cities* (Penguin Random House India, 2019), *So Many Leaves* (Pratham Publications, 2021) and *Shades of Blues: Connecting the Drops in India's Cities* (Penguin Random House India, 2023).

**Harini Nagendra** is the director of the School of Sustainability and Climate Change at Azim Premji University, Bengaluru. She uses social and ecological approaches to examine the factors shaping forest conservation, urban biodiversity and resilience to climate change. Her books include *Nature in the City: Bengaluru in the Past, Present and Future* (Oxford University Press, 2016), *Cities and Canopies: Trees of Indian Cities* and *Shades of Blue: Connecting the Drops in India's Cities* (with Seema Mundoli). She is also the author of the Bangalore Detectives Club historical mystery series set in 1920s colonial India.

**Vishnu M.J.** is a researcher and practitioner in the domain of the 'Urban'. He has more than twelve years of experience working across sectors, including mobility and public transport, water, sanitation and environmental services, and climate change adaptation. He is particularly interested in the interactions of society and the State with these sectors, and how these could be channelled towards a just and sustainable future.

**Kavya Michael** is an environmental social scientist with expertise in analysing the 'natural environment' through a social science lens. Her research and professional experience broadly lie in examining global environmental change and energy-related issues through a human rights and justice lens. Within this domain, questions of class, caste and gender have been central to her analysis. She also studies the multiple intersections of climate change/environmental hazards, urban inequality, informality, and inter- and intra-regional migration with a special focus on the Global South.

**Tanvi Deshpande** is a research fellow at the Birmingham Institute for Sustainability and Climate Action at the University of Birmingham and a visiting fellow at the LSE–Fudan Global Public Policy Hub, London School of Economics and Political Science. Her research has primarily focused on urban governance and justice in the Global South, particularly South Asia (India, Nepal and Bangladesh) and parts of Africa (Kenya). She is interested in decolonization and contextualization approaches that highlight the local (ideas, knowledge, practices and organizations) to address structural discrimination and dependencies. She is a co-founder of the Frontiers for Just Cities in South Asia network led by early career scholars working on urban issues such as climate change, disaster risk reduction and sustainability in the region.

# About Samruddha Bharat Foundation

The Samruddha Bharat Foundation (SBF) strives to forge a resurgent and strong India that is a global superpower, a cosmopolitan beacon of democracy and accommodative of every Indian. It does so by constructively reshaping India's

- *Software* (transforming mass consciousness, public discourse, popular and social culture, education as well as by forging principled coalitions); and
- *Hardware* (reforming policies, institutions and governance to reorder India's polity, economy and society).

In breathing life into these goals, the SBF works closely with India's progressive parties, the nation's foremost thinkers, activists as well as a plethora of organizations and movements. The SBF thus serves as a clearing house for all progressive forces to collaborate in furthering the constitutional idea of India. For further details, see:

🌐 Website: www.samruddhabharat.in

X (formerly Twitter): @SBFIndia

🅕 Facebook: Samruddha Bharat Foundation

📷 Instagram: @SBFIndia

Scan QR code to access the
Penguin Random House India website